Siam Was Our Home

A narrative memoir of
Edna Bruner Bulkley's
years in Thailand in
the early 1900s,
with added
memories
from her
children.

Mary Bulkley Stanton

Published by
Hara Publishing
P.O. Box 19732
Seattle, WA 98109
(425) 775-7868

Mary Bulkley Stanton
Post Office Box 1865
Bellingham, WA 98227-1865

ISBN: 1-887542-14-0
Library of congress number: 2003112356

Manufactured in the United States
10 9 8 7 6 5 4 3 2 1

Editor: Lynn Moen
Cover Design & Maps: John Moen

Note: The figure on the cover is a reproduction of one of the leather
cut-out figures used in the Nang-talung shadow plays of the Ramanaya
stories. Traditional figures are intricately carved from cow hide and
have more movable parts – joints at the elbow, wrists, etc. I got this
less-intricate reproduction in the 1990s on a visit to Thailand. See page
46 for more information. – M.B.S.

Contents

Preface and Acknowlegements

My mother used to hold her dinner guests spellbound as she told dramatic tales of her early years in Siam, as Thailand was then called. We lived in Trang in the Malay Peninsula near the border. My father ran the Presbyterian Mission hospital – one of only three doctors in the whole peninsula. Mother had gone to Siam in 1903, three years after she graduated from high school, to work in a missionary girls' school. Through the next 31 years and the reigns of five Siamese kings Siam was her home. She married Father in 1910. They had seven children – I was number six – and Siam was our home.

About 30 years after Mother's death in 1962 I learned that my brother Dwight had Mother's old trunk. In it was a manuscript she had written about her early years in Siam. I decided to enter it into my computer and print it out for an impending family reunion. A friend at church, Dawn Groves – author, computer instructor and yoga teacher – formatted those 22 chapters plus a final story, "Jungle Grandma" which Dwight had written about Mother's return to Thailand in 1947 to 1950. I had these printed for family members and made extra copies of the chapter "Epidemic" which I sent to a number of friends.

Somehow Lynn Moen – a published author, former bookstore owner and desktop editor – saw a copy, read it and offered to put it into publishable form, which I readily agreed to. When working together, we realized that Mother's manuscript was incomplete. There was very little about Father or us seven children. But the trunk also held a treasure trove of letters sent to Father's family which had been returned to her, and her notes and early drafts. I found more intriguing stories that cried out to be included. I also gathered some perspectives we children had about growing up in the Orient, and I changed the title from "Siam Was My Home" to "Siam was Our Home."

In editing Mother's manuscript I have used her language as much as possible to reflect the tone of her era. Occasionally her words would not be considered "politically correct" but I thought they should stand as written. Siamese words – and others – are italicized in the text and are defined in brackets the first time they appear, and/or in the Glossary/Index in the Appendix. We learned that the spelling of some place names have changed over the years – we used the old names. I accept full responsibility for any errors or inconsistencies in the book. Some of the old pictures were in poor shape. We did what we could with computer technology, then included them anyhow.

In the ten years I have worked on this book I have had much help, particularly in the last three years. Many people were crucial to the successful outcome of this book, and I am grateful. There would have been no book without it. My sincere thanks to you all.

My brother Dan has supported and encouraged me the whole way and added his recollections. My niece Anore Jones allowed me to include portions of my sister Dorothy's yet-unpublished story – those about her years in the Orient. My nephew Brian Bulkley sent me Dwight's sketches and other pictures. My niece Lynn Paul took the photo of the pendant and lent us my sister Peggy's albums. Other nieces and nephews have also made their store of family pictures available. This is their heritage and I am glad to make it available to them and their descendents.

Kathy Allen was the first to read and evaluate the manuscript. Dawn Groves helped get the first 22 stories in shape for the family reunion. The late Charlotte Smith read the manuscripts and cheered me on. Lynnette Allen and others counseled me when I had computer problems. Ken Mallikamas – whose first language is Thai – helped tremendously with the Glossary. John Moen created the cover and the maps. Martha Eby line-edited with an eagle eye. And Lynn Moen has worked tirelessly with me for the last three years as we made this collection of stories into a book. I am deeply indebted to her for her skill throughout, for never letting me let up, and her unrelenting commitment to see this project through to the end with me.

My mother, Edna Bruner Bulkley, was truly a most remarkable woman, and a great storyteller. Her stories come alive for me with each rereading. May you enjoy them as I do.

Mary Bulkley Stanton, Bellingham, Washington. August, 2003

Introduction

It was only two and a half years since I graduated from Sacramento High School at seventeen. I was too young, my father said, to go away to the University at Berkeley.

To fill the time I studied shorthand and practiced typing with the secretary in my father's law office. At night school I took up charcoal drawing and perspective. I kept busy making pen-and-ink sketches for party prizes, menus and score cards on order.

To please my father and grandmother I joined the Odd Fellows Lodge and to please my Sunday School teacher, Mrs. Hatfield, I reluctantly joined her Presbyterian church. Then, because theater, playing whist and dancing were indulgences frowned upon by church members, I gave them all up and started a new life in which playing the small church organ became an absorbing interest.

In a rebellious mood one day the following year, I

confided to a friend that I was haunted by the unwelcome idea that I must be a missionary.

"Don't be silly," she chided, "we wouldn't let you." However much I was comforted at the time by her reaction, something happened later to reverse my attitude. I accepted Mrs. Hatfield's invitation to attend Presbyterial as her guest. This annual conference of the Presbyterian women's groups in northern California and eastern Nevada was being held that spring of 1903 in Chico, a city I had never visited.

The opening address was given by the Rev. Dwight E. Potter, a leader of the Pacific Coast Laymen's Missionary Movement. He told about the many missionaries killed in the recent Boxer Rebellion in China and described the death of one, a woman sent out and supported by this very Presbyterial.

"Who," he challenged, "is going to take her place?" By the time he had finished his address my decision to volunteer was painlessly made.

There was great rejoicing, and several of the older church members spoke affectionately of my Methodist grandfather, Ashley Bruner, who, it seemed, had been their pastor in the original church building, which had since been destroyed by fire. They were sure their former preacher's spirit was present and had something to do with my decision. I agreed. They told me also that my father and his three brothers had sung in the choir.

From that day I had a feeling of being carried along by Destiny, willy-nilly. The Harriet House Boarding School for Girls in Bangkok, Siam, called familiarly Wang Lang, had priority in its request for someone young and willing to do anything. So I was to be sent to live and work in Siam, not China. Five months later I was on the *S. S. Korea* bound for Hong Kong.

Edna Bruner Bulkley (circa 1958)

1 - A Bit of China on the Way to Siam

Four weeks after leaving San Francisco on the *S.S. Korea* with my bride-and-groom chaperones, Grace and Robert Franklin, who were to teach at the Christian high school in Bangkok, we arrived in Hong Kong. The interlude spent there while waiting for unscheduled and infrequent sailings to Siam held no fond memories. The damp heat and accompanying rash, the mosquitoes, the ants and the crickets at night, the pavilion-like bathrooms the size of ballrooms, the English cooking, strange fruits and unfamiliar atmosphere – all combined to make us long for the coziness of a ship's cabin and ocean breezes.

Yet there seemed to be a conspiracy against our leaving. Siam sailings were wrapped in secrecy; all we could learn was that we should be ready to leave at a moment's notice.

It was a relief, after days of waiting that might have been more happily spent in sight-seeing, to be tipped off that we might hunt for a cargo boat somewhere out in the harbor with steam-up. Hastily we filled several *rickshas* [two-wheeled carriage, pulled by a man] with trunks and suitcases and started off in a single-file procession through miles of the native quarter of the city, through streets densely crowded with Chinese celebrating the harvest moon festival. Then came an anxious search for one vessel out of a score or more, widely scattered in the busy, crowded harbor.

We had been fearful during the *ricksha* ride and now we felt helpless in the painful knowledge that failure to reach it in time would mean going back to begin all over again. Robert was in the larger boat with all the trunks. Grace and I, in the smaller one with the suitcases, were fearful we would get separated from him. We implored, we gesticulated, we shouted frantically. The Chinese boatman, standing in the stern of our *sampan* [small boat worked by oar at the stern], wielded his oar in and out of traffic as unconcerned as a stone idol.

We neared the gangplank of the *S. S. Pitsanulok* feeling that the doxology was in order. It happened that the Captain was at that very moment swearing at sight of our approach. He hastily summoned his two officers to a meeting in his quarters. The First Officer was then sent to tell us that the ship was going up the China coast, and that we must take some other vessel.

That fair-haired, good-looking young German officer had not expected to face three attractive young Americans! He was shy and embarrassed, but orders were orders and he probably felt the eyes of the Captain and Chief Engineer boring the back of his head. "This ship is going first to Swatow [now Shantau]," he said, a bit breathlessly.

"We were told that the *Pitsanulok* was listed for Bangkok," Robert replied, puzzled, while Grace and I looked deflated, to say the least.

"Yes, but later."

"How long will you stay in Swatow?"

"It is uncertain. But I am sure you will find a direct sailing for Bangkok tomorrow."

Then Grace spoke up with her sweetest smile, "Could you give us some idea of the time we would lose by going along with you?"

The First Officer relented, "It may be a matter of a few hours or, at most, three days in Swatow."

Robert, remembering the cable he had sent in those last few moments at the hotel, reminded us, "We shall be expected in Bangkok at the end of a week. Shall we risk complications?"

I said whatever they decided would be all right with me. He looked at Grace anxiously.

I was glad when she said with feeling, "Even if we were sure of a direct sailing tomorrow, I'd rather not go through this again."

Robert turned to the officer grimly, "We'll stay on board if we may."

We could not understand the officer's hesitation and embarrassment and were relieved when he signalled to the boatman below to bring up the luggage. We were encouraged when he led us to the saloon and said more graciously, "Please be seated while I tell the Captain."

A few days later all three laughed as they admitted that they had not wanted to be bothered with passengers – that they were not compelled to do so if they could manage discreetly, without involving their company.

"None of us," the Captain said, "likes to carry passengers. There are so many queer and querulous people, so we try to get out of it if we can."

During our twenty-one days on the tiny, twelve-hundred-ton cargo boat the officers made up for that initial cold reception with every kindness and consideration in their power. We had jolly times at meals. We had evenings of music around the piano. We told stories on deck in the moonlight.

Our two cabins opened off the small dining saloon on each side of the piano. We shared our bathroom with the propeller mechanism in the rounded stern. The days were lazy and pleasant enough, but the nights were a horror. I found that I had a vulnerable spot of squeamishness in my makeup the very first time I started to go to bed.

Cockroaches! Giant winged ones, darting out from curtains and cushions. Huge crawling ones on couch and bunk and dresser. Of course everyone knew about it and the Chief Engineer, especially, delighted to tease, and would describe at breakfast the antics of his "pet" cockroaches who crawled over his face and tickled his ears.

When we anchored in the broad river at Swatow we learned about the *coolie* [unskilled native laborer] and cargo-trade competition going on between the British and German steamship companies. Our British rival for the contract to carry the Chinese *coolie* laborers to Siam was anchored nearby, and we were told that neither vessel would leave till the bottom price in the bidding for the privilege was reached.

A *dhoby* [Indian of low caste, usually washerwoman or man] promptly appeared alongside in his little *sampan* fully expecting to take away our soiled laundry to wash in the city. The captain forbade it – we might leave any minute! On the third day we were allowed to go ashore on condition that we would return immediately at a signal blast from the ship's whistle.

For the remaining eleven days that we were in Swatow we had tea and tennis with the English Presbyterians on the north shore day after day, and visits with the American Baptists on the south side, and were always saying goodbye. We managed our laundry as best we could in hand basins.

About noon of the eleventh day at Swatow there was suddenly a great commotion. The Germans had won the bidding with fifty cents Mexican per head for the transportation to Bangkok. [Mexican currency was often used as a standard in the Orient.] Twelve hundred peasant men from poverty-stricken inland villages disturbed our peace as they stampeded over the main deck, taking complete possession. They were going to Siam to work hard to better the living conditions of families left behind. We were finally on the last leg of our journey to Bangkok.

Our cabins had breast-high windows on two sides. The deck passengers covered every foot of space up to and under them, making it necessary to pin our curtains when dressing and undressing. It was like walking on a human carpet whenever we stepped from the saloon door to the stairway of our small awninged deck, where we spent most of our days.

Here was a bit of China spread out on a ship's deck. Each man's home was the spot where his box and bedding-roll was placed, and he used only as much space as his narrow mattress took when unrolled at night.

They chattered from morning to night, inoffensively, and I felt that we were amusing objects for their conversation and jokes. Some of them smoked long gurgling pipes. A few gambled. They played chess and they drank pale tea from quaint teapots. They spent hours oiling and combing their long heavy tresses with handmade wooden combs and braiding each others' *queues*. Twice daily at mealtime they separated into a score of circles with individual bowls of rice placed around center pans of soup, vegetables, and fish.

They may have appeared a bit wild at first sight, but from early childhood I had been used to the kindly Chinese laundryman in California who brought lilies at New Year, and my father's cultured Chinese clients who sometimes met him in our home on their way to and from Paris and London. I had learned to like and trust their countrymen.

It was an endless fascination to study them for counterparts of familiar types; to fancy resemblances to Charles Dana Gibson characters, orientalized; to imagine that I was seeing certain prominent Occidental gentlemen squatting there, shovelling rice with chopsticks.

During the nine days of our voyage from Swatow to Bangkok, the sultry sun beat down upon twelve hundred steaming, unbathed bodies in varying states of exposure. The Chinese-lantern odor of their scant clothing mingled with the smell of rancid *copra* or coconut, from the ship's hold.

This was my real initiation into the orient, and never, never, would I forget the smells – and the cockroaches.

Young Edna Bulkley

2 - Arrival in Siam

It was a Sunday in October 1903, fifty-two days since leaving San Francisco. Our small twelve-hundred-ton freighter *Pitsanulok* was slowly making its way up the Menam river from the Gulf of Siam. Since daylight, except for breakfast, I'd been watching our approach to this foreign land, my new home. We passed desolate mangrove swamps stretching as far as the eye could see, whose only inhabitants seemed to be crocodiles, mosquitoes and fireflies. Once a Chinese *junk* [vessel with very high poop deck] with a strange, slate-blue sail passed like a ghost on its way to the sea.

During the hours of slow progress my thoughts turned to what had brought me to this new turning point in my life. I could almost echo the words of the little old woman of Mother Goose, "Lawk-a-mercy-on-us! Can this be really me?" Then I saw a lone *pagoda* [Buddhist tower or shrine], guarding a lovely island temple and it seemed to offer a welcome and promise of adventure in the "Kingdom of the White Elephant, Land of the Yellow Robe."

After inching our way to the dreary dock, we were within the oriental city of King Chulalongkorn at last, and the throbbing engines silenced. The lonely sea and inhospitable river were replaced by a kaleidoscopic scene of activity and color. The Menam became the "Broadway" of Bangkok, literally the highway of Siam. I was facing the west bank, the ancient half of the city – miles and miles of fruit gardens without roads or electricity. Moored along the edge were floating shops and houses, with quaint roofs edged with intricate carvings. They danced to the tune of the restless river.

A string of ancient *Laos* boats was tied up between trips to the far north. Anchored midstream was the old *Deli* waiting for its next voyage to Singapore. The river, like any busy downtown street was alive with activity. Launches raced back and forth, tugboats towing paddy barges chugged against the tide. *Sampans* were everywhere, ferrying passengers or delivering anything from pigs to bricks, while tiny canoes darted in and out of traffic, selling food or sweets. A few *rua-pet,* or "duck boats," [small native house boats] passed by – part of a large floating population – mother rowing, father steering, with grandmother minding the children and cooking.

Dreamily I turned from the river scene and crossed the deck to join Robert and Grace Franklin. I had seen little of my bride-and-groom chaperones on the Pacific crossing, but the many days of shared experiences in Hongkong and Swatow and three weeks on the tiny freighter cemented a friendship that endured.

As we three stood at the ship's rail on the lower deck, one thought was in our minds. We were three weeks overdue. Would we be met? We anxiously scanned the figures on the dock. Far back we saw a lone foreigner standing, dressed in dazzling white from pith helmet to canvas shoes.

"Wouldn't it be nice if he has come for us?" Grace said.

"Yes," replied Robert, "but how could anyone expect us without advance notice?"

"He is staring at us," I commented.

"Why shouldn't he? Two good-looking American girls must be a rarity in this part of the world," he replied.

At that moment the man moved closer, cupped his hands and called up, "Which is the bride?"

Robert, with a chuckle and a roguish glance at me, shouted down, "The best-looking, of course!"

Bounding up the plank just laid to our deck, the stranger made straight for Grace, saying with Irish-American heartiness, "I can always spot a bride!"

"I'm Snyder, by the way, the Mission treasurer and business manager. Am I glad to see you! I've been haunting both the British and German shipping offices every day for news that some ship had crossed the bar, and I've met each one in spite of rumors that you might have been lost in a typhoon."

"You can't imagine how we have felt," Robert interjected, "being unable to let you know." He proceeded to explain why we were delayed.

Grace and I negotiated the inclined plank with the aid of a helping hand and followed the two men around the warehouse to a narrow lane, fenced with rusty sheets of corrugated iron. Deep ruts showed that the monsoon rain was not long over. We had to pick our way to the waiting carriage. The Malay owner-driver, in *sarong* [skirt-like garment worn by men or women], white jacket, black velvet pants and round cap, was standing beside the *gharry* [horse-drawn cart] swishing flies from his sleek, small horses.

"I thought this was the land of boats!" I exclaimed, at the sight of the Victoria and pretty little horses. I had read in *The Heart of Farther India,* by Mary Cort, published in the 1880s that Bangkok was described as the "Venice of the East," all waterways and boat travel.

"Not for us on this side of the river," Mr. Snyder replied, "but quite true where you will be living." This was the first news about my new home. Grace and I were seated and the two men took the drop-seat. The driver climbed to his high box and shook the reins.

"We're going north on New Road now," Mr. Snyder said as we turned at the end of the lane, "just to help you get your bearings. It parallels the river for miles." He went on to explain that it was begun by King Mongkut and was Bangkok's one, long, land thoroughfare. Short roads, bordering *klongs* [canals or water thoroughfares], led away from the river into a vast area of rice fields.

People filled the street as far as we could see. Dogs and pigs, chickens and ducks poured out of the dark cubicles that were shop-homes. Our horses kept their smart pace and space opened up magically.

A single-track electric tram ran along one edge of the narrow road and siding spurs at intervals narrowed the road even more. The tram moved slowly, one foot of the motorman constantly pumping a bellows that sounded like a raucous squawk. He called out to his friends and swore at those who got too close; and once I saw him lean out and push a pedestrian out of the way with his foot.

Tram

Weaving in and out of the crowds were Chinese *coolies* pulling *rickshas.* Those seeking fares sauntered dazedly, the shafts almost perpendicular. Those with fares, bent over with eyes on the ground, darted in and out of the traffic with amazing skill. A family appeared to be moving its entire household possessions in two huge baskets, slung from a pole and resting on the shoulders of husband and wife. The children followed with the dog.

We passed a number of shabby one-horse *gharries,* one with a sheet draped over sagging springs, its harness patched with string. Their drivers were Chinese with unkempt *queues,* and bare torsos under open flapping jackets. When they lashed their horses with whips I winced and wondered, would I ever get used to such cruelty?

"Traveling restaurant" on the move.

Here and there people were standing at the traveling restaurants. These consisted of two cabinets and a charcoal brazier under a large brass basin. Shelves in the cabinets held bowls, chopsticks and ingredients for a quick meal. On the move each cabinet was suspended from either end of a pliable, split bamboo, balanced on one shoulder as the proprietor jogged along.

At *Klong* Payome, the first tidal canal, our *gharry* turned east on a narrow pike, built from silt of the *klong* on one side and from the swamp on the other. It was tree-shaded and quiet.

"Here we are," Mr. Snyder called out as we clattered over the *klong* on a wooden bridge and entered the mission compound. "This is our house on the left. The one on the right is the press and the other buildings are further back."

The Snyder house was built on high pillars with covered veranda on all four sides. The space below was paved to make a children's playground safe from snakes and stinging creatures of the tropics. Looking up at the house as we clattered over the bridge I saw four children, the oldest a girl of twelve, watching critically at the verandah railing.

A Siamese teacher who spoke English was waiting to take Robert and Grace to the Christian High School, so we said goodbye. At the top of the stairs a slender little woman greeted me with outstretched arms and a lilting welcome, "Edna Bruner! Here at last! Come here, children."

The children came eagerly. Just as I was thinking how nice it was to spend my first day with such a friendly family, a brittle voice loudly demanded, "What made *you* come to this God-forsaken land, Miss Bruner!"

Conscious that I was surrounded by Mr. and Mrs. Snyder and their children, I bit my tongue to avoid retorting and merely nodded. This was my introduction to Mrs. Harrick who I soon learned was their house guest. Almost immediately Mrs. Snyder called the house-girl to serve dinner and I was escorted by the whole family to the table at the far end of a very long room.

Mrs. Harrick was seated beside Mrs. Snyder at the other end of the table. Looking baffled and explosive, as soon as she could break into Mr. Snyder's conversation she shrilled, "I want to know what made *you* become a missionary!"

"Well," I said, "I suspect my dear-departed grandfather is to blame. When I was a small child, out walking with him one day, I slipped under the swinging door of a saloon and the horrified old gentleman had to go inside and drag me out. He is probably using his influence up-above to see that I go straight." There was no comment, and Mr. Snyder's face was almost in his plate.

Hungry after the long trip and fascinated by the unfamiliar food served to me I plunged in with gusto, discovering it was quite delicious.

Just then I was startled to hear the children clap their hands and cry out, "Goody, goody! Now you'll stay a long time."

At my questioning look Mrs. Snyder laughingly explained, "We have a tradition that the new missionary who eats all the first large helping of rice and curry will like Siam and stay a long time. So few do. We say that there are more Siam missionaries in America than in Siam."

"Thank you, children," I said happily, "I hope I shall indeed."

Rising from the table after we finished, Mrs. Snyder sang out, "Nap time!" and the children raced for the far side of the house. Mrs. Harrick went to a shaded corner of the verandah to wait until Mrs. Snyder would be free for a gossip fest. Later I learned that Mrs. Harrick was one of the misfits that every mission must have had to put up with at some time. An only child, married in haste and on impulse, she had found no liking for the loneliness of an up-country mission station. She had come down from the North Siam Mission with her caustic tongue and unhappiness, for dental work and shopping. The following year it was arranged for her to live in the States with her two daughters. Her doctor husband lived on in Siam until his death.

I was led to the guest room and Mrs. Snyder lowered the mosquito net and tucked it in all around, saying, "Undress and sleep as long as you can. You must make a daily nap your most important habit if you want to live long in this climate."

Gratefully I took her suggestion, and I must have dropped off to sleep the minute my head hit the pillow for all too soon I woke abruptly to the children's whooping as they scrambled for their baths.

My "bathroom" was like the one in the Swatow hotel — an airy veranda corner typically furnished with a waist-high clay jar of water on the tin-floored section, and a shelf with dipper and basin. I had already been introduced to this method of bathing while in Swatow, soaping myself and then dipping water out of the clay *ong* [large porous jar] to rinse off. Dressing in the humid heat, I looked at my wool suit with deep distaste. As if they penetrated my thought, both ladies came in to talk about clothes.

"Give your suit to someone going home, Miss Bruner. By furlough time it will be moth-eaten, mildewed and entirely out of style," Mrs.

Snyder began. Yes, I realized, it would be seven years before I'd wear it again in the States, since the mandatory furlough or leave time for missionaries was every seven years.

"Canvas shoes are quickly and cheaply made," Mrs. Harrick cut in, "and you must buy white stockings because black attracts mosquitoes. Oh they are dreadful!" And she rolled her eyes.

"There are lots of Chinese tailors to make cotton dresses," Mrs. Snyder continued. "Camisole, drawers and petticoats are all you need underneath!"

I looked from one to the other, amused as they proceeded to indoctrinate me in correct dressing for the tropics. Both ladies were wearing long, full skirts that swept the floor. Mine was ankle-length and snug at the hips.

"Don't tell me," Mrs. Harrick said disgustedly, "women in the States are wearing skirts that tight!"

"Not all, yet," I laughed.

The children began to clamor for their tea and we went to the veranda where a table was set with blue and white Willow-patterned cups and saucers. Each child's cup was almost filled with milk, topped with enough tea so that they felt they were having "grown-up tea". They sat demurely, wide-eyed as they watched and listened intently to the adults. At a signal from their mother after finishing their tea, they left to play under the house.

As Mr. Snyder got up from the table to go to his study, he said, "Be ready at six o'clock and I'll take you to Wang Lang."

A huge tamarind tree on the front lawn shaded the veranda corner where we had tea. A faint breeze coming across miles of tidal swamp from the Gulf of Siam stirred its lacy leaves. A red hibiscus hedge separated the lawn below from the *klong* where a *rua-pet* was stranded in the mud of low tide. The family was squatting on the little deck having their evening meal. Over a high brick wall was a very old Chinese cemetery, completely covered with jungle growth. The rear of the compound impinged on the densest quarter of Chinese in the whole city. Yet there was no roof in sight where we sat, peacefully undisturbed by the children's voices or the clangor of New Road.

As in a dream I heard snatches of conversation between the two ladies. "I hear Miss Cole is thankful to have someone at last, young enough to train in" . . . "Poor Miss Cole; she has been disappointed so many times." . . . "It's just too bad Miss Bruner is to have that small verandah bedroom when it isn't necessary". . . "Miss Cole is too Spartan; the school is like a prison." Soon, as I showed no apparent interest, their talk turned to the recent arrivals for the North Siam Mission whom Mrs. Harrick would join on the long river trip.

When the *gharry* again clattered over the driveway-bridge Mrs. Harrick had gone to her room and I did not see her again. I said goodbye to Mrs. Snyder and the children, feeling I had found a home-away-from-home in Siam.

From the time we left the compound and headed up New Road, where we turned north, Mr. Snyder kept up a running commentary about our surroundings and the road, which was more congested than in the forenoon. Here, the populace was entirely Chinese, while the lower district had been *Mon* [an original Siamese tribe] and Malay. People were pouring out of dark, airless holes by the thousands for the coolness of evening. This Chinese district, which Mr. Snyder termed a constant fire hazard with its bamboo and thatch, ended at the second *klong*.

Here, in contrast, were uniform, two-story, brick and plaster built shops with living quarters above. This was the foreign business and shopping district with a Sunday-deserted look. Here were the British and American legations, the British and French banks, the two British clubs, a large German firm and the sedate India dress-goods stores.

Crossing the third *klong* we were in a stretch of New Road where my senses were assailed on every side. Iron mongers and tin beaters raised a din to high heaven. Messy leather-workers spread out into the street with their odiferous hides. Teak and rattan furniture in the making spilled out to the gutters from their dark holes-in-the-wall with incessant hammering and sawing. Beyond all these were the goldsmiths and silversmiths and the notorious "thieves market," Mr. Snyder said. Finally I asked, "Why is Siam so little known? Crossing the Pacific I was teased about the 'jumping off' place I was going to, 'the end of the earth!'"

"Because the country is peaceful and nothing happens to make news abroad, I suppose," Mr. Snyder said. "And," he continued thoughtfully, "Siam gets few tourists because Hongkong and Singapore have long presented such a devastating picture of Bangkok that few have the courage to come."

Mr. Snyder continued, "And yet, the Thai, – 'Free people' as the Siamese call themselves – are a great people; probably the oldest unabsorbed race on earth, still doing business in the modern world! Millenniums ago they possessed the region north of the Yangtze River in China. When the two small, Chinese states along the Yellow River had to expand and couldn't move north or west because of fierce tribes, nor to the east which was swamp, they began infiltrating the easy-going, cultured Thai to the south. The 'Tali Kingdom', their last stand in China, was conquered by Kubla Khan. The Thai leaders then joined their predecessors and wrested their present kingdom from the Cambodians."

I asked where the name Siam came from. Mr. Snyder answered, "Probably, from India – Cyama, or Syama Rastra, abbreviated to Samarade by the Greeks of Ptolemy's time."

While listening to this bit of history I was thinking of all the types of costumes I had seen: Chinese men had *queues* and wore bag-trousers; river men and dock coolies wore a loin cloth. The Christian teacher, who met Robert and Grace, was dressed in a brilliant blue silk *panung* [lower garment] with white military coat. The Snyder's housemaid had short hair like the men, and wore a *panung* with a camisole; their cook wore nothing but a breast scarf above the *panung*. Indians wore long white *dhoties* [loincloth worn by Hindu men] with black jacket and the Malays wore *sarongs*. I had been trying to identify women on the street by the breast-scarf.

"Something is missing in all these crowds," I said. "Where are the Siamese men and the Chinese women?"

Mr. Snyder grinned. "There are no Chinese women in Siam! Chinese women are not allowed to leave China. Chinese men take Siamese wives and send their earnings to their families in China.

"As for Siamese men," he continued, "you will find few downtown on the streets. A large percentage are in the rice fields outside the city and the fruit gardens across the river. Then, besides royalty, the nobility and their retainers, there are teachers, clerks and government officials. Thousands wear the yellow robe in the monasteries, but there are no

A busy Bangkok klong, or canal.

Siamese men in businesses. Chinese men and Siamese women carry on most of the business in the country."

Crossing a wide *klong*, congested with traffic, I saw the Golden Mount, built from the mud of the canal and said to have been dug as a shortcut to the Cambodian border. A winding brick-paved path led to the *pagoda* on top. Here we passed through a jagged breach in the old fortress city wall built for protection against enemy war elephants and sharpshooting arrows.

Still following the tram line we crossed a clean, quiet *klong* with grassy banks. I had been watching a flaming sunset. Suddenly we came to the high crenulated wall of the King's innermost, royal city; it was almost dark. The last faint red streak betrayed the mysterious skyline of palaces, temples and *pagodas*. My breath caught in my throat. I longed to stop a moment, but the ponies trotted inexorably on. Mr. Snyder assured me that I would be able to see it from Wang Lang. A broad boulevard circled a vast oval space – the *Premene*, or royal cremation ground. Cutting across the *Premene* we drove down a long narrow road between crenulated walls to the river. The wall on our right bordered the old palace city of the former Second King.

3 - Arrival at Wang Lang

Outside of Bangkok, at the beginning of the century, education for girls was a project as yet undreamed of except in the few places where there was a mission school. The Harriet House Boarding School for Girls, widely known as Wang Lang School [its name translates to "behind the palace"] had a long waiting list and never an empty bed because of its reputation for discipline and character training. It had another distinction. It was the only girl's school in the land whose curriculum was in accordance with the Government standard for boys.

We left the *gharry* at the end of the lane. Mr. Snyder told the *syce* [driver] to wait for him. A bridge-walk extended out over the water. It was now quite dark. A coconut-oil taper on a table under the roofed middle section illuminated the ferry manager, an old native woman. Her teeth were black from a lifetime of chewing *betel nut* [the areca nut]. She wore the typical market-woman breast cloth and *panung*. She gave a grunt as Mr. Snyder put down a few coppers, and called shrilly to the boatman across the river. We walked down the cleated gangplank and stood on the bobbing float. "See those lights there?" Mr. Snyder said, "that is your new home!"

We boarded the ferry, a *sampan* propelled by a single long oar at the stern, Chinese-style. I was given the one seat in the middle. Mr.

Wang Lang School from the water

Snyder took the small triangular space in the bow. Other passengers sat on their haunches. Because of a strong down-tide the boatman made a wide arc upstream to finally land neatly at another float and bridge landing diagonally across river. This was Wang Lang School. I had a feeling of deep peace and of belonging, as if I had lived in Siam in a former life and had now come home.

A vine-covered fence topped a bricked embankment. From the arched gateway a raised walk led to the broad, front stairs of the residence. A lantern on the gate and hanging lanterns in the front rooms beamed a welcome to us. Many open double-doors gave the effect of a lighted pavilion. As we entered we could see someone get up from a desk and cross over to meet us.

This was Miss Edna Cole, principal of Wang Lang School, known affectionately as *Mem* Cole [*Mem:* the address for non-Siamese women]. She was known and respected from the Malayan border on the south to the northern boundaries of China and Burma – wherever her former students, the wives and daughters of high Siamese officials in government service were living.

This was Miss Cole's year of distinction. The government now recognized her school for the high standard of its curriculum. Four senior girls had been permitted to take the King's scholarship examination in company with boys from the government school. The young men who were outstandingly successful were sent to Europe for advanced study. All four girls passed.

Miss Cole was small and very, very thin after twenty-five years of activity in the tropics. Her dainty, crisp white dress with high, choker collar and long, tight sleeves accentuated her bony hands and sallow complexion. Her graying pompadour was lopsided and inclined to be unruly. From her perfect nose and eyebrows one could see that she had been a pretty young woman. Her pleasing voice and wide, straight mouth could not conceal a rare sense of humor that fascinated me as long as I knew her. We clasped hands in greeting and her discerning gray eyes met mine. I knew immediately that I was approved, and that I wanted to be her loyal supporter.

After the introduction, Mr. Snyder told me *Nai* [mister] Heng would bring my trunks by boat the next day, then he left. Four Siamese teachers came in to be presented. Each gave the customary *wai* salute in greeting — palms together as in prayer. Tiny, vivid *Kru* [teacher] Suwan [heaven], alone came forward to shake hands and say, *"Sabai mai ja?"* [Are you well?] Then, in English, "How-do-you-do?" with each word spaced and rising in scale like tinkling notes of music. *Kru* Suwan was Miss Cole's right hand and dearest friend. In contrast to the other three, who seemed soberly critical, her greeting was accompanied by a warm, friendly smile.

All four were dressed in the height of palace fashion – white high-necked muslin blouses with peplums and long sleeves, elaborate with lace or embroidery, and worn over pink *panungs*. This was the decreed palace color, except on the Buddhist Sabbath when it was red. They all had short hair cut pompadour-style, stiff with pomade.

Miss Cole's teachers and pupils were the only Siamese women in the land with white teeth because she loathed betel-chewing and would not tolerate it on the compound, except for the kitchen cook and her helpers. From an early age *betel nut* was chewed by Siamese women, making their teeth ebony-black, the height of fashion. In truth, some of the teachers' teeth still showed a hint of pink, in spite of much vigorous brushing.

The teachers returned to the school building and Miss Cooper, Miss Cole's assistant, came into the room. She was tall, broad and generously curved, bearing out a saying in the tropics: "thin people become thinner and stout people become stouter."

I was to learn that the two women were opposites in every way. Miss Cole warmly casual, Miss Cooper mathematical and unbending. Her fifteen years in Siam had not tinged her pretty brown hair nor caused a wrinkle. She wore pince-nez, which served to heighten the appearance of severity. The two women never had an argument. Each respected the other's merits just as each supplied the other's lack. Miss Cooper would state her views without fear or favor and yield graciously for events to take their course. I only knew her name Larissa from her mail, for it was never spoken. Both women scrupulously observed the use of the prefix *"Maa"* to names of all females and *"Nai"* to males, except the *"Kru"* for teachers of both sexes and titles for nobility or royalty.

Maa Chuen, the housemaid appeared to announce dinner. As soon as we were seated at the long table, a tall, dark-complexioned girl entered from the kitchen veranda and slumped into a large armchair opposite me.

Miss Cole introduced her, "This is Berta, back from school in India, helping me until we go to the States for her further schooling in a few months." Then ignoring the girl's sullen silence, she added, "Berta sleeps near me in one of the dormitories and has most of her meals with the school. Tonight is a special occasion."

She appeared to be close to my age, so I had hopes that we might become friends.

As dinner progressed I became aware of creaking boards, whispering and rustling sounds in every direction. I noticed the agitation of *Maa* Chuen, eyes down, biting her lips. Miss Cole, the disciplinarian, was having a struggle within herself. Finally, after speaking quietly with *Maa* Chuen, she decided to overlook a situation she could not control and turned to me. "It seems that the whole study hall has left their desks without permission to get a look at you. Poor *Maa* Chuen is being mobbed every time she goes down the veranda to the kitchen." Then chuckling, she added, "I asked her if she thought you pretty and she is so upset she answered, *'Mai roo,* I don't know!'"

Suddenly as we rose from the table, three loud, long, thundering notes from a huge bronze gong shattered the night air, instantly scattering our unseen audience.

"What in the world is that!" I asked.

"That's our clock in the hospital compound," Miss Cole said facetiously. "Nine o'clock – time for *Maa* Chuen to close the doors and turn out the lights." Then she said seriously, "We hope you will be happy here with us, and be able to sleep in spite of the gong every hour. Miss Cooper will take you to your room. Breakfast at seven."

I followed Miss Cooper up a wide stairway. In the small hall at the top she pointed to her room facing the river, and showed me the bathroom off the rear veranda, which she also shared. Then we went the length of a small dormitory where the youngest children, some little more than babies, were sleeping.

"Good night," she said as we reached the double doors to my room. "Please remember to open your doors so the children will have ventilation!"

This was the room Mrs. Snyder had mentioned. It was to be my happy sanctum for three years. The two outer walls of the ten-by-fifteen foot corner veranda were of whitewashed boards that did not reach the steep, sloping ceiling of plaited bamboo. In that open space a bat was soon disputing my occupancy by flying in and out to test my nerves. A thin half-partition gave me further space as a dressing room. Its outer wall was actually the veranda railing with a *moolie* [bamboo screen]. Here stood an *almirah* [large, old-fashioned teak wardrobe].

The bedroom had three small, high windows – two faced north with a glimpse of the river and the other looked down into the tree-shaded hospital compound. I could just see the roof of the house of the resident doctor, Dr. George McFarland, an American missionary's son, born in Siam. *Maw* [Doctor] Yawt, as he was called, and his wife were the only other Americans living on the entire west bank. Always good friends, they later became associate members of the Mission.

Besides a cane chair and a table with a mirror, my room contained a four-poster teak bed with a snowy mosquito net firmly tucked in all around. When I carefully crawled inside I found two small thin, Chinese mattresses that had a tendency to slide apart and pull the net askew. The only bedding was a sheet folded at the foot. It was all I ever needed.

I slept fitfully that first night. Every hour I woke and counted the deep penetrating strokes of the great gong while they throbbed across the sticky, hot night. Six notes shattered the air at midnight, nine at three o'clock, then twelve long, slow musical tones at six in the morning. At every beat of the gong all the pariah dogs in the area joined in a crescendo of howls.

At seven o'clock breakfast, while Miss Cooper worked on a stack of class papers, I saw how Miss Cole, all starched and frilled, brisk and cheery, set the pace for the day, dialogue-fashion. I learned how life was lived at Wang Lang and what was expected of me – how promptness at meals, always fully dressed, was obligatory. Asking

"How are you?" or "Did you sleep well?" were taboo, as was conversation about one's "feelings" or health. "Sickness is selfishness and 'nerves' indulgence," she said.

She yielded to the Mission's rule that a daily nap was urgent for newcomers to the tropics, but she hoped I would discipline myself to only twenty minutes sleep. I would find it enough and a useful habit all my life.

Use of first names was not permitted, and I thought, "never hear my name spoken – that's hard!" Yet, because her discourses were delivered casually, humorously, I accepted them as wise.

Breakfast over, Miss Cole promptly turned to the practical matters I needed to know about. "Miss Cooper is anxious to be relieved of organ duty, therefore you may as well make your first appearance before the school today playing for chapel." Well, that gets me off to a fast start, I thought.

"Next week," she continued, "because it is time to prepare for our annual Christmas bazaar, I will turn my senior English class over to you whenever I am busy. Wang Lang has been invited to include an exhibit of school work, along with the government's exhibit at the St. Louis Fair, and we need your help with map drawing and embroidery designs."

Already I could see that my days were going to be very full, with little time to settle in.

"Miss Bruner should have time to meet the other Americans in Bangkok, don't you think?" Miss Cooper suggested.

"A good idea," Miss Cole agreed. "Tomorrow you can take Miss Bruner to the American Legation [Embassy] 'At Home,' and to the Hays's 'At Home' on Thursday." Turning to me, she went on, "I will go with you to Prayer Meeting at the Snyders' on Wednesday – I have to see the Treasurer anyway – and to dinner at the Boys' School on Friday, where you will see your friends, the Franklins. There are only about twenty-five Americans here now."

It was immediately apparent to me that there would be many obligatory duties besides those at the school about which I had no choice, but they would make life interesting for me socially. I wondered

Student princesses at Wang Lang – Note panungs

if there were any eligible bachelors, or how long it would be before I met any. Obviously this was not a question to ask now.

A girl entered the room to deliver a message and knelt beside Miss Cole's chair. I inferred that this was the customary act of deference to age and position among the Siamese people. The girl was small for a twelve-year-old and vividly alive. Her eyes penetrated mine.

"This is *Tanying* [princess] Nart," said Miss Cole to me. Turning to the girl, she said, *"pradio pai"* [soon I will go], whereupon *Tanying* Nart rose like thistledown and vanished. By that long moment's look I knew that I would have an ally in her should I need one.

Suddenly Miss Cole was reminded of something. "We're forgetting the most important matter of all – your language study!" she all but wailed. "Now where am I to find a teacher for you? None of the staff can be spared until after the Christmas holiday." She mused a few moments, then suddenly exclaimed gaily. "It's never been done before but I believe I could get a teacher from Suan Kularp, the government boys' school. They have an English headmaster." Quite pleased with herself, she added, chuckling, "A young man teaching at our girls' school would really be something."

Rising from the breakfast table Miss Cole continued. "Come with me. The whole school is just bursting to see you in daylight."

I stood in the archway between her room and the drawing room, conscious that knots of older girls out on the lawn were trying to appear uninterested.

As time went on I discovered that Miss Cole's room, which faced the river, was the most loving spot in the whole city, where there was never a harsh word or look. Here she admonished her students, treated or cared for them when they were sick or hurt. She listened, counselled and comforted troubled students struggling with life's problems and buffeting. She also helped many financially.

Miss Cole had crossed the room to her desk chair, greeted teachers and servants by name. Seated on the veranda floor in one of the doorways was *Maa* Ouan the school cook; beside her was *Nai* Krern, her husband, carpenter and jack-of-all-trades. One teacher gave orders for the day and counted out the marketing money. Another, holding a bottle of medicine, spooned some liquid into a child's mouth. A third teacher bandaged a finger. A constant coming and going went on, and to each person Miss Cole gave patient, loving consideration. When the big school bell rang for classes the room emptied quickly.

"Now," Miss Cole said, "I will show you everything until it is time for chapel. But first, get your pith hat. You must never go in the sun without it.!"

Dutifully I went to get it and put it on for the first time.

On the rear veranda Miss Cole pointed to a small two-room shack in the near corner of the compound wall, where lived *Ah* [Chinese servant] Bea, the Chinese boatman and water-carrier from Swatow. He served faithfully for more than thirty years.

Moving on down the veranda we stopped at the kitchen, a separate building with a short runway. This was the domain of the good-natured, easygoing *Ah* Muie, our cook from the island of Hainan who had already done his early morning marketing before coming to work. The kitchen was rather a mess to my eyes. A hen, with its feet tied together and apparently about to be slaughtered, pecked frantically at its feet. It was surrounded by a litter of string beans, tiny Java potatoes, eggs, meat, rice, a coconut and jars of spices for curry.

After introducing the new *"Mem"* and some questions and answers in Siamese, Miss Cole said to me, *"Ah* Muie is very unhappy because Miss Cooper locked up his frying pan and he just loves to fry things!" She spoke to him soothingly in Siamese. Then, as we were leaving, she said gaily in English, "Be good, *Ah* Muie, and you'll be happy!"

The school building was a long "L" shape, separate from our residence. We cut across the lawn to the far diagonal corner of the compound. Here, on the river's edge was the school's kitchen, adjacent to the simple platform landing with its ladder steps. *Maa* Ouan had not yet returned from market. Her family quarters were above the bath house, our next stop. It was a large square room with cement floor, gutters and runoff. Around three sides of the room were benches holding about thirty basins and dippers. Down the center was a double row of *ongs* which *Ah* Bea was refilling with water from the river. This was for the daily bathing.

Wang Lang School

At the dining pavilion, Miss Cole sat at one of the long tables for a talk. Although all the work at the school – except cooking – was done by the older girls in rotation and it was a condition of acceptance, there was always a long waiting list.

"Most of the girls," Miss Cole said, "do their chores cheerfully. Some from the palaces evade working by permitting others, whom they consider were born to serve, to do their work for them. It is my dearest wish to teach the dignity of labor to a class to whom any personal effort is abhorrent. You can help by being willing to do your own laundry."

I said I would be glad to do so, not knowing then about the primitive charcoal irons, with their noxious fumes in the tropic heat.

"One of the girls has asked to do your room work. Her name is Muen," Miss Cole continued. "She is part Malay and has been a charity pupil from babyhood. You can pay the school as Miss Cooper does for her helper."

Having always taken care of my own needs all my life, I wondered what it would be like to have someone do work for me. Some months later after a bout with fever and facial neuralgia I was happy when Miss Cole told me to let Muen do my laundry as well. Yet it wasn't clear to me why I should pay the school rather than Muen directly. I finally accepted that such rules must be followed.

Continuing on with our tour, we passed a large tank with a network of troughs "That's our most precious possession – from Montgomery Ward," Miss Cole said with a wave of her hand. "You must see where our drinking water is kept." Under the rear veranda she unlocked a door.

The entire latticed-in ground floor of our residence was filled with *ongs* of rain water from the tank, each with a wooden cover. "*Ah* Bea and *Maa* Chuen are the only ones permitted to enter. *Maa* Chuen fills the many small clay carafes for our daily use upstairs and *Ah* Bea gets what is needed for the kitchen. Six months ago in the hot season, there was cholera in Bangkok. The river – the only source of drinking water for people – was low and brackish. We were able to furnish rain water to all who came for it."

Maa Chuen came to announce a visitor. An exquisite, bejeweled little mother of one of the pupils was seated on the veranda. Her heelless, embroidered slippers had been left on the stairs as was the custom, and her feet dangled from the cane chair made for "foreigners." Beside her, on the floor, sat her servant, custodian of her mistress' umbrella, betel box and tiny cuspidor. During her visit with Miss Cole the servant took a sira leaf from the *Niello* [beaten silver] box, spread it with a pink lime mixture, a few strands of tobacco and a section of *betel nut*, rolled it deftly and proffered it for her mistress to chew.

After her visitor had left, Miss Cole explained to me that most Siamese did not like two-story houses for fear someone might walk overhead. That accounted for the many chairs I saw up and down the long veranda. "You must be careful not to walk on the upper veranda unless you are sure there are no visitors," she warned.

That afternoon, in spite of my resolve to take a brief nap, I slept long, as if drugged, waking to the chatter in the dormitory. I longed to be lazy but I knew I mustn't miss Tea.

The tea table was in the north end of the long veranda against a background of plants and hanging baskets of ferns and orchids. Little children played games on the lawn. Some girls sat in groups on the raised walk or on the steps with books or fancy work, while others walked back and forth as far as the two landings, forbidden to go farther.

Miss Cooper brought some reading, Miss Cole did not stay long, and Berta seemed restless. I thought of the royal palace across the river. By leaning far over the railing in the corner I could see a *pagoda* – the rest was hidden by our big Pradu tree and two travelers' palms.

Afternoon tea on the verandah at Wang Lang

At intervals throughout the day the scene against the sunset the evening before had been drawing me to the landing like a magnet. But I was determined to wait until evening when I could be alone. As soon as the school bell rang and the compound cleared, I walked down to the landing and sat on the long bench overlooking the river.

Once, when I was young, I had made a wish that I might always live with a view. It was the summer of my thirteenth year while I was staying in Pacific Grove, California. I had sprained my knee and ankle jumping from a hay mow to the slippery barn floor. I spent my days in a hammock under the pines overlooking Monterey Bay. Now here was the fulfillment of my wish beyond my dreams.

A broad panorama of the royal palace-city of King Chulalongkorn spread diagonally across the river, above the floating houses and a low fringe of trees. From the temple of the Emerald Buddha near the *Premene*, to the royal landing at the bend in the river below, the fantastic skyline continued across the river to the nine prong-towers of *Wat Aroon*, Temple of Dawn.

The evening before, this majestic spectacle was silhouetted, black against a darkening red glow. Now the almost horizontal rays of a brilliant sunset bathed the whole lovely scene in a warm light. In the center of my mural-like view, the palace roof and delicate spires glittered like cut-steel. A great, shining golden *pagoda* stood among others of porcelain tiles and scintillating glass mosaic. Massed closely were many temples with the most beautiful roofs in the world – roofs rising in overlapping tiers colored blue with orange borders or green with rose, all sparkling, their multiple gables edged with gold leaf carving and every cornice and ridge tipped with gold-crested *naga*-serpents.

I was filled with a deep sense of gratitude to God for this gift of so much of the beauty my soul craved. I sensed what the peace of this time and place could mean to me for meditation and prayer, for strength of body and mind. Here I might find solace in aloneness, compensation for family and friends I missed. This view of mine could be the mystery promised by the little island *pagoda* – a key to understanding the wonderful race of people I had come to live among.

Night comes suddenly, without twilight in the tropics. As I sat on, enchanted in the warm darkness, lights from boats and houses began

River view from Wang Lang

to dance on the water. From a distance the music of a native orchestra floated, like rippling water. Nearby I heard a reed flute pick out a quaint air in five notes of the scale. Someone was playing a lively strain on a coconut-violin. The *sampan*-ferry slipped back and forth to the hospital landing above, the voices of its passengers sounded strange. Wavelets from a passing launch slapped at our embankment and set the float jerking crazily. Six bells rang out from the royal yacht in the bend below – seven o'clock and an hour to dinner. Thankful that there seemed to be fewer mosquitoes here by the river, and not quite as voracious as those during dinner the night before, I decided to remain for a while and think.

Why was I here? I couldn't get over the wonder of what had happened in my life so suddenly and effortlessly. Yet inevitable perhaps, considering that my four grandparents had braved the sea-voyage around South America in the 1850s to pioneer in California. Or that I seemed to be the only one to continue the tradition on my father's side, of a minister, a musician, and a lawyer in every generation. I had cousins in music and law but no one concerned with religion.

My mother's wedding present from her father was the home where I and three younger sisters were born in Sacramento. After finishing high school following the Spanish American War, I made my first journey alone to San Francisco to visit our friends the Van Pelts. While I was there, the largest ship ever to sail the Pacific – the brand new *S.S. Korea* arrived in San Francisco. The Van Pelts took me with them to a reception aboard and we were conducted over every part of the beautiful vessel. I imagined what it would be like to take a long voyage on it. That was on September 5th, 1902. On September 3rd, a year later, I was a passenger on that ship on my way to Siam.

In those days, to people outside church circles, a foreign Missionary was a curiosity, to some a freak. To my maternal grandfather, Daniel Sivarsey Flint, I was a traitor to family tradition. Although I was the eldest and favorite of his fourteen grandchildren, he never forgave me. My father, though hurt because he saw the making of a lawyer in me, was kind and understanding. My mother, bless her, took the same stand she took when she gave me permission to ride a certain vicious bronco against the protestations of a whole family gathering. She said, "I trust Edna." On that occasion I was on my grandfather's hops ranch south of Sacramento. I had been told not to pull hard on the reins which were old and untrustworthy. Uncle Will was watching while the horse bucked and raced with the bit in its mouth, making straight for the river. Seeing the danger, he broke some branches off a tree and stood in the road to turn it off from what would have been a fatal plunge, stopping it just in time. I was white and trembling at my close escape.

"Do you feel like trying again?" Uncle Will asked. "If not, the horse is master and you may never be able to ride it again."

"I'll try," I answered weakly. I was not sure I wanted to, but was fearful my uncle would be terribly disappointed if I didn't.

Although badly shaken, I mounted again and this time the horse behaved like a lamb and the half-mile ride to the house was serene. I was able to enjoy my ride and marvel at the change. It was a valuable lesson I learned that day.

At this point of my reveries the deep throbbing tones of the big Mandalay gong reminded me of the dinner hour, and I left the landing.

4 - The First Week

Tuesday at four, dressed in my tan lawn suit – with hat and parasol to match – I was ready to make my duty call at the American Legation. Miss Cooper joined me at the landing which was barely above water and we had to go up an incline to reach the float where Ah Bea was steadying the school boat, a glorified *sampan* with comfortable seat and back rest. Earlier in the day *Nai* Krern had been sent to order a carriage. It was waiting at the public landing on the other side of the river.

The moment we started I sat on the edge of the seat, in anticipation of seeing my "palace view" close-up, in daylight. As we burst out upon the Premene from the narrow lane between high, crenulated walls, the great North Gate of the palace city was open, showing a street lined with artistically-sculptured trees leading to the Grand Palace. The entire area sparkled with exquisite color in the sun. Again I felt the thrill of an exciting discovery.

I settled back in my seat as Miss Cooper began a lengthy explanation. "You will want to know something about our Legation family. The Honorable Hamilton King is now in his fourth presidential term and is Dean of the Diplomatic Corps. He's rather bluff, but very friendly and fun-loving, and both Siamese and Europeans like and respect him and Mrs. King also.

"Their three daughters, Helen, eighteen, Marie, seventeen and Coralee, twelve are all adored. Mrs. King will be taking them to Switzerland in a few months to attend school and live with an aunt. Then you will be the only young American woman in Bangkok!"

My thoughts momentarily strayed to absorb the full impact of her words. The only young American woman in Bangkok! What an enviable position for any young woman, I thought.

Miss Cooper continued, "The city is full of young bachelors of all the continental varieties, with the British predominating. The only American, Mr. King's secretary and part-time tutor to his daughters, is on the point of leaving. There are few diversions for men aside from their club, playing tennis and drinking, and quite a number of them appreciate the opportunity for social contact at the two American 'At Homes.' But don't get any ideas, Miss Bruner. They are all under rigid contract to remain single for a term of years as you, yourself, are mildly restricted."

The term "At Home" began to have more significance as I fantasized about meeting these eligible bachelors, even if I wasn't supposed to "get any ideas." Somehow I knew that both Miss Cole and Miss Cooper would keep watchful eyes on me.

We turned down a dirty lane toward the river, past a small, neglected temple. I don't know what I expected after I passed the imposing British Legation compound, which extended from the road to the river. Certainly not the small, crowded place with no wall or railing at the water's edge, or the one-story wooden building with legation and consulate offices on the low, dark, ground floor.

Miss Cooper led the way through a little gate in a low, white picket fence to the farthest corner, skirting lively players on two badminton courts, end to end. Mr. and Mrs. King were sitting under an immense banyan tree, surrounded by guests, to whom I was soon introduced. Two Chinese "houseboys" were serving tea and sandwiches, cake and ice cream. Helen and Marie dashed over between sets and offered to teach me the game.

It was a happy hour and I began to understand what the cordiality of that simple home meant to many in this faraway, oriental land.

On our return in the *gharry,* our way was blocked by an accident. Two *rickshas* had collided, spilling the women passengers out into the dust with their marketing – branches of betel nuts, cabbages, squash and string beans mingling with live chickens and squirming fish. The women were unperturbed as they replaced their breast scarves and tightened the twist in their *panungs* before stooping to pick up their belongings. The *ricksha* pullers, on the other hand, put up a hilarious act of screaming and swearing at each other for the benefit of the bystanders. I laughed aloud, and was surprised when Miss Cole rebuked me gently.

"I must advise you, Miss Bruner, never to laugh that way in public."

"Oh, my apologies." I quickly said. "What a hilarious act they are putting on for the bystanders. Why is it inappropriate to laugh?"

"There's an old Buddhist maxim that disapproves of showing amusement publicly, and since we are guests in this land it is seeming for us to conform," she explained.

"But of course!" I agreed. I felt a twinge of embarrassment. Thinking of my friends in the States and their spontaneity I wondered if I would always be able to keep a straight face every time a spontaneous laugh wanted to erupt. I could guess what I was going to miss most in this land. There was so much to learn!

It was good to be in the Snyder home again – minus Mrs. Harrick, their guest who had left with a group for the long river trip to the far north – and to see Robert and Grace with their infectious good humor.

Besides their principal, Reverend Eakin, leader for the day, and his wife, there were two others whom I met for the first time, Canon Greenstock of the London S.P.G., and Reverend Carrington, both elderly widowers. With one couple on furlough, another on a long six months' tour of the provinces, and one on duty at each of the schools, there were few left to represent Christianity and to share with a million or more Buddhists a different way of life.

As the Mission had no church service in the English language, this weekly meeting was especially important to the women. As long as I was in Bangkok I found myself looking forward eagerly to the days when I was free to attend. I had not been brought up in a religious atmosphere, so to follow the prevailing custom of kneeling at one's chair for the long, closing prayer was distasteful for me. I did

Siamese market woman in panung and breast scarf.

not mind, however, after I found the group all had a tolerant sense of humor. Little Walter, at my side, looked up as I looked down. He said, "My, but your eyes are green!" It was a smiling group that adjourned to the veranda for tea with a real American layer cake made by Mrs. Snyder in honor of the newcomers.

Miss Cooper liked making these rare social calls. When we started out on Thursday she visibly discarded her Wang Lang mood in an effort to be companionable. The Hays' "At Home" was the Legation's rival. Each had its coterie of "regulars." Missionaries were welcomed at both but were too busy for regular attendance.

On Friday evening Miss Cole and I attended the dinner at the Boys School, along with my friends and traveling companions Robert and Grace Franklin. The other guest was the senior member of the Mission.

"Since you're a newcomer, Miss Bruner, perhaps you'll permit me to tell you a little about the Mission's beginnings in Siam," he began.

"I would like that!" I replied eagerly.

"Well, in 1828 the Reverend Doctor Gutzlaff of the Netherlands Missionary Society and the Reverend Jacob Tomlin of the London Missionary Society sailed from Singapore to Bangkok, a distance of perhaps 1,000 miles, spending twenty terrible days at sea. Because at that time the king was hostile to Westerners, the only ones here were an English merchant, a French priest and the Portuguese consul. The consul permitted the two men to live in a shack on his property. Working night and day on the language and bible translation, wracked with fevers and dysentery, they barely survived, but were able on their return to Singapore to have missionary tracts made by the Baptists in India.

"Both men appealed for help to every known agency. In time the Congregational and Presbyterian churches responded, but a family spared from the very new Burma Mission was the first to arrive in Bangkok. Thirty missionaries were sent by the three Mission Boards in the twenty years that followed.

"At the end of that time there were but seven left. The rest had died of tuberculosis, dysentery, fevers and childbirth. One succumbed to brain fever and a wife was stricken with paralysis.

They went through a cholera epidemic that took forty thousand lives but touched no missionary or native Christian."

"What an astounding story! And how do you account for their immunity?" I asked.

"I suspect that the converts lived close to the missionaries and had the benefit of what medicines were available, and probably much prayer. I don't remember the dates, but over time the other two Missions dropped out leaving the field to the Presbyterians."

On the long drive back to Wang Lang that night, I tried to learn more about Miss Cole's early life. In answer to my questions, all she said was that she graduated from the St. Louis Missouri Normal School and Western Seminary in Oxford, Ohio, and she first came to Siam in 1878. She did not elaborate further and I did not press her. I could only try to picture conditions twenty-five years earlier, when young King Chulalongkorn began to inaugurate Western ideas. Later I learned that Miss Cole had been appointed to the Northern Mission, then in its infancy, and was transferred to Wang Lang five years later.

Saturday of my first week at Wang Lang was my initiation into the dread institution of "Duty Day" which, like the laws of the Medes and Persians, was not to be excused or evaded. It began at 5:30 a.m. with the ringing of the big bell on my dormitory veranda and ended at nine o'clock at night, after the two-hour study period, fighting mosquitoes and drowsiness. Only one thing was worse – Wednesday "Work Day," when a hundred teak beds had to be kerosened!

I rose at one of the after-midnight hours when wakened by the hospital gong, and dressed that I might not be a moment late ringing the bell. The first relay of twenty older girls was waiting when I reached the farther dormitory to precede them to the bath house. Each was in her night *sarong,* to be exchanged for the fresh one she carried after their "dipper showers."

Back in the dormitory, the girls folded their mosquito nets into the frame above, smoothed the single sheet and light, cotton blanket, then put on their *panungs,* carefully considering the color for the day. This piece of cotton or silk, a yard wide and three yards long, had to be draped smoothly over the buttocks, twisted to hold in front, the rest of the material precisely folded and drawn between their legs, tucked in at the waist and held in place by a silver belt.

It was quite a sight to see all those girls bent over double, backs toward me, absorbed in their meticulous task – twenty "behinds" looking like ostriches. A sleeveless, white camisole completed the costume for the day. Their short hair took little time to comb with some pomade to stiffen it. The final touch was the face-powdering – a few crumbs of rice powder, moistened with perfume, patted on so the powder dried in wavy streaks. This ravishing aid-to-beauty took me some time to appreciate.

A royal decree in the succeeding reign of Rama VI ruled an end to the mannish haircut for women and the wearing of the men's garment, the *panung*. The old custom, slow to die, and never given up by the older royalty and palace women, had a historical background that shows the caliber of the Siamese women.

In one of the many wars with Burma when the Siamese army was sadly depleted and the enemy nearing the city, the women begged to be permitted to go into battle, dressed like the men. Their action contributed to a victory. The women petitioned the king and were granted the privilege of continuing to wear the *panung,* the men's costume.

Sunday morning, at the usual seven o'clock breakfast I was wondering what Sunday would be like. Miss Cole, as if reading my

Wang Lang school children

thoughts, said, "Sunday is a busy day too. Sunday school is at nine and church service at ten when Mr. Eakin comes from the Boys' School. Then this afternoon" – a long pause – "I will take you to English Church down river near the dock where you landed." Miss Cole was like that – a reward for my first bewildering duty day and morning service in a strange language. It was a sacrificial act on her part, because she had a constant stream of visitors and it was an effort to take the long drive a third time within the week.

Daylight was fading when we arrived a little before six o'clock. The church, close to the river's edge and shrouded by great tamarind trees, had all doors open on three sides. At first I studied the English ladies in the choir. Then I found the Rector's Oxford diction took concentration.

After a while the sounds outside claimed my attention. I thought, I may have a lifetime of going to church, but never another first time like this. A peacock shrieked in the trees overhead and a bullfrog kept chiding the padre. A rumbling rice mill lent an undertone to the whine of a saw mill while a cicada competed with both. An anchor clanked. A tugboat chugged slowly against the tide with its heavy burden of barges. In a lull I could hear the subdued voices of the Malay *syces,* as they swished mosquitoes from their harness-jingling, stamping charges. A ship's bell on the half-hour stirred memories and a reminder that I should write my first letter home after dinner.

Silence on the long drive up through the city provided a fitting climax to my first week in Siam. As I wrote my letter in the heat of my room later that night in my nightgown, I was damp from neck to floor. I resented the loathsome, rumpled, flannel abdominal band I had been ordered to wear next to my skin, "guaranteed to prevent intestinal disturbances."

Five months later, after pouring my heart out weekly in letters home, I received a frantic letter from my mother asking why they had had no word from me since my first letter from Bangkok. I cried bitterly at the anguish my silence must have caused her. Miss Cole informed the Legation of the circumstances and Mr. King requested a Post Office investigation.

The result? A pile of my letters was discovered at the home of our local letter carrier, torn for their stamps! Fortunately the letters were recovered and sent off to my mother with the explanation.

I reached the front veranda next morning at six o'clock where Miss Cole was already waiting. *Nai* Kaao, the teacher from he government Boys' School, was walking up from the landing. After the introduction Miss Cole left us and we started my language studies, using the tea table as our classroom. With a worn, paperback primer like those used by all the children in the land, we spent the next two hours that day, and for five days a week observing sign language. I parroted the forty-four consonants and twenty-six vowels, then wrote all forty-four consonants so perfectly that he asked me to repeat them in his notebook to show his friends. I couldn't explain that I had been drawing things since I was old enough to hold a piece of chalk at a blackboard.

It was nice to have my teacher pleased, but when I failed to immediately distinguish between the different tones of a simple word such as *"kao"* [rice], his pained expression showed me how wrong I was. What I did not learn until my third year was that the Siamese language was like three different languages: one the servant, marketplace and jail language, one for the middle class, and one only for royalty. And the incredible spelling! *"Sai"*, meaning "left" spelled aloud, is actually pronounced "I saw my toe sigh" with the emphasis on the last word. I had to be so careful what inflection I gave to the simple word *"mah"* for there were five sounds possible, level, depressed, period, rising, emphatic, and I could be calling someone a dog or horse when I simply meant "come."

At the end of the lesson, I managed a gracious *"chern"* meaning "thank you," to his formal leave-taking. I waited until he reached the landing, then made a dash for the dining room and a warmed over breakfast.

While I was eating Miss Cole came in and asked, "How do you like your teacher?"

"He has a nice voice and manner and seems very much in earnest."

"Did he look at you?"

"Why, I don't believe he did. That's odd."

"Well then, that is because he is just out of the priesthood. I noticed his hair and eyebrows showed recent shaving. Monks are not supposed to look at women. While he was in the monastery, a neophyte attended him wherever he went, and kept a large, long-handled fan before his eyes."

"Teaching me ought to be good practice for breaking that habit," I replied.

After a pause, Miss Cole said. "Now, I must give you some idea of what lies ahead. Tomorrow you can start helping with the maps for the St. Louis Exposition. Each of six girls has one ready for coloring. That is where you come in. I'm sorry it has to be done on the floor of the guest room."

After a word to *Maa* Chuen about getting the room ready, she continued. "I'd like you to give piano lessons to Beatrice, an unhappy Eurasian. Her father, a high British official has returned to England and her mother, a native of Laos, is dead."

"How sad! Yes, I'll be glad to teach her."

"I want her to feel this is her home. Being the only girl to have music lessons will give her importance. Now our annual school bazaar is three days before Christmas. Every girl is making something for the sale, as they have been all year. Krern is off today getting lumber for the stage and booths. There will be a cantata – remind me to give you the music score. Berta has a pretty ball drill she has been working on and I would like you to put it to music. The sewing classes need working designs enlarged from small illustrations. You see how much we need you! This will be a banner year for Wang Lang."

And a banner year for me with so much to learn in addition to the language classes and everything else she had enumerated. I thought I enjoyed challenges, but the list of duties was getting longer and longer. Yet how could I disappoint her?

A few nights later as we were leaving the dinner table Miss Cole announced that it was time for me to think about taking my turn at housekeeping.

"Oh no, please Miss Cole," I said without thinking, "I'm not ready yet." Then, catching Miss Cooper's startled, amused, possibly approving glance, I wondered at my temerity. I justified myself in the belief that Miss Cooper enjoyed housekeeping, and I had already superseded her at the organ.

In spite of my reluctance to plunge in so quickly, it was obvious that whatever Miss Cole wanted, Miss Cole got, and one didn't question her. However, she did allow me a few more weeks grace to settle in and adapt, for which I was grateful.

Upriver view from Wang Lang

5 - A Royal Fair

I was scarcely settled in my second week at Wang Lang when Miss Cole made an announcement after breakfast. "You have come at the right time, Miss Bruner. Mr. and Mrs. King and their daughters have invited you to attend King Chulalongkorn's royal fair tomorrow night. He has decreed one each decade since 1883."

"Yes," Miss Cooper added, "and this one celebrates the thirtieth year of his reign."

Miss Cole smiled at this interruption, and seeing my questioning look, continued, "He has constructed a beautiful park with lagoon and knoll outside the city for it."

Miss Cooper again interjected, "You must wear your prettiest frock! This night is reserved for diplomats and Buddhists monks from all over Siam."

"I shall. What can I say? I'm thrilled!"

The next night we approached the bamboo fence which enclosed the park. It was studded with millions of tiny flickering lights, produced by tapers in coconut oil in glass tumblers. All the booths and pavilions were also outlined with them, and over all, like a canopy, were strung thousands of colored paper lanterns. It was enchanting.

Knowing I would be full of questions, and because neither Helen nor Marie had attended this fair before, Mr. and Mrs. King gave us a running commentary of everything we witnessed and often answered our questions before we asked. More than a guided tour, it was a history lesson.

Thousands of Buddhist priests could be seen everywhere in their saffron robes. Released from their seclusion during the rainy monsoon season, they were plainly entranced, although quiet and dignified. Each ranking priest had a tall fan, embroidered in gold and silver to denote his rank, carried by a neophyte. All the King's court was present in what was for them a rare excursion outside

43

their inner, royal palace walls. Each queen, surrounded with her treasures and glittering with jewels, held court seated on the carpeted floor in her sumptuous pavilion,

Under a thatched roof, a full Siamese orchestra played: drum, tom-tom, *flageolet* (sets of basso and alto gongs set in circular frames) and xylophones – the most interesting and beautiful instrument I'd ever heard. I could see that they were made of bamboo pieces, strung over a carved sound box, with intricate ivory inlay. Its sound evoked visions of forests and waterfalls. I felt as though I would never tire of listening to it.

Out under the stars the Royal Orchestra of *Kaans* was playing. Dressed in the ancient garb of the former Siamese kingdom of Tali in Yunnan province in south China, these Shan-Siamese musicians stood at their tall reed instruments as they played, the strains soft and haunting.

Strolling through the grounds that night, we saw the court dancers performing barefooted on the lawn, their exquisite slow-motion "Lotus" ballet. The two-score dancers held illumined lotus-shaped lamps in either hand. In the final movement alternate girls,

Siamese dancer

kneeling to let the others step to their shoulders, rose slowly to form a radiant human lotus blossom. It was breathtaking. With their chalk-white faces and fantastic long curved, silver finger tips, they were an unforgettable sight.

We moved with the crowds from one show to another, or sat on the grass to watch or listen. In one show called *Khon*, a man recited a tale from a *Ramayana* epic while the performers, who wore fantastic head-masks of *Yaks* [enemy forces] and monkeys, pantomimed the action.

On another stage a performance called the *Nohra*, taking its name from the *Nang Manora*, was taking place. Five singers told the story of the heroine accompanied by bamboo clappers. The three actors were men – one as a comic relief, one as the hero and one as a heroine. Often, I was told, they were trained in their roles for many generations. The hero's dancing and gestures exhibited all the acrobatic coordination and exquisite grace of the Russian ballet, in extremely slow motion.

The most popular and elaborate stage performance, the *Lakon*, more closely resembled an opera ballet, and was made up entirely of women, except for one – a male comic. In this one, the costumes, unchanged since ancient times, were as rich and dazzling as they were different from anything conceived by western mind. A long skirt of gold brocade, falling in heavy pleats, was held by a wide jeweled belt. A shoulder-cape of gold and jewels covered the bare shoulders and breasts reaching to the belt in front and falling to the hem of the skirt in back. A jeweled coronet, rings, bracelets, armlets and anklets, made the ensemble utterly gorgeous. The feet were always bare. Their chalk-white paste makeup, made their faces rigid and emotionless.

Mr. King explained that few Westerners ever stayed to see the whole performance, unless they knew the language and the story. The action was too deliberate for most restless foreigners. As for me, I was enthralled.

Siamese dancers

Finally, we ended our evening watching the shadow play, called the *Nang-talung,* (meaning "leather from Patalung," a city in the peninsula). It is one of the oldest forms of Thai dramatic art and is believed to have come from India originally, although it is unknown there now. Java is the only other country with a similar form. In the thirteenth century a young woman wrote her memoirs from the court of King Phra Ruang, Siam's King Arthur, in the ancient city of Sukothai. Presented by her

Nang-talung figure

father as a concubine to the king, she rose to the position of favorite through her artistic skill and cleverness. Accompanying the king to all the fetes and ceremonies, she described the many entertainments and mentioned performance of the *Nang* after the annual military review of foot-soldiers, horsemen and war elephants.

We made our way to a large group sitting on the grass. Moving closer, I could see the *rong,* or small stage was a platform built of bamboo roofed with thatch, five or six feet above the ground. The two side walls were also thatched, and a large muslin sheet covered the front. Brilliant gas lamps highlighted the sheet. Performers manipulated large, intricately carved and colored leather cutouts of the characters with thin wooden sticks to control the movement of their jointed arms, hands – even jaws – as they swooped and leaped silhouetted against the screen. The figures battled furiously to the accompaniment of an orchestra of clamoring gongs, primitive string and percussion instruments and cymbals. Throughout the performance people moved around, women nursed their babies, and food vendors plied their wares.

The stories enacted were from the *Ramayana,* the classic Hindu epic which tells the adventures of the deified hero *Rama* and his friend *Sugrieve,* and *Hanuman,* the monkey god and his retinue of monkeys. There were exciting skirmishes and mighty clashes with the enemy *Yaks,* in their efforts to recapture the abducted *Sita*, *Rama*'s wife. The kindly *Rishi* (hermit) always helped *Rama*, giving him the power to take another form in order to escape the avenging, pursuing *Yaks*; or enabling him to help a princess in distress by concealing her in a crystal ball.

The Kings said these performances could go on night after night until the early morning hours. At intervals – to give the players a rest from their cramped positions – clown figures would be shown with pertinent dialogue to keep the audience entertained. The Nang-talung was tremendously popular in the country districts, whenever there were festivals. I found it entrancing.

My sleep that night was crowded with imagery. And this was only the beginning. The following week the city of Bangkok was cleaned up and decorated with flags and lights for His Majesty's birthday. Every compound along the river's edge had some kind of illumination, and ships were strung with paper lanterns. It was the custom for the king to go out in the royal launch to view this act of homage.

Between the leaf-shape crenulations topping the palace walls were the same little glass and oil-taper lamps we had seen at the Royal Fair with their lovely, soft, flickering effect. Fluttering above them red, green and yellow pennants alternated with three-tiered paper umbrellas.

The school landing decorated for His Majesty's birthday.

The *Premene* was crowded with people and carriages and *rickshas* day and night. Scores of food stands, each lighted by the resin torches made from the gum of the yang tree, filled the grassy spaces beside the palace wall.

The masses of people were dressed in bright colors. Women, loaded with jewelry, roamed around quietly. I marveled that whenever I saw large crowds there was a total absence of noise and rowdiness. I never saw drunkenness or police in evidence.

We drove through these crowds of pleasure-seekers to the Foreign Office ball, held in Maha Chakri Palace, within the palace grounds. It was transformed with little flickering coconut oil tapers into a place of unearthly enchantment. The ballroom glittered with court uniforms and the gold-and-silver coats and spangled sashes of Siamese princes and nobles.

From our vantage point I could see King Chulalongkorn, ever gracious and smiling, walk up and down the lines of bowing, curtseying guests. He had announced that this would be his last appearance at the annual function, so it was a very special occasion.

On another night I heard an urgent call from Annie. She and *Tanying* Nart stood in the gateway to the landing.

"*Mem-ja,* please, can we come out? Tonight is *Loi Kratong* – no study till finish."

"Yes, of course." Miss Cole had told me this was a yearly festival of propitiation to the river spirit for the people's abuse of the good water, a very old rite from India. "I know this is a special occasion for you. I shall be pleased for you to show it to me. What have you there?"

"We have float carved by *Kru* Krern. See?"

Carved from a banana stalk, its silvery green seemed to glow. On it a candle, a flower, some betel nut, a copper coin and some *kanom* or sweet cake had been placed.

Maa Cham joined us then and explained, "See? On other side too. Everybody in Bangkok is on the river bank to celebrate. We make offerings to *Maa Nam*, what you call Mother Water." Her arm swept out to indicate what looked like a fairyland flotilla – tens of thousands of lighted candles bobbing on the river. Annie carefully placed the float she had been carrying into the water and, with her hands together in a prayerful *wai,* released it to join the other points of light, now more dramatically punctuating the darkness which quickly surrounded us.

"We watch it until we no longer can see it. If we can see for long time, that means very good luck!" The group of students and teachers on our landing stood in silence for some time, watching the tiny, flickering crafts until they blended together in the distance, then made their way back to their studies.

By this ancient and lovely custom each November did the people celebrate the change of season, affecting a profound transformation in their whole way of life: from six months' humid, rainy season of the southwest monsoon to the six months' dry northeast monsoon. It was a change from total absorption in rice fields, business and the seclusion of the priesthood, to a time of celebrating the rice harvest with temple fairs, feasting, courting, weddings and merit-making – a whole nation at play.

This was followed by the most important and impressive festival of the year, *Taut Kathin,* when his Majesty took gifts of new yellow robes to the monks of selected chosen temples on four successive days, setting an example for faithful Buddhists from all over the kingdom to do the same.

Miss Cole and Miss Cooper had seen the processions many times, so they arranged for *Kru* Suwan, Miss Cole's "right hand" and favorite teacher, to accompany me to see two of the four processions. I was especially pleased because she was filled with Siamese lore and had enough English to explain it with contagious enthusiasm. Her high-pitched musical voice reminded me of tinkling bells.

Tiny *Kru* Suwan with her short hair pompadour style was the perfect model of the old fashioned, palace-type Siamese lady. Babies of her day and station in life had received a novel treatment. The back of the head had to be flattened straight up from the neck by daily massage. The elbows and fingers were double-jointed by daily snapping.

As we waited at the edge of the *Premene,* opposite the north palace gate, *Kru* Suwan told me that the king went by royal

Walking in the procession.

limousine the first day of this celebration, and by state coach on the second day. In former times he had gone by elephant on the third day.

The great crowd was quietly expectant, as a steady drum beat interspersed with single drum notes heralded the approach of the procession. Then the scores of drummers, dressed in purple with fantastic hoods, came into view, followed by a waving sea of royal, tiered "umbrellas," the bearers garbed in ancient Siamese costume. Then came the army units, followed by the King's Lancers in sky-blue uniforms, and finally the King's body guard in bright scarlet coats with black-plumed white helmets.

When handsome, kindly King Chulalongkorn passed close by in his gilt *palanquin* [covered litter] borne by porters in scarlet, I tingled with the reverence that I felt in the people all around me.

As we walked back to the river haunted by a simple tune played by a piper, I asked *Kru* Suwan, "Why were the people so quiet? Their heads were bowed as the king passed."

"Well, you see, *Mem,*" she replied, " there was an old Cambodian custom that no one should look upon the king. Some of our kings followed that custom. Our king now has been to

Europe and does not want the people to be afraid, but they are slow to change."

The grand climax of the *Taut Kathin* festival, was the procession of royal barges on the river, seen only this one day each year. I was happy when *Kru* Suwan was permitted to go with me again. We drifted down river in the school boat with Ah Bea at the oar, and found a good place where we could see everything from our boat.

Royal procession celebrating
the king's birthday

I had a close-up view of King Chulalongkorn as he walked from the pavilion onto the landing stage, and entered the royal barge, the *rua pratinang*. It was one hundred and fifty feet long and eleven feet wide, *Kru* Suwan informed me. He sat on the throne in the center under a golden canopy draped with gorgeous gold and silver brocade. The throne was surrounded with the tall jeweled fans, seven-tiered umbrellas and other insignia of royalty.

At once the barge moved off down river, all crimson and gilt, its prow a high carved and gilded *naga*-head, a tassel of waxen blossoms suspended from its mouth. The tail of this sacred serpent of the Cambodians formed the high graceful stern. The sixty oarsmen were in scarlet from hood to ankle. Their gilded paddles flashed in the sunlight as they dipped rhythmically in perfect pattern and cadence. The Prince Patriarch followed in a similar barge, seated on an altar, then the Queen and Crown Prince and highest Princess, each in a gilded barge according to rank.

The Royal Barge

As this lovely sight rounded the bend beyond the Temple of Dawn I felt as if I was in another world. Wang Lang was the dream – the oriental pageant, the reality. This last decade of King Chulalongkorn's long reign was as nearly utopian as our world has seen. There was no poverty as in other lands; no one could freeze or starve because the monasteries afforded free shelter in their *salas*. There was reward for intelligent endeavor. The humblest born could earn a title of nobility. The aged were honored and cared for. Children were taught to honor priest, teacher, and parent in that order. Their heritage from ancient times was a gracious dignity and charm inherent in free people. They were at peace within and without their borders. They were friendly to the stranger and tolerant of foreigners' outlandish ways, whether Hindu, Muslim, Chinese or European.

A few years later when King Chulalongkorn had passed away and his remains were in the beautiful Amarindr Hall, I was with a group who were given an audience there by his successor son, Rama VI. Dressed in black from head to foot, we walked down the long hall and stood before the new king, while scores of Thai women sat on the floor, dressed in their native mourning white.

Leaving, we backed across the width of the great hall, stood a moment in the arched doorway of another chamber to view the magnificent jewelled urn containing the body of the late King. Then, two by two, as we had entered, we stepped backwards the long length of the hall, eyes on the young King. Fortunately, we were not wearing court trains or overly-long skirts.

6 - A Christmas Eve Excursion

I almost never heard my given name spoken, one of the absurd conventions of time and place, as were all the formalities between men and women. Possibly I felt the artificiality of the conventions more than others because I was from California, "the wild and wooly west." Once, near Christmas, I rebelled. A middle-aged couple was visiting us and as we watched the smoke of a great conflagration down in the city, I exclaimed impulsively, "How I should like to see it."

The husband replied, "Let's go!"

After watching the fire, it grew dark on the long way home and my companion became more and more quiet. I could imagine his reaction – dreadful, dreadful. What must his wife be thinking? What would people be saying? He had run off with a young lady, had behaved like a schoolboy.

However, whatever disapproval I might have earned was lost in the shuffle the next day when the whole school packed up and left for the holidays, all but the half-dozen girls who had no other home. I had to stay and was exhibited to the women who came for their daughters. I dreaded the empty days ahead. I must get away! Miss Cole gave her consent.

On the morning of Christmas Eve I started out to visit Grace and Robert Franklin, venturing out alone for the first time. As I walked down the long tunnellike road between the high palace walls and crossed the *Premene*, I found a waiting tram and took a seat in the first class section behind the motorman. It was a tiny caged-off section. As the other part began to fill up with the people of many nationalities, I found myself getting attention that the school withheld, and I began to feel free and ready for adventure.

Traveling by tram was far more interesting than by carriage, but alas it was also a daring venture. Miss Cole had agreed that I might try it, since I was young and new to the country. I hoped I might persuade my friends to try it for a day of fun.

Street venders

Fortunately they too were at loose ends and quite open to adventure. I wanted to get inside the palace wall of "my view" to see the Emerald Buddha. Robert and Grace were particularly interested in going to the Sampeng section of Bangkok. We consulted Mr. Eakin, who sent one of the Siamese teachers to get a permit to see the Buddha. He was to wait for us at the main palace gate in the late afternoon. We decided to go to Sampeng first and end up at the palace and from there I could walk home.

The *ricksha* I had taken at *Klong* Silom bridge was waiting and my "puller" was sent to get two more. It was about a mile and a half in distance – too far to walk in the middle of the day. A teacher instructed the "pullers" where they were to take us first. After that we were on our own with the few words of Siamese we had picked up in two months.

We found ourselves in one of the most fascinating sections in all Bangkok – where the Hindu section of the city began at a break in the old city wall. We were told it was like some of the alleys in Canton, China. It began with a lovely flower market on a wide bridge. We saw a profusion of jasmine garlands or leis – all sizes to fit a lady's wrist, encircle her neck or drape a buffalo's horns. With their tassels of waxen *chumpa* and *frangipani*, they were overpoweringly fragrant. Coxcomb, roses and lotus held their own among the exclusively

Small shop

tropical blossoms, of which the green, night-blooming flower was the most exotic.

From here we plunged into the miles-long dirt lane, narrow and shadowy, cast in semi-daylight by the crude awnings of burlap and matting hung over it. We were in and out of large Chinese shops with rolls and rolls of more beautiful silks than we had ever seen in the States.

At a small shop Grace and I decided to buy the long-handled, heart-shaped feather fans, replicas of the larger ones carried by neophytes who walked before priests to prevent their masters from seeing women. When we couldn't understand the price, the crowd that gathered produced a young man who knew English. After helping us make our purchase, he followed us into an apothecary's shop and explained about the medicines compounded of tiger's teeth and whiskers, turtle blood, cobra venom, and all parts of a rhinoceros, including the horn, tail and liver.

As I began to buy sugarcoated peanuts and the *glacé* fruit slices which look like cartwheels, my friends said, "Think of the hands and flies and insects that have touched them." We had been told not to eat anything that was not boiled or fried before our eyes. But I knew Miss Cole ate everything and had never been ill. I had heard her say, "What

Street vendor

you don't see, won't hurt you," and I was inclined to accept her philosophy.

The large cauldron of boiling rice was tempting. We sat down on stools at a bare table so close to the passing crowds that we were occasionally jostled. The rice was poured onto a raw egg in a deep bowl. It had bits of pork and other things, including greens and was immensely satisfying. For dessert we had banana fritters fried in coconut oil, and glutinous rice and banana steamed in banana leaves.

At one time we found ourselves out on a bridge over a busy *klong* filled with many small boats. We were glad to leave the heat and glare there, and return to the dark lanes with their intriguing smells. A crowd gathered around a stall where Siamese fighting fish were sold. Each fish was in a separate bottle. When the bottles were placed close together, the fish began to gleam with brilliant red and blue and green. We understood that when put in the same bowl the fish fought to the death. We did not want to see that. But it was interesting to see how each fish bought was placed in a lotus leaf pinned with slivers of bamboo.

The Temple of the Emerald Buddha

From Sampeng we proceeded to the temple of the Emerald Buddha. Built in 1782, it is the most interesting and elaborate of all the many thousands of temples in the land – the King's own royal chapel within the Grand Palace area. We were met at the main palace gate by the Siamese teacher, armed with a permit to get inside.

The temple was surrounded by nine *Prangs,* the Buddhist type of tower, of glazed tile, each *Prang* a different color. On one side of the magnificent Pantheon, stood statues of all the Kings; on another side, a model of Angkor Wat in Cambodia. Adjacent was the royal library of Buddhist scriptures – all the cabinet bookcases built of the finest specimens of lacquered teak, inlaid with mother-of-pearl.

The marvelous, dazzling bell-shaped Buddhist-type of tower, the gold *Stupa* could be seen close by. A covered gallery around the temple courtyard had murals of the great Hindu epic, the *Ramayana.*

The temple building was typical. The long, narrow nave, separated by pillars from the side aisles, reached the high roof with its massive beams decorated in black, gold and vermillion. It sloped inward toward the top, as did the outer colonnades that supported the roof overhang. Doors and windows, deeply recessed, also sloped inward with heavy ebony shutters and mother-of-pearl inlay, also representing episodes of the *Ramayana.*

The ridge of the temple roof was in the form of the Buddhist *Naga,* or Serpent. The four stages or levels of the temple roof were a rich blue with gold border, each edged with gold filigree and flame tips. The gables were of glass mosaic as background for the carved golden figures of *Garuda Krut*, vehicle of Vishnu, which was used as the royal coat of arms.

The outside temple walls, pillars and porticoes were of pastel tinted glass mosaic on a ground of pale gold. Inside the temple, wall frescoes, like lovely old tapestries, represented stories in the life of Gautama Buddha.

At the top of a very high altar under a gold canopy, on a carved throne overlaid with gold-leaf and inset with glass mosaic, sat the famous jade image called the Emerald Buddha – said to have diamonds, rubies, topaz, amethysts and sapphires blended into the pure gold of the hair and cape-collar. When, where, and by whom it was made is a mystery of the dim, distant past. In the first half of the fifteenth century a pagoda in Siam's northernmost city, Chiang Rai, was struck by lightning, exposing the golden image. Later, little by little, the gold leaf covering the image flaked off revealing the green jade – its true nature. The idol was moved from city to city and finally stolen and taken across the eastern border where it remained for two hundred years, until the first King of the present dynasty brought it to Bangkok.

The grand palace area in the northeast corner of this famous temple, is a walled town of more than a square mile within the walled city of Bangkok. In former days a large part of it was exclusively occupied by women. Probably every noble man of importance in the realm had presented a daughter to serve one of the queens or many concubines or scores of princesses, and she would be accompanied by an old family retainer to look after her. Few foreigners ever entered this area with its woman gatekeepers and guards, woman police and judges, and its hosts of servants. In earlier days there had been vast numbers of slaves as well, but King Chulalongkorn worked during his long reign to abolish this odious system, thus fulfilling the hopes of his boyhood English teacher, Anna Leonowens. Margaret Landon, later our neighbor in Trang, wrote her story in *Anna and the King of Siam*, the basis for the musical and movie, *The King and I*.

7 - Cutting of the Topknot

One day Miss Cole received an invitation to attend a "coming out" party in high society for one of our boarding students, Charoen, and I was chosen to go with her. The invitation came from her father, the Governor of one of the provinces. He had come to Bangkok to make the complicated arrangements for the celebration at the family home. The occasion was the Tonsure Ceremony or the "cutting of the topknot." This event must occur in the eleventh or thirteenth year of every female child. Originally it proclaimed to the world that the young girl was of marriageable age. Now, however, very few married so young in Siam.

Charoen, the Governor's daughter

Astrologers were paid to ascertain a lucky day. Money had been saved for years and some recently borrowed, and all loans called in to pay for three days of feasting and fun. It was the most important event in a woman's life, for even a wedding was much simpler, and besides, on that occasion she had to share the honor and attention with a man. Her cremation might cost more and last as long and give as much fun to others, but she was not there to enjoy it.

As the day approached I became more and more thrilled that I was privileged to attend, for, as Miss Cole informed me, very few foreigners had ever been permitted to witness this kind of occasion.

Maa Chuen had tea and toast ready for us at half-past four in the morning. *Ah* Bea, grinning at the prospect of a long day of leisure after depositing us at our destination, rowed us upriver against the tide in a fog that made our tiny lantern look ghostly. He had miscalculated the tide somewhat and we found the *klong* we were to enter an expanse of mud. There was nothing to do but watch the mist lift with the sunrise and wait for the incoming tide to fill the canal. The early morning had been cool, but when we reached our destination the heat became oppressive and we were cramped from sitting in the boat for so long.

This was the third and last day of the traditional ceremony. On the preceding nights, the compound had been filled with crowds watching jugglers and a Chinese puppet show in one corner and a *Lakon* [native dance] in another. Food and betel nut vendors were cleaning up and preparing for another day and night of good business.

Early as we were, the Governor, dressed in royal blue silk *panung* and white military coat, greeted us and at once escorted us to the dining room for breakfast. Other guests began arriving while the *klong* was navigable. Soon it would be a mud lane again until the afternoon tide. During the long interval until the ceremony was due to begin, Miss Cole talked with every one, but since no one knew English, it was a day of silence for me.

When we were ushered into the room prepared for the ceremony, seven priests in their yellow robes were seated cross-legged on a narrow platform the length of the room. They chanted prayers while holding in their hands a cord that completely encircled the house – to prevent any encroachment of evil spirits that might mar the good luck of the young girl on this special day.

After a while Charoen came in and sat on the floor without speaking or glancing at anyone while the monks kept on chanting prayers. She wore a hand woven cloth-of-gold skirt, and was bare from the waist up except for a magnificent jeweled cape collar that covered her breasts, and the heavy broad bracelets of red-gold that circled her arms to the shoulder.

Later her mother made her first appearance and placed Charoen on a low stool in the center of the room. She then began to separate the girl's topknot into three strands. From babyhood until now, that tuft of hair, about 3 inches in diameter, had never been cut, while the rest of the head had been kept shaved. The topknot had been oiled and coiled, and decorated with flowers or a jeweled pin.

At the ceremony.

Every motion throughout the whole day's proceedings was calculated, deliberate and took endless time. The droning of the priests went on continuously. First the prince-brother of the former Second King stepped forward, and with a curious pair of ancient scissors, cut one of the three strands of hair; the queen of the late Second King severed the second, and lastly a lesser wife of King Chulalongkorn's father cut the third strand. Whereupon Charoen retired to her room.

When she reappeared she was dressed in another even more gorgeous skirt and more jewels. Again she was placed in the middle of the room and a professional barber began to dry-shave the topknot circle to conform to the rest of her head, after which a soft silk roll was placed to circle the crown. The thirteen-year-old girl sat there motionless, without a twitch or quiver – I did the squirming – and the monks chanted on.

It was half-past ten. Charoen disappeared again and we were led to the dining room where a banquet was spread for the guests – rice and several kinds of curry, salads and condiments and sweets and fruit. At the same time the seven monks were being served where they sat on the platform. They were not supposed to eat after eleven o'clock. When they had finished they returned to their temple.

About one o'clock another part of the ceremony began. It was presided over by a Brahmin priest in a white silver- spangled net robe. Charoen, the young daughter of the house appeared again, dressed in a long white skirt. She was carried down to a tiny *sala* or platform built out from the stairs over the garden, and lifted on to a table. Then each guest stepped up in turn, dipped the conch shell into a jar of consecrated water and poured it on to the head of the girl. Sitting motionless, eyes downcast, Charoen could not quite control the fit of shivering from the cold bath.

For the final *wien tien* [blessing], the guests and family sat in a circle on the floor around Charoen. A lighted candle was passed from person to person, each one waving the hand three times around the flame and then toward the girl in the center, repeating a formula of good wishes.

Some time in the future the hair of the severed topknot would be carefully divided into two parts. The shorter part would be put into a small float of banana leaves and allowed to drift away on the river, carrying with it any undesirable traits of character. The longer hair would be kept until it could be taken on a pilgrimage and left at the great footprint of the Buddha at Prabat.

At the next high tide, the long ceremony over, *Ah* Bea met us at the landing and we embarked for our journey home. I had time to muse over these strange customs in my new adopted land, where school life would continue as before for 13 year-old Charoen until the next major event in her life, her wedding, probably again at a time propitiously ordained by astrologers.

Procession of priests

8 - Princess Cherchome

During my first week at Wang Lang I frequently heard of a Princess Cherchome, the only daughter of the last Second King. The Princess lived in one corner of the old palace area across the river from Wang Lang. I wondered about her and how she lived because there was no gate or sign of life in the wall we passed. All I knew was that she was Miss Cole's friend, and about her age, and that she was not allowed to leave the walls of the palace without the king's permission.

One day I was told that Princess Cherchome had received the necessary permission, and had asked Miss Cole to take me with her to see her that afternoon.

Instead of crossing to Ta Prachun as usual, *Ah* Bea ferried us to Ta Wang No, opposite the Bangkok Noi railway station, terminus of the line to Petchaburi. Here at the northwest corner of the former palace city, a servant was waiting to open a small gate within the large one, and take us to her royal mistress.

It was a lonely life the princess led with only two noble-women friends to share it and a few servants. She could not marry because there was no prince of her rank. She was taller than most Siamese and had the aristocratic bearing one would expect of a princess.

Her face was strong, and would have been beautiful but for the disfiguring black teeth, the result of years of chewing *betel-nut*. When I looked into her eyes with their mingling of humor, sadness and the eager curiosity of a child, I wanted her to like me.

While we had some *kanoms* and a curious perfumed drink, Miss Cole and the princess had much to talk about. When she learned that I had brought my camera she was delighted, and called her friend to help arrange a bench for a good light. One minute she was primly self-conscious, and the next minute laughing gaily.

After that she would occasionally send a servant to ask me to visit her. She was learning English and studying the Bible, and because I was a beginner in her language she enjoyed practicing conversation with me, which she would not do with Miss Cole. The princess was

Princess Cherchome and Miss Cole.

farther along in English, however than I was in Siamese, and our mutual attempts to understand and be understood would have been amusing to a third person.

Slowly, haltingly, she told how occasionally the king gave her permission to visit the royal palace and would then devote some time to chatting with her. She said his favorite subject was religion, always getting down to Christianity, in which he knew she was interested through her Christian friends at Wang Lang. Some years later she sponsored the first woman's club in Bangkok, after she received the king's approval. Nearly all the early members were Christians, women graduates of Wang Lang.

One afternoon Princess Cherchome took me over the silent, deserted grounds to the former palace which was later turned into a museum. All the many long paths were paved, but cracked and uneven.

It was a sultry July day in the rainy season, and as we passed through gate after gate of inner walls, the air became more and more stifling. The farther we went from the river, the less breeze there was, and damp waves of heat seemed to push up from the ground and sap all my energy, until I wondered if even seeing a king's palace was worth the effort.

The walls and buildings were gray and green with mildew and moss, and here and there plaster was broken. As we passed a temple the princess said deprecatingly, "It is not used now." It did not matter, really, that the inside was dark and forsaken, for the beautiful roof was still lovely, its colors unfaded. The gold-leaf of the carved figure of *Garuda* in the gable façade was untarnished. The solid ebony doors and windows were exquisite in their mother-of-pearl inlay, and the little bells high up under the eaves all around the great building were tinkling sweetly in the faint breeze above.

As we went up the narrow, steep steps of the throne hall, the princess tried to prepare me by saying, "It is very dirty, *Mem*." When the attendant opened the massive creaking door with a key like a cable and I stepped over the high sill, I had the shock of my life! Immediately the dim, dingy interior became alive with hundreds of screeching bats, frightened at the unusual disturbance, all darting and swooping over our heads. The carpet on the floor was almost indistinguishable from the long accumulation of their excreta. The atmosphere was oppressive. I had a vague impression of some shrouded furniture at the far end of the long room before I hurried outside for some fresh air and to get away from the bats.

The princess explained that the Crown Prince would have to spend a night here before he could become King, possibly in connection with his novitiate as a monk.

Thirty years later I visited the princess just before leaving for the States. She was no longer confined to this old palace and was tasting freedom for the first time in her seventy years. She was gay and talkative as she described one of the highlights of her new life – the cinema. She had just seen one of Cecil B. de Mille's classics, *The Cross* or *The King of Kings*.

9 - Elephant Show

On one of their visits, the Franklins talked about a trip to Ayuthia for the last day of the three-day *krung kao,* or elephant show.

"This is the first one for us," Grace announced, "because it's only every ten or twenty years that the King orders one. Would you like to go with us?"

"Sounds like quite an adventure. I'd love to! I've heard some of the teachers and older students talking about it but had no idea there would be a chance for me to go."

"Actually the hunt has been going on for many months," Robert added. "They've been rounding up wild elephants in over a hundred miles or more of jungle in the Eastern area, and this three day celebration is the culmination. I've been told that few hunts in the world are so bound up with superstition, tradition and spirit-warnings. The nature of the animals, their intelligence and sensitivity, make them extremely difficult to lure. The faintest movement, the slightest sound at the crucial moment of nearing the camouflaged stockade wedge, they say, has been enough to cause a herd to stampede and undo days and weeks of heart-breaking anxious effort."

Arrangements were made, and at

Elephants with their mahouts.

six o'clock one morning in March I met the Franklins at the little railway station on the Lampong Canal. Grace and I were dressed in our thinnest frocks – we knew it would be a long, hot day. I felt sorry for Robert, required to be dressed in his starched white drill coat with military collar. The train was crowded to capacity by the time we reached Ayuthia, the former capital of Siam.

From my study of the history, I knew that the city, built in 1545, had had a population equal to that of London at that time. After the Burmese destroyed it by fire, and the pervasive jungle took possession of its temples and palaces, it was never rebuilt. A crude village grew up near the railway station and along the river within sight of the ruins. However, it took us another hour from the train station by *sampan* to navigate the canals with their floating houses and shops moored to rise and fall with the tidal water, and to reach the elephant stockade.

Two pavilions had been built at right angles at one corner of the *kraal* [large enclosure for elephants] by the stockade. We went to the one reserved for officials and foreign guests and at once met a nobleman in the Government Service who had a son in Robert's school. This was great good luck for us. He had been educated abroad and spoke English, so was able to explain the events to us.

The other large pavilion was filled with royalty in full view for us to see. His Majesty, an amateur photographer, was already busily taking pictures. The women in his entourage were like exquisite dolls, bejeweled and dressed in colorful costumes. The lesser queens and favorites, and the princesses, were each surrounded with their special coterie of women. Some were proudly unconcerned, others plainly bored, and a few unashamedly excited by the brief freedom from their restricted harem life in the royal palace-city with its amazon guards, spies and intrigues.

My attention was drawn from watching the fascinating Court scene, to the area around the stockades, the colorfully arrayed people, accented by the monks, in robes of varying shades from dark orange to light yellow.

"There must be thousands of people here!" I exclaimed.

"I'd say closer to tens of thousands," Robert put in.

"I'm still fascinated by the variety of costumes I see."

"So am I, Edna," Grace agreed. It sounded so good to hear my name! Only when I was with the Franklins was I called by my first name.

Inside the *kraal* a hundred enormous wild elephants milled about constantly. Tame elephants, each mounted by two men with long lances, moved among the wild ones.

"Would you tell me about the tame elephants and their riders," I asked our nobleman friend.

"Those are *mahouts* [elephant trainers], *Mem*," he explained. "and the elephants they are riding are indeed tame and have been trained for many years. They are like police, and they prevent fighting and disorder among the wild elephants."

The Elephant Kraal

"Still, it must take a great deal of courage to be among so many wild elephants."

"Indeed, *Mem,* they are brave men, trained from childhood as were their fathers and grandfathers. They come from distant places, far from towns, and spend their lives with elephants in the jungles."

"What about their families? What is the effect of all this on them?"

"They will be glad to get home after the many months of hardship and danger and their wives will be glad to see them. For," he went on to explain, "binding taboos are put upon the women for the protection of the men's homes. From the day the *mahout* starts out on the long, dangerous expedition, his wife must sleep on a bare mat. She may never sit with her legs over the door sill. She may not allow wood or trash to accumulate under the house, and she is not allowed to use any cosmetics. She is solemnly pledged to observe all these conditions. Failure to do so in any single case would cause her husband to fall and be killed, and every one would know that she was to blame."

"Very clever!" Robert looked at Grace mischievously. "We American men should have something like that when we leave home."

"You'd love that, wouldn't you?"

Not quite understanding this repartee, the nobleman went on. "It is too bad, *Mem*, that you did not come the first day. All the *mahouts* burned incense at that shrine you see in the center of the *kraal.* The leader made his elephant kneel and salute the King several times. It is a great honor to be leader of the hunt. His Majesty will reward him."

My attention was drawn to the stockade itself. I could see that it was built of stout tree trunks about twenty feet high. The double gateway between the two pavilions formed what looked like a pen.

Noticing where I was looking, he continued. "That is the pen where single elephants can be captured for training when they herd them out to bathe twice each day. Only a few are chosen. All the other elephants are returned to the jungle to roam free again. See there. The double gates that make the pen are loose logs that are raised and lowered by the men standing on the framework above."

In the middle of the forenoon as the herd began to file out to a pond a few hundred yards away, the mass of spectators parted to form a wide swath for their passage. There was visible excitement as

Elephants in traiining

the largest tusker approached the gate-pen. It's keen intelligence had kept it from getting caught thus far.

There was a tense moment as it neared the gate-pen hemmed in closely by other frightened animals being driven by the tame elephants in their rear. But in a flash it had bolted ahead so close to the one in front that it could not be isolated. Again, on the return to the stockade, it was too clever to be caught alone in the trap.

When the herd was being released again in the afternoon there was intense excitement, because all knew that the capture of the giant tusker would have to be the final triumph of the hunt. As the animals were let through the gateway, a few at a time, the trained elephants and their *mahouts* were working inside. There was perfect coordination between them and the men on top of the stockade gates. The pen was cleared in time as the mammoth tusker's turn came. It could not move backwards to avoid it, being too tightly wedged in – their lances saw to that. As it was forced through the first gate into the pen, a baby elephant slipped in, unseen.

When the gate logs crashed down and the huge beast saw that it was at last a prisoner, there was an exhibition of appallingly savage rage. There was not the usual cheering and laughter from the crowd now, for with ear-piercing screams and furious trumpeting, the huge tusker stood on its hind legs and plunged with all its weight down on the innocent youngster, again and again, goring it with its powerful tusks in concentrated fury.

A hush fell over the crowd as they witnessed this brutal display. I felt as if I had been hit in the pit of my stomach. I caught Grace's eyes. I knew she had tried not to see it.

Gradually the caged beast became calmer and seemed to accept its fate. Heavy rope cables were attached to all four feet and its training began then and there along side the royal pavilion, with four tame elephants and their *mahouts* leading the prisoner back and forth, to the great delight now of the court and the crowds. The show had culminated as they had all hoped.

We did not stay to see the other elephants released, or to witness any other of the festivities surrounding the *kraal*, knowing it would last well into the night, as was customary. What I had seen would remain in my memory a long, long, time.

Working elephants

10 - Challenges and Adjustments

The Men in My Life

1904 was Leap Year. Early in January I received a letter from my sister. She was worried that I might do something impulsive, and at the same time, she showed considerable interest in a subject that I seem to have neglected writing about – *Men!*

So I wrote to reassure her:

> "Dear Leslie,
>
> Since I detected curiosity behind your concern for me in your latest letter, I am hastening to enlighten you. Don't worry! I find life so very exciting and the business of getting used to the tropical way of living so absorbing that there is not room for thought about changing my status of "Single Lady"– yet!
>
> Besides, I contracted not to marry for at least two years, and I'm told most of the young men out here have a much longer time than that to wait before "settling down."
>
> Perhaps I should describe what the situation is here. Many women my age might envy me, being the only unattached American woman in this huge metropolis. In the first place, there is only one unmarried American man in Bangkok right now and he is very stuffy, not my cup of tea.
>
> There is another American, working up north in the teak forests. He's good-looking, and a bit on the wild side, with a dragon of a mother. After meeting him at the legation, an English friend, whose husband is director of the Royal Mint, planned a dinner party at the Oriental Hotel where we danced afterwards. A few days later we were having a wonderful time together at a party when his mother felt an attack of "Nerves" coming on. He not only had to leave with her immediately, but was kept in constant attendance upon her until they returned north. So that was the end of that.
>
> I did meet a gorgeous young Dane not long ago and have been running into him in unexpected places. And there is a titled Belgian with whom I occasionally play badminton at the

American Legation. He is so handsome that I can scarcely keep my eye on the shuttlecock for watching him.

Somehow, I have a feeling that no matter how strong the pull, it would be impossible for me to marry another nationality. I am too American, and of the Western-ranch-and-wide-open-spaces type.

Of the scores of unmarried British men whom I see at church and festivals, most of them drink heavily, which I would not know how to cope with. And many of them keep native women to run their establishments, more or less on the quiet.

I am not quite sure what I should do were I to marry one of them and learn afterwards that a native woman had preceded me and been bought off, but who was probably hovering around, nevertheless, perhaps with some fair-skinned children! I would not have the nobility of character of a German woman I know about, who faced that situation by bringing the whole family into her household and lovingly devoting herself to them.

There actually are three Britishers who come to Wang Lang fairly regularly. We call them the Three Musketeers as they "batch" together. One seems to prefer American society and I am reasonably sure to see him at the legation Teas. Another, Manning, is very faithful in coming here to the school three days a week for an hour of badminton at six o'clock in the morning. All three call quite regularly on our "At Home" day, but the last of the trio does not like women and is either coerced, or comes to keep an eagle eye on the other two.

Manning has a fine voice and likes to sing the sentimental songs you send, especially that one *Deep down in my heart I have a feeling for you*. One beautiful moonlight night Ralston, the other one, was inspired to suggest a boat ride. The setting was perfect for romance. Then suddenly *Ah* Bea, our boatman, started showing off by dipping his oar in such a fashion that little fishes splashed out of the water into the boat and on our feet! If that wasn't enough, Miss Cooper who was chaperoning us kept up a running conversation that demanded a certain amount of attention.

So you see, Leslie, life has it's lighter moments, but there is almost a conspiracy to assure my life doesn't become complicated by a love interest.

Love, Edna

I came to understand why it was said that there were far more Western women who had spent a brief sojourn in the Orient and then returned home, never to return to Siam than the number who actually stayed. Living in a totally different culture in a stilted social atmosphere, adjusting to monsoons, stifling heat, and unusual foods posed incredible challenges. Add to that dressmaking problems while trying to keep within a year or two of western Fashion was more than many could endure!

Pests

My first three years in the Orient, without the modern conveniences which came gradually over the years, were training me for a life of cataclysmic accidents and changes, all to be appropriately dramatized and stored in memory. I knew I must learn willingly or leave, for no matter how much I might like the people and thrill to the pageantry, unless I could take the hardships with a little faith, hope and fun, I could not belong. Just living on the surface was an unthinkable, pitiable compromise.

Although Bangkok at the turn of the century was a Shangri-La of peace and plenty, with the splendors of court life in its very midst, royalty going in and out unprotected and unselfconscious, it was also totally devoid of the sordid and distressing poverty common in most of the other great cities of the world. Nevertheless the physical conditions of the tropical climate could be downright cruel to the Westerner.

It seemed as if all Nature joined in a conspiracy to torment every newcomer to the tropics, forcing him to make certain adjustments if he contemplated remaining any length of time, healthy and happy.

There was the perpetual dampness during the rainy season and the fight against mildew. There was the continual battle against mosquitoes necessitating sleeping always under netting, often tempted, when prickly-heat rash was at its worst, to forego the net for the fresher air and freedom outside and risk the danger of malaria.

At night when lamps were lit there was little peace at the piano, desk or dinner table, reading or visiting, because of the constant distraction from mosquitoes and other winged creatures that occasionally descended in clouds. The lovely looking silver moth left a burning rash where the dust of its wings touched the skin.

A small house lizard called a *chinchook*, darting back and forth across the ceilings, could fall and leave a wriggling tail on the floor. Larger spotted lizards called *tookaas* had a quaint way of popping out from behind picture frames or cupboards when least expected, emitting their outrageous call, usually a number of times in succession, very loud at the start, and each successive one softer - **TOOK**-Kaa ...TOOK-kaaa... took-kaaaa. We always counted the number of times, because seven of them meant good luck.

Loathsome big cockroaches scurried about after dark and there was no known method of control or extermination except by personal hand-to-hand combat. No Buddhist servant would take the life of even so filthy a scavenger, because of the remotest possibility that it might have been an ancestor in some former incarnation.

Then, too, there was always and forever the ant pest. One variety invaded wardrobes and dresser drawers, another kind marched in close formation endlessly, forming a wide black track across the floor or wall. The swift little sugar ants were a perpetual nuisance and could be kept out of food only by screened safes standing in bowls of water.

One day while taking my turn at housekeeping I unwittingly stood over a fire ants' nest which was under the pantry floor. In a matter of seconds the ants were traveling rapidly up my legs, and as if at a signal, all began stinging at once. As if pursued by demons, I tore upstairs, ripping off my clothes as I ran to the sanctuary of my room to get the bottle of ammonia always kept handy for such emergencies.

"Elephant" scorpions haunted dark places, villainous three-to-six inch centipedes curled up under potted plants, and snakes were as liable as not to investigate a sheltered spot inside, to be discovered at the most unexpected times.

After dinner one evening while we were still talking at the table, I felt something drop in my lap. Instinctively I jumped up, holding out my skirt. A four-inch centipede was clinging to the silk. Our dinner guest, an Englishman with the railway construction, was holding our Siamese cat on his lap. He quickly used the cat's paw to brush the centipede off.

Another night I went to a church meeting without the lantern I usually carried, and was first to leave after the service. No sooner had I reached the road than there was a noise of shouting and beating the ground among those who had followed me out. A cobra was coiled in the middle of the path, just where I had been walking.

Ladies at an Annual Meeting in Bangkok.
Edna is in middle of back row, wearing a hat.

Annual Meeting

Each year in September, the missionaries came to Bangkok for Annual Meeting. Although they were allowed a vote and had equal privileges, for all the women the event had a deeper significance. This can be fully appreciated by women who have lived in an isolated place among people of different race, language and customs.

Books were few, pastimes fewer, and of pleasures – as we think of the term – there were none, no social occasions beyond this annual formal function, no entertaining, except when there were guests from out of town. Oftentimes there would be but a single family member in attendance, while the other was absent on furlough, for fifteen months.

At the Annual Meeting a woman could enjoy the change of food and see new faces and clothes. Being in Bangkok meant shopping with an infinite variety of materials to choose from. It meant an opportunity to have a year's supply of canvas shoes made to order at the Chinese cobblers'. To some, Bangkok meant spending hours in a dentist's chair in the days before novocaine, and to others a physical checkup and consultations. Perhaps the biggest treat was attending a church service in the English language.

I had looked forward with keen anticipation to meeting the rest of the Mission and joining in the round of dinners and parties. Fate decreed otherwise.

On the very evening they began reaching Bangkok, a large group arrived from the States on their way to the northern *Laos* Mission. Every home overflowed with guests and the air was filled with sociability. And I had *dengue fever*. After three days of headache, a curious red rash broke out. My eyes, ears, nose and mouth swelled beyond belief. Every joint was stiff and agonizingly painful, which is why it is also – and appropriately – called "breakbone fever." It is probably the only disease that is considered funny – it is always laughed at – while the patient wishes he could die and be done with it.

I had a language examination coming up to complete my first year's study. I decided that will power and exercise might help me to keep that date, so I staggered downstairs at intervals all day to play finger exercises on the piano, and – it worked! I was able somehow to get through it.

Then two days later I had an accident that sent me to bed again. On my way down through the city to attend meetings, I had stopped off at the East Asiatic Company's pier to see the group leaving for the north. The American Minister and Mr. Brown of the British American Tobacco Company were waiting in front of the Oriental Hotel next to the pier.

Three *Laos* boats were lying side by side, separated by a foot or two of water, as the river current moved them back and forth.

Laos Boat

These strange craft were about fifty feet long, exceedingly narrow and low in the water. They had a small forward deck, not more than ten feet in length. The higher rear deck had an improvised cabin built up over it, about eight feet square. Between the two was about twenty feet of storage space with a rounded bamboo top. Running along the outside of this middle section, was a plank used by the boatmen when poling in shallow water. We jumped from the landing flat to a barge; from the barge to the middle *Laos* boat, and then across to the third, where several others of our party were already seated on the floor, swapping stories.

To return, we left one by one. I was walking slowly along the plank, leaning sightly inward, touching my fingertips to the low bamboo roof, when, just as I was maneuvering around to the deck, someone jumped across, assuming I was safe – a second too soon! The boat lurched violently, and threw me off balance. I wrenched my weak knee as I fell into the water up to my neck. Providentially I grasped the oar-stake before I lost consciousness, and I was rescued. The river at this point was deep enough for oceangoing vessels, and was swift and treacherous as well.

Mr. Brown got blankets from the Oriental Hotel next door, and Mr. King sent for the legation boat to take me upriver to Wang Lang, after Dr. Crooks and Dr. Walker set my twisted knee. The Bangkok Times noted the accident with the heading "Who saved Miss Bruner's Life?"

River boat on Menam

Lonely days followed when I watched river life from the upstairs veranda. Once a floating house took advantage of a strong up-tide to change to a new mooring – moving-day for a pretty little teakwood home with carving and three quaint gables. The family continued living as usual while moving. The children enjoyed the attention they were attracting. The youngest stood naked on the front platform, having his bath by pouring water over his head from a palm-bark bucket, dipped into the river. I wondered if they would keep going till the tide turned and then drift back to the site they had chosen on the way up.

Aches and Pains

Bangkok had only two doctors, both in government service and no hospital or nursing facilities for "foreigners." What with the long distances, slow transport, and the uncertainty of messages getting through, one had to bear aches and pains as well as one could. On one occasion I had a painful ear abscess and sent word for Dr. Hays to come. Finally on the third day I was taken down to his office in the British Dispensary to have it lanced, and learned that my message had never been delivered! On another occasion I had a fever after a night of delirium and was taken in to see Dr. Hays. Forgetting to ask if I had ever taken quinine, he prescribed eighty grains in two days – what he might have prescribed for a tough old sailor. The result of the treatment was more uncomfortable than the unchecked fever. For months afterward I was constantly drenched with perspiration, and had to change my clothing many times a day.

During that time I experienced a "jumping toothache" and was obsessed that I had but a few months to live. Fortunately I made it through the school's Annual Bazaar and then was able to recuperate for ten days in the lovely home of some friends.

Exotic Foods

I used to wonder if I would ever again see a lowly carrot, cabbage, cauliflower or celery. Did the monotonous diet and scarcity of vegetables lead to tooth decay? In the eighteen months I had been in Siam, I averaged a filling a month – without the benefit of novocaine. Blaming the diet made me feel guilty of treason, for didn't we have the delicious curries, and the chicken *pilau* dish, made with rice cooked in chicken broth with raisins, smothered with ground peanuts?

Whether or not the Snyder children were right when they remarked I would stay a long time because I ate the curry that first day, I observed that those who preferred it to European-type foods seemed to settle down and adapt themselves to living in the tropics more readily. For me, the variety of flavors of curry dishes made the meat dishes I had been accustomed to at home seem uninteresting and boring. I could eat curries day in and day out and never tire of them.

As the seasons changed, so did the varieties of fruit, and I had to admit that the tropical fruits almost compensated for the apples, peaches, pears and berries I'd been used to. There were many varieties of banana, that could be boiled, baked, fried or preserved as apples are used elsewhere. Green, unripe mangoes made a sauce that was better than traditional apple sauce; and in my estimation, ripe mangoes were more delicious than the finest peach. There were also papayas, pineapples, small green-skinned oranges, persimmons, and guavas. Other fruits were totally new to me: *pumelos, mangosteens, jack fruit, custard apples, luknot,* and *durien.*

The *durien* is like no other fruit on earth, with its murderous spikes and obnoxious odor. I had heard it said, that it often divided families as if perpetrated by the devil, for one either loved it or loathed it. While its short season lasted, *durien* could be more important than the weather as a topic of conversation, in accents of rapture or disgust depending on the point of view of the speakers.

One morning Dr. Hays stopped at Wang Lang after his regular visit to the Naval Academy. He had just purchased a fine large *durien* from a passing sampan and was seeking a place where he might eat it in peace, since Mrs. Hays would not permit the fruit on their compound. The doctor walked straight into the dining room, with his *durien* dangling from a heavy cord, and asked in a professional manner: "Have you learned to eat *durien* yet?"

"No," I replied.

"Well, you are going to now, do you hear?"

"Yes," I answered meekly, wondering if he was likely to use force.

Chuen took the fruit to the kitchen to be opened with a hatchet, returning with a plateful of the creamy pulp, napkins, plates and forks.

"Sit down and eat!" he ordered. "You must eat until you like it. I won't let you off! Hold your nose if you must." With that he pounced upon his plateful with a grunt of satisfaction.

Obediently I complied, taking the first tentative bite, feeling repelled by the wave of its unfamiliar, nauseous odor which seemed to smack me in the face. How could I possibly get another bite down, I wondered.

"Eat!" he ordered again, leaving me no time to even think. The second bite was almost as bad as the first. There was something about the texture, too, which revolted me. I forced another forkful down.

"That's right. Keep eating!" With his eagle eye on me, ready to pounce if I so much as hesitated, I forced myself to keep eating as many sections of the fruit as the doctor dictated.

With each bite there was an undeniable urge to take another, and another. Dr. Hays nodded his approval and continued to eat his share with obvious relish.

By the time I finished the last mouthful he was beaming. "Good girl!" he said. "You're one of us now! You see, there's no other way you could have done it!"

11 - Stella

I heard how many foreigners who came to Siam suffered from illness or homesickness or disillusionment too great for adaptation. I was very fortunate because that was not part of my experience. The first season I was in Bangkok, the total population was around eighty thousand. There were comparatively few foreigners [not Asians], and only five of us were unmarried women between 20 and 25 years of age. I was the only American.

One was the daughter of the Russian ambassador. There were three English girls: one was connected with a British firm who had no social life with her compatriots because she was "in trade." To her Wang Lang was a friendly refuge until she decided to break her contract and return to her homeland. Another was a governess, and then there was Stella.

Stella had been living with her uncle in a quiet English village when she met and married *Nai* Liem, the young secretary to the Siam legation in London. He died a year later. Soon after, she received a letter from his older brother living in Bangkok. He offered her the hospitality of his home and passage money for the voyage, and urged her to leave as soon as convenient. Stella accepted gratefully.

She knew nothing whatever about her husband's family or of life in the Orient. On her arrival at her brother-in-law's home, she learned he was a nobleman, and as was the custom of all men of wealth or rank, he had a number of wives. She could neither speak nor understand the language, and the fair-haired, pretty, young widow found herself in an intolerable situation.

She found her way to the British consulate, and was directed to Wang Lang as a temporary haven. Miss Cole found her a position as a governess to the two daughters of a prince where she had a delightful cottage to herself and was happily independent. When I came on the scene and met Stella she was being swept off her feet by the audacious wooing of a handsome and fascinating young Siamese nobleman. Poor

Miss Cole, realizing the sorrow ahead for the girl if she married him, was in a state of agitation, almost holding her breath. She maneuvered to have me included in some of their excursions, but to no avail.

Stella did not understand the oriental culture, and her longing for companionship and security made her blind to any warnings, and she paid dearly by marrying the nobleman.

Her first child died suddenly after a convulsion, and there was little one could do to comfort her. They lived in an out-of-the-way district, difficult to reach, and we knew that her husband, although seldom at home, did not care to have her friends visit her.

It was not that he neglected her deliberately, but that he was utterly unable to resist the pull back to his former associates and manner of living. Her first husband had been able to accommodate himself to her British environment, but she could never hope to meet the demands of her Siamese husband in his surroundings.

The following year, after the birth of boy and girl twins, Stella had a long illness and was moved to the English nursing home for care. Stella died there.

The Queen mother had asked to keep the twins as her wards. Occasionally, when crossing the parade ground by the palace walls, I would see a Siamese nurse on an outing with two fair-skinned little children, exquisite as dolls.

12 - Four Siamese Girls

Each year in Bangkok there was a King's scholarship examination. The boys who were successful were sent to England to be prepared for Government posts. The four girls who graduated from our Sixth Standard [English plan] at the end of my first year in Bangkok, made history by taking that highest test. Miss Cole's determination to win that privilege – never before granted to women – had met with opposition, naturally. The gratifying result vindicated her faith. All four passed successfully, and three of them, who were Christians, became teachers at Wang Lang.

Kim Chuang, one of the famous four who took the King's Scholarship Examination, was a second generation Christian. Her father was a Chinese teacher. She earned her way through school by extra service to the staff. Because of her home training and long contact with Americans, she taught at Wang Lang after graduation, and in time rose to the position of Head Teacher. She later had charge of the language school for new Americans, helped edit a magazine for Siamese, and became a leader in the formation of the National Christian Church. She never married.

Suwan [Siamese for "gold"], another of the famous four, also became a teacher at Wang Lang. A typical girl of the nobility, she was presented to a princess by her family in infancy, and lived in the royal palace precincts for many years. She was petite and vivacious. She liked to tell me about life in the palace city where night was day and late afternoon was the time to wake and dress and go visiting. She told of the city of women, carefully guarded, where no man might enter. Police women kept order and women judges meted out punishments. The queen was served food in state by a long, long line of her favorite attendants, who sat on the floor the whole length of the pavilion, passing the many dishes from hand to hand up to where Her Majesty sat alone on the floor of a raised dais.

Women lived only to make themselves beautiful and desirable, caring only to hear some new gossip or find some new interest. It was a world where the latest fad became a passion. Fortunes were won and lost in its pursuit, such as in the collecting of orchids or other exotic plants. Ladies in the palace did exquisite embroidery work in pure gold and silver thread that never tarnishes – on slippers and cushions and fans.

I taught the older girls at Wang Lang how to weave bead belts and chains. Suwan had the school carpenter copy my loom and then introduced the fad into the palace where it had a momentary vogue.

Tong Dee [good gold] was the prettiest girl in the school according to our western standards, with her large starry eyes, her vivid, flashing smile, shy yet whimsical. However, by Siamese notions of beauty, she was not pretty at all. Tong Dee was generous and impulsive. She sent to her home for some ripe cocoa pods from the tree in their garden, and we spent one Wednesday morning drying them in the oven and pounding them to a paste with mortar and pestle, then left the finishing process to the cook [to make hot chocolate]. It was delicious.

Her father, a wealthy Chinese from Canton, was farsighted. Recognizing that Siamese officials would want educated wives in the future, he was providing a few out of his own family. They would bring high prices, and the money paid by the bridegroom would become the bride's dowry. He was an ardent supporter of our school, came frequently with gifts of jewelry and fruit, and made a fuss over Tong Dee and her younger sisters. Their mother was Siamese, of course, because Chinese women were not allowed to leave their country in those days.

The thousands of immigrants who poured into Siam every year were too poor to support families, even if they could have brought them with them. They did the lowliest, hardest work and practiced the utmost economy, looking toward the day when they might be merchants, contractors, mill-owners, men of substance and respect. Siamese women as wives were distinct assets in reaching their goals. They were industrious and ambitious. Their children were brought up in the custom of the country – Siamese in all respects, and eligible for positions of rank and honor.

These Chinese were the bulwark of the commercial world of the Orient. Although the Siamese were of the same stock as the Chinese originally – even the older of the two peoples – they have mixed with other races and cultures in this area to such an extent that there is a vast difference in their ideology and religious philosophies. The Chinese think in terms of family and business – the Siamese in terms of ease and prestige. The feudal custom of presenting sons and daughters as wards of royalty and nobility still held during my early years in Siam, but it died out after King Chulalongkorn's death.

Jarun was perhaps the brightest girl in her studies. She was capable in all areas, and spoke English exceptionally well. Her mother was *Mon*, one of the original tribes in this land before the Brahmin Davidians came from India. Jarun's father was a retired government official of the lesser rank of nobility. Her home life was not very happy because her mother had been discarded for a younger wife. As long as she was a pupil in school, her father refused his permission for her to become a Christian. Like Kim Chuang and Suwan, Jarun began to teach at Wang Lang after finishing her studies. Then her father removed his objection. When I went to Petchaburi to superintend the school there, Jarun volunteered to go with me.

One day, while still a pupil, Jarun invited me to visit her home. We went downriver some distance in the school boat and then turned into one of the canals that dent the west side of the great city. It was bordered by trees that met overhead in places, a refreshing retreat after the heat and glare on the river. The houses along the canal were almost concealed in greenery. Almost every Siamese home had its own tamarind, mango, pomelo, and orange trees. In addition, many other kinds of fruit trees, sugar cane, banana clumps, papayas and pineapples, coconut palms and bamboo are found.

Along the way, typical teak houses with thatched roof and pointed gables, were built up high off the ground. The ladder in front led to a veranda, kitchen and open livingroom, beyond which was the sacred inner sleeping room.

Jarun's home was a more imposing place of brick and plaster, built in the foreign manner, but now showing signs of age and neglect. She had probably sent word on ahead, because her father met us fully dressed in a *panung*, although men at ease in their own houses often wear *sarongs*.

Chinese tea and biscuits and fruit were set on a tea table by a maid, and then Jarun acted as interpreter for us both. I marvelled that this gentleman of the old school had seen the value of a modern education. Had there been an older brother she might not have been so fortunate.

The respect that Siamese children showed their parents always impressed me. And Jarun that day, on arriving and leaving, got on her knees and gave the national greeting – palms together, thumbs against the chin, fingertips level with the eyes. In addition she offered the extra respect due to rank and age by bowing her head at the same time.

Twenty years after their graduation I was visiting in Bangkok and the four "girls" planned a get-together with a few others. They brought a feast of rice and curry, salad and condiments, fruit and *kanoms* to the house where I was staying and we sat *pap-piep* on mats on the floor around the spread tablecloth very much as they had celebrated my first birthday at Wang Lang.

I heard that Princess Nart [see pp 25, 48] had died quite young, and that Annie's marriage to a titled government official, after a two-year courtship and some misgivings, ended unhappily after a few months. His former common-law wife planted herself in their home. Annie then went to Singapore for nurse's training. After volunteering to a call for help in a cholera epidemic, she met and married an Englishman.

One former student had married a prince, several were wives of titled government officials, and nearly all had children attending the new Wattana Witiya Academy [roughly translated, "the spreading of knowledge"], the successor to Wang Lang school. Over the years it outgrew its quarters and moved to a large site in the northern section of Bangkok with its new name.

13 - Berta

Ever since my arrival at Wang Lang and my first introduction to Berta, I had been baffled by her behavior toward me. Because we were so close in age, I had hoped I might win her friendship over time, and that she would call me by my first name. When I suggested it, she had said Miss Cole would never allow that.

Instead of the companionship I wished for, her antagonism had only increased since that dinner on the evening of my arrival at Wang Lang. At first I thought she might have resented my status as an appointed missionary, but why should she resent my being at Wang Lang, when she had a favored status as Miss Cole's protege and was an assistant teacher of the youngest children?

She always seemed to be sullen around me. When I attempted to make friendly overtures by inviting her to accompany me sight-seeing, on walks in the evening or to any special events, she declined with a martyred air. Yet she was popular with the older girls and always seemed to be attended by a group of them. Around them she was carefree and gay.

I made allowances for her diffidence after Miss Cole told me about Berta's background. Her parents, a German couple, had both died in Bangkok, leaving two little girls. A Scottish lady adopted the younger, fairer of the two and took the child to her parents in Scotland to raise.

Miss Cole had taken Berta as her ward, had been sending her to school in India, and planned to take her to the States for college when she turned eighteen.

During my third week I finally admitted to myself that something was wrong, either with me or with the school. For not only were a hundred girls aloof and unsmiling but I was being deliberately ignored by the older girls.

The *how, when, where, why* and *what* began to absorb my free moments – became my last thought at night and first on waking. Several times, when I was unable to keep the girls' attention in class, I found that if I gazed dreamily, unconcerned, into the distance or interestedly out upon the river, this intrigued them into respectful attention, at least temporarily. They did not like being ignored!

I felt the strain of watching my every word, look and act. Sometimes, alone on the landing in the dark, I did some soul-searching. Was I too young, too "foreign?" Yet I had felt at home while driving up through the city on my first day – felt as if I had lived here in a former life!

I loved the school, the girls and my work. I vowed I would let nothing spoil my happiness in being here. Pride forbade that I should speak of it to anyone. I could only wonder if Miss Cole and Miss Cooper were aware of the situation and how long it would last.

That Berta was in some way party to the school attitude seemed evident one day during the rehearsal of her ball drill. She had trained sixteen older girls, each with a small rubber ball, to stand in a square and bounce them rhythmically back and forth in patterns. For the piano accompaniment Miss Cole had requested that I use parts of the operetta *Robin Hood* that I knew by heart.

On the first trial with music, what had been a perfect performance before, became a scramble. Berta had a tantrum and complained. But when Miss Cole came to watch the drill, such was the girls' habit of loyalty to her that there was not a single mistake and no further trouble. After this the girls made a great show of their devotion for a while and it was good to see Berta laughing happily.

One little incident was both puzzling and comforting. I tried desperately to understand. At the organ one day, I happened to catch the eye of a lovely girl from the royal palace in a wistful, half-smiling, adoring look that instantly froze into a frown, caught off-guard. Often when I felt sad or troubled by the mystery of the school attitude I would ponder that girl's expression for some slight comfort.

Gradually four girls aligned themselves on my side and were promptly and completely ostracized. Such a strangely assorted group: Muen, the orphan from birth, who did my room work and always seemed near-bursting with importance, or a secret! Little Princess Nart, the vividly beautiful child who had looked penetratingly into my eyes the first morning at breakfast. Annie, the merry, bumptious Eurasian girl who, like Muen, had no other home. *Maa* Cham who had passed the King's scholarship examination and would stay on as a teacher next term. She spoke English fairly well and told me happily that her father with a lesser title of nobility – had at last given his consent for her to become a Christian. Although *Maa* Cham could have explained the school's conspiracy of rejection, she never revealed the cause, nor did she complain of what she suffered because of her friendliness to me. These four showed their sympathy in little ways. On my desk I would find some exotic, tropic flower, such as a lotus or a Siamese rose – so different from ours in the West – or perhaps a handful of heavenly-scented jasmine buds on my pillow. (*Maa* Cham left her world of Bangkok to go with me to a lonely up-country station, Petchaburi, raised a large family and remained my devoted friend.)

Life at Wang Lang became hectic about the middle of March. Miss Cole was going on leave as soon as school closed, taking Berta with her to attend college in the States. All the hectic week before their departure, I witnessed a demonstration of the devotion that Miss Cole had inspired in a host of friends. Christian and non-Christian, men and women in all strata of life, and school patrons of several generations, all came bringing gifts according to Siamese custom, principally eggs, fruit and sweets of every kind.

I felt desolate at the thought of a year without Miss Cole. How I would miss her – her gaiety and her humor as she recounted day by day incidents at meals. She had us laughing at her tale of Krern's alibis when she had been mildly scolding him. Mildly, because it was almost impossible for her to be stern and was never necessary. I never heard her voice raised.

How I would miss her advice on shopping expeditions such as the time I wanted to buy a beautiful green and gold *panung* to make a dress. She informed me that a *panung* could only be used for the lower part of the body and was not suitable for a dress. I was grateful for the times she took me with her when making calls at the home of some high titled official or to the palace of some prince who had a daughter in school.

And all the time I wondered what Wang Lang would be like without her. I would miss her most at meal time when she was rarely silent and always stimulating. If she was ever tired, no one heard her admit it. Tired in spirit occasionally, she might be self-reproachful in a bantering way, talk less, or give voice to a mood of disillusionment, as once, when she demanded of no one in particular, "What *is* Faith?" At times she bubbled over with mischievous humor, and when there was agreeable company she sparkled.

Her wit could take a sardonic turn on occasion commenting on missionaries or Mission matters. She might treat them lightly with wit, but not with outright criticism. And never would she criticize a Siamese or Eurasian friend whose faults and failures she defended like a guardian angel. It was said that Miss Cole was "as famous for her wisdom as Solomon." All sorts of people came to her for advice, sympathy or assistance and to each she gave herself as if it were the most important matter in the world and she had nothing else to do. Her integrity, in which trust could be placed and confidence never betrayed, was the secret of her very special place in the hearts of all who knew her.

I wondered, too, how Berta would fare in a strange land where everything was different. Would she be able to adjust? Would she find friendships in her new life?

The morning after Miss Cole and Berta left, when I went down to breakfast, and throughout the day as I went about my duties meeting the teachers, the older girls, the servants, I was bowled over by the different atmosphere. Everyone was smiling and effusive. My relief after the strain I'd been under while Berta was there was enormous. It was like the sensation I had when I was enveloped in a blinding, crackling flash of light while pulling a silk slip over my head in the dark during a rainstorm on the California desert.

Wondering about the different atmosphere at Wang Lang, I went upstairs after breakfast to go over my wardrobe. Muen, the girl who did my room work, was prolonging her duties unnecessarily instead of leaving at once when she saw that I intended to remain. This was a sign that she wanted to talk – meaning a lot of questions in stilted English that got nowhere, were sometimes embarrassing, and always to be avoided if possible.

Miss Cole had assigned Muen to me with the remark that she was the most difficult pupil in the school. She then explained that the part-Malay child was left with her when she was an infant and had never known any other home or family, thus enlisting my sympathy.

Far from being difficult, however, Muen was only too obsequious to suit my Western upbringing. While not understanding all the implications, I had followed Miss Cole's instruction to discourage any intimacy or show of devotion. Muen had learned to be unobtrusive, as a caged wildcat might be said to be. Actually she was biding her time until fate would give her a chance to perform some act of devotion, and she was clever enough to know how far she could go.

Her attachment to me had improved her position in the school family and given her importance. She could enter the *Mem's* room and handle her personal belongings, and even Princess Nart sought her out to learn all my secrets. Muen knew she was supposed to leave the room when I entered, but she went on dusting my photographs in a deliberate way. I decided to ignore it and sat at my desk to study. Then came the sly question.

"Is *Mem* glad Miss Berta gone?"

"I don't know why I should be glad," I answered.

"Does *Mem* like Miss Berta?"

"I think she did not like me," I evaded.

"Miss Berta hate *Mem*." This was the bomb she had been longing to explode for months, yet it was dropped in a caressing tone.

After a moment I responded, "Surely you do not mean that?"

"*Ching, ching* (it is true), *Mem*!"

"Why do you tell me now?" I asked.

Teasingly she replied, "*Mem* not know why all the girls afraid to be friendly? I tell *Mem*."

I busied myself in the wardrobe considering the shock of her words and did not answer. Not fooled by my pretended indifference, Muen judged that the time had come to be bold. Leaning in the doorway, and without attempting to dramatize the story particularly, Muen spoke softly, as she might relate a pleasant dream:

"I tell *Mem*. In here, one night before *Mem* come, Miss Berta light candle, send for girls, one by one, swear not tell, swear not have anything to do with *Mem,* must make *Mem* unhappy and go away, promise love Miss Berta. Miss Berta make hard, angry face. Girls frightened."

So that was the reason I was ostracized, the cause of my anguish. Muen now had her triumph. I was looking at her, thoroughly interested. While I tried to grasp the full significance of what she had revealed, there was one question I had to ask. "Did Miss Cole know about this?"

Blandly but convincingly she replied, "Miss Cole know everything!"

I think I must have expected her answer for it was not too upsetting. My reaction was that now nothing mattered, the nightmare was over.

I sat down at my desk and smiled acknowledgment of my debt to her as I said, "Thank you for telling me. I did not know why the girls were unfriendly, and I am grateful that you were my friend when the others were not."

I ignored the fact that although she had been left out of the conspiracy and not taken the oath, still she had been afraid to tell me until after Berta had left the country.

I hoped that she would be satisfied and leave me alone, but Muen seemed to think something was lacking, for she asked quickly and confidently, "*Mem* hate Miss Berta and angry at girls?"

"No indeed," I replied. "I am sorry it happened but I do not blame the girls."

She seemed unable to comprehend, hesitating with some inward struggle for just a moment before deciding further discussion was futile and left the room.

I knew that Muen would now be the center of attention with the girls as she embellished her tale of devotion to the *Mem.* I, on the other hand, had a solitary struggle trying to digest this devastating trait of personal loyalty that had such a hold on the Siamese people.

14 - Vacation at Sriracha

Life in Bangkok at the turn of the century was a bit on the grim side for most of the foreigners in Siam and it was not possible to run away for a weekend for a change of scene. There was not a mountain or a sizable hill in any direction. The whole central plain was a vast rice region, under water much of the year, and without a single road reaching out from the city for even a few miles. Travel by river or canal was interesting if one had unlimited time. However, north a short distance by rail was Ayuthia, Siam's former capital, filled with fascinating ruins. But nowhere outside Bangkok was there such a thing as a hotel. Foreigners camped in the *salas* of temple grounds. Officialdom could stay at government buildings. The king had a palace, Bang-pa-in, near Ayuthia whenever the court desired to get away from the life of Bangkok.

Before 1893 King Chulalongkorn had a palace under construction on the island of Koh-Sichang in the gulf, but it was never finished because of an infamous event. It seems that the French Colonial

The King's summer palace

government at Saigon ordered a gunboat to Bangkok in defiance of a treaty between France and Siam, claiming that an officer had been shot by Siamese soldiers on the border. When the Siamese fired at the gunboat, French cannon answered and seventeen Siamese men were killed. For the one French soldier who died, the French demanded a terrible indemnity. The Siamese also had to surrender Cambodia and the Angkor ruins, previously a part of Siam.

Siamese people did not need vacations. They had the whole six months of the dry season to enjoy one festival after another if they wanted pleasure and they understood the art of relaxation without leaving their homes.

Sriracha is on the east coast of the Gulf of Siam across from Koh-Sichang. An enterprising Siamese nobleman had started a vacation resort there for Europeans who desired a change from Bangkok. As a financial investment it was a disappointment, mainly because of the transportation problem. As he became more involved in a lumber company working in the Sriracha forests, he lost interest in the project, with the result that the place was shockingly neglected and rundown.

A genial Britisher, retired from government service, had settled here with his wife and had a lovely garden of roses and English flowers seldom seen in the tropics. They were popular with all members of the foreign colony who could manage to get down there. Transportation was practically impossible without "pull" from someone high in the government, but Miss Cole had always been accommodated. The year after Miss Cole & Berta left, she had requested passage as usual for the school family with Miss Cooper acting in her absence.

The first of April saw a queer-looking crowd step off a small government boat onto the pier at Sriracha-by-the-sea, after a sleepless night on the open deck. Miss Cooper was taking the school family for a vacation. There was *Maa* Ouam, the fat school cook and *Nai* Krern, her carpenter-husband who would have to forage for firewood, carry water, do heavy work and empty the W.C. buckets daily, unless he hired some Chinese to do it with his bonus. Their young daughter, Mien, was along. Also two new pupil teachers, *Maa* Cham and *Maa* Teardt, and four Eurasian girls who had no homes – Lily, Minnie,

Annie, Milly – and myself. There were baskets and boxes of cooking utensils and crockery, lamps and floor mats, eleven bedding rolls each with a mosquito net inside, each mattress with its sleek black oilcloth facing. Trunks and tin traveling boxes of all sizes contained clothing, bed and table linen, books and personal needs for a month.

Our house was a huge, whitewashed, barn-like shell, foursquare, with four bedrooms opening off the long living room. Miss Cooper and I had the two corner rooms facing the sea and each new teacher had two girls with her, all sleeping on the floor as they would have done in their own home.

I had an ancient iron bedstead with wide-spaced steel strips instead of springs. The soft mattress was continually making pockets in the spaces. We each had a faded rattan table and chair, long ago discarded from somebody's veranda – you could always tell that weather-beaten look. The living room had a teak table and some rickety bent-wood chairs. We covered a packing case with a sarong and placed it between the two front windows as a table for the kerosene lamp and a few books.

The bedroom partitions only reached about a third of the distance to the high roof, there being no ceiling. Above our heads was a vast region of dark thatch and bamboo poles, the abode of rats, lizards, *tookkaas* and bats. If there were snakes, centipedes and scorpions, they did not come down to bother us. The *tookkaas* were very noisy, shrieking at intervals day and night. The rats carried off our stockings and handkerchiefs, the bats had me ducking, unconsciously, whenever they came abroad at night, swooping for insects.

The un-planed wall boards once had a coat of whitewash which was now yellowed and sloughed off at the slightest jar. On long, hot afternoons, lying on the bed, I noted the changing designs where the wash continually flaked off and powdered the floor.

We had an improvised kitchen on the ground floor under our living room, with its *ong* for water and charcoal *anglo* for cooking. This was most unorthodox, for it was the custom in Siam to have the kitchen and servants' quarters entirely separate from the dwelling. Living over charcoal fumes was not healthy even though the windows were always open.

Soon after sunrise we ran down to the beach for a swim. Breakfast immediately afterwards was a hot drink and Huntley and Palmer biscuits, with rice and curry at ten o'clock and tea at four.

During the day I did some studying of the language in preparation for the second quarter's examination, perhaps some writing or sewing.

The hour from five until six, when the sun was sinking behind the hills of Koh-Sichang across from us, was the loveliest part of the day. We always spent it in the sea. We might take a walk before dark, but after dinner what with the uncomfortable chairs and the lamplight swallowed by the cavernous roof above, we went to bed early.

Sea bathing was restricted to a very small area because of the sharp "oyster" rocks. Several of us got scratches or cuts which were slow in healing. Farther out, of course, there was always the danger of sharks and crocodiles. Our chief amusement was riding astride banana stalks which are buoyant enough to float the weight of several persons. Sometimes, when we could get several banana stalks, we had a race, paddling with our hands.

One evening I was wishing I knew how to float. Just then Judge Wilkinson, an Englishman visiting in one of the rooms above the water, called down from his window, "Do you want to float?"

"Yes," I answered, "You must be a mind reader."

He leaned his elbows on the sill and said, "Well, then, it is quite simple. Stretch your arms out and throw yourself back as you would on a bed and don't mind if your ears are under water."

I did, and floating was just as simple as the telling.

Sometimes on dark nights we walked on the little bridge to watch fish and eels making lightning streaks in the water. When we bathed in the warm sea at night, every motion in the water was like striking a match in the dark. Our bathing dresses would be aglow and studded with tiny phosphorescent creatures like spangles, even when removed in the bathroom afterwards.

The girls had their hearts set on going to some hot springs and when Miss Cooper refused to go, they concentrated on me. Knowing that the sun was my poison, they promised to hire a buffalo cart – the only vehicle in the region. Had I even seen one of the native farm carts close-up, nothing in the world could have persuaded me to consent, for they are built to carry the long sheaves of rice. The floor was about a foot wide and the rack sides sloped outward. The wheels must have been at least six feet high. The only alternative to sitting or standing on the narrow bottom of the springless, jolting contraption, was plodding through the burning sand. I had padded the crown of my pith helmet with cool banana leaves for extra protection from the sun, and had a two-thickness umbrella besides.

There was the merest cart track through sand all the way to the village Bary Phra and beyond to the springs. The boiling water dribbled lazily from mounds of yellowing earth built up around each spring. There wasn't a green thing about, and the heat was intense. Although I survived, never did four walls seem more welcome than our crude house when we got home that evening.

One morning a native sailboat brought some visitors from the island of Koh-Sichang, and after a cup of tea, they asked me to join them on a sail up the coast to Anghin. The wind died, the sea was like glass. The sun beat down as we rolled in a ground swell. That evening I suggested cutting straight across to the island instead of going down the coast, as we had come, which they had dreaded. There was a stiff wind and we made good time. Even so, it was after dark when I left them at Koh-Sichang. Standing in the bow, wet with warm spray, I sang with the pure joy of my adventure as I sailed at racing speed back to Sriracha alone, except for the silent old fisherman at the stern.

Miss Cooper had written for permission to return to Bangkok at the end of April when the little government boat would be making its biweekly trip down the coast with mail and supplies. On the day it was due everything was packed and ready to be carried to the end of the pier. Someone shouted that the boat was in sight. The cook's husband ran to the village to call *coolies* to help with the stuff. While the girls scurried about, we watched the boat slow down, deliver a mail bag to the waiting sampan – and glide away.

Then I saw a new side of Miss Cooper. Down on her knees, leaning out the low window, she waved her hand and blew a kiss to the disappearing boat. But she was serious enough when she stood up to face us.

She was needed at the school as principal in Miss Cole's absence. Miss Galt, who was being loaned to Wang Lang from the boy's school, had been alone there all month. The monsoon was due to change and jeopardize sea travel in small boats.

Miss Cooper called the family together, told us to unpack as little as possible and to spend every spare moment inquiring in the market, and searching along the beaches, for fishing boats to take us to Koh-Sichang where ships and lighters stopped on their way to Bangkok. I was to go first.

Three days later while we were eating dinner, Mien rushed in breathlessly, knelt down beside Miss Cooper, said "*Mem-ja*, there is a fishing boat, a very small one. It is going to Koh-Sichang. Shall I tell the man to wait?"

Miss Cooper asked me, "Are you willing?"

"Yes, indeed!"

Then to Mien, "Tell the owner we will come along soon." Immediately we set about carrying our things downstairs in the dark, over to the edge of the market place and then down the long pier to its end where the little boat was tied up.

It was about ten o'clock when Miss Cooper said good-bye and left me to get four girls safely to Bangkok. There was just enough room under the low rounded roof for the girls to lie down close together. After all the rush, a breathless calm kept us there most of the night.

I sat out on the tiny deck and watched a grand electrical display. Vivid sheets of lighting in a complete semicircle to the south and west, flashing incessantly, was the advance skirmishing of the approaching monsoon. It lit up the jagged mountains of Koh-Sichang and turned the dark glassy sea into a radiant mirror. With each illumination I saw marvelous things and awesome, unearthly shapes revealed in the massive cloud banks, piled up in battle array along the horizon, flaming a brief fraction of a second, constantly changing.

Our boat was a round-bottomed *rua pet,* about fifteen feet long, covered over in the middle for shelter from sun and rain. The owner, a wiry old grandfather, curled up in the bow. His grandson sat in the stern and sang, improvising words from old tunes, using only five notes on the scale, repeating the refrain endlessly in a high-pitched nasal falsetto. Suddenly I heard the lad quaver, "rot'n *farang.*" I was a *farang*, and two of the girls with me were wearing foreign dress.

What did he mean? I asked the teacher, *Maa* Cham, who had joined me, what the boy was singing about – "I heard him say 'rotten *farang*'."

She laughed. "He doesn't know a word of English, *Mem*. He is just a country village boy and never saw any foreigners before. He is telling the story of the trip and how happy he is to have this exciting thing happen to him."

We reached the customs landing at Koh-Sichang about daybreak, where Miss Cole's friend took us to his small bungalow for the day and promised to make all the arrangements for our passage on a lighter in the late afternoon.

All day the heat had been singularly oppressive. One felt that nature was hushed and expectant, scarcely breathing as it waited for the promised rain. A few hours in the lighter brought us to the bar, where we spent the night. Shortly after anchoring, the monsoon "broke." I was glad to let the girls stay in the small cabin which one of the ship's officers had vacated for our party.

I tried to relax in a deck chair wherever I could find shelter from the rain. The prelude of the night before had been on a grand scale, but compared to this night of terrifying tropical war of the elements, it was somewhat like comparing Bach with Wagner.

Wang Lang students going on a picnic by boats.

15 - Leaving Wang Lang

It was widely accepted by everyone in foreign service in the Orient that the third year was the most difficult for a non-Oriental to tolerate. Six months leave was the rule after one had put in three years in government service, the legations or foreign firms. The Presbyterian Board of Foreign Missions granted a year's furlough after six years of service to its missionaries.

I had heard that a British official in India, while advising a newcomer how to cope after striking a native in anger, confessed that in his first hot season he had felt like committing murder. He had given himself up to despair in his second hot season, and only begun to feel again like an Englishman after his third hot season. He added, "People begin by losing their patience, then their sanity – only the exceptions recover both, having learned to use them."

My third hot season was a devastating experience. I had planned to stay at the school through the vacation, but Robert and Grace invited me to share a cottage with them and two other couples, each with

Playing in the waves at Sriracha

babies, at the beach at Sriracha where I had vacationed before with our school girls.

From beginning to end the days were a succession of woes. The moment we crossed the bar, the little tub of a boat began to toss about like a cork, and every one in the party was immobilized on the deck. As seasickness has never been a problem for me, my spirits rose proportionately with the violence of the boat's motion. This necessitated my taking on the role of nurse for the babies as well as their parents.

Some time after midnight, anchored offshore, mosquitoes found us easy prey for torment, and little fire ants discovered our lunch baskets and stung anyone in their path. Without the slightest breeze for relief, there was little sleep for any of us as we tossed through the long night, stretched out on deck, until we could land at daybreak.

Soon after getting settled in Sriracha we found out that our Chinese cook, engaged for the month, was an opium addict and could not be depended upon. We women were forced to take turns by the week, to prepare all the meals in a kitchen about fifty feet from the house, going back and forth in the fierce April sun. The village well was very low. All water had to be boiled and we had to exercise great economy in its use.

One of the babies cried, it seemed, almost constantly. Sometimes at night I would take the child from its mother's or father's arms and soothe it to sleep, because their distress of mind made them ineffectual. I preferred walking the floor with the child to listening helplessly as it wailed, hour after hour.

Halfway through the month Mr. West had to return to Bangkok, and Robert incurred an injury that compelled him to use a crutch in order to get about. A very rough sea on the day we were to leave Sriracha climaxed our unhappy vacation. With Robert virtually helpless and the two women beginning to feel ill at the very sight of the high waves, I had to receive the babies from a Siamese sailor while balancing myself in the rocking craft at the pier and deliver them safely in the same manner at the steps of the anchored ship. The two mothers looked on terrified as their infants were seemingly being tossed in midair.

I had lost much sleep during the month, and ten pounds I could not afford to lose. Moreover I was disillusioned about cooks, babies and vacations. The cumulative effect of the heat and the strain and the immediate resumption of school brought on a nervous breakdown and I was a useless creature. Miss Cole was noncommittal about my illness, having made it very clear many times that illness was not to be tolerated. It could only mean one thing – return to the States. Fortunately the Mission doctor in Rajburi, Dr. Wachter, persuaded Miss Cole that I should recuperate in his family's home for a month, knowing Wang Lang's hectic atmosphere would not be conducive to my recovery.

Day after day in the quiet of my room in their lovely home I faced the question: Is this the end for me in Siam? Am I mistaken in my feeling of identification with the people of this land, that here lies my destiny? My soul, my whole being, cried out against giving up. I picked up my Bible and turned at random to the story about the woman who touched the hem of Jesus' robe and was healed.

Then as suddenly as three years before in California, when a lightning conviction had made me volunteer for foreign mission service, so now something happened. All the terrible tenseness and fear and sadness vanished, bringing the assurance that I could have all the strength I needed, by the simple act of claiming health from the Source of Life itself. In a few moments my entire outlook was changed and I was eager to return to Wang Lang.

The Wachters were astonished when I announced my decision. I learned later that in a letter she wrote to a friend that evening, Mrs. Wachter wrote: "We don't understand what has happened, but Miss Bruner is suddenly quite well and is preparing to return to Bangkok."

So I returned to Wang Lang, freed from the pall that had enveloped me – body, mind, and spirit – like a heavy blanket. It was August, the height of the rainy season. Wang Lang was home and the school was friendly. There was nothing to indicate that I would not continue on indefinitely. I was looking forward to the social contacts of Mission Meeting.

A few days prior to the Annual Meeting in September, I passed my third-year language examination making me a full-fledged member of the Mission. Then in the course of one day's deliberations my world was again turned upside down.

Dr. and Mrs. McDaniel had come from lonely Petchaburi to make a desperate appeal to the Mission, and to me personally, to join them. The two other families who had been their associates had gone on furlough and on their return would be transferred to another station.

They were alone now. Mrs. McDaniel, a trained nurse, helped in the one-man, rundown hospital which had no native nurses. She herself had one small child and was expecting another. The school needed someone in charge or would have to be closed.

The Mission listened, sympathetic but helpless. Leaving Wang Lang for any reason other than health or marriage was inconceivable. It had never happened before. Wang Lang had taken from other stations, but never given.

Because I had been specifically appointed to Wang Lang by the Board, the Mission would not arbitrarily transfer me or ask me to make the change. I felt a "pull" while the doctor was speaking, and the idea appealed to me more and more as I thought about it while the Mission was taking care of other business. Within a few hours I knew that I wanted to go, and announced my decision. The Mission declared a recess to give me time to make sure I knew what I was doing before putting it to a vote.

Miss Cole must have received advance notice, for she had absented herself from the meeting. I found her lying on a couch in the next room where she obviously could have heard the whole proceedings through the thin walls.

"What do you think of this, Miss Cole?" I asked. "Am I doing the right thing?"

Her reply was characteristic of her pride and her honesty. "You must follow your own intuition and guidance."

"But how do you look at it?"

"Please, Miss Bruner," she said, turning her face away. "I have such a headache. I'd rather not discuss it now."

On reconvening, the Mission voted my transfer. Miss Cole, in the next room, wept.

I was to leave Wang Lang on the 25th of October, three years from the night of my arrival. I went about my duties with mixed feelings, in a sort of daze.

One morning about the middle of the month I awoke feeling different, wholly alive, eager! Overnight the monsoon had changed. The festive northeast, dry-season monsoon had come down gradually from Alaskan regions to send the exhausted, southwest rain monsoon back to its base in the African region, there to gather its allies of thunder and lightning for the countermarch and challenge six months later.

I breathed deeply and stretched my arms, smiling in anticipation. I decided I must begin at once to make some new clothes with the muslin I had, by the fitted pattern Mrs. Hays had made for me.

A few days later I was irresistibly drawn to the landing to watch the long, low counterpoint of the King's royal barge on its first, practice trip upriver in preparation for *Taut Kathin*. Nearing the school on its return, the sixty paddlers always gave us a good show, chanting *"hey-lo, sar-ra-par, hey-lo, hey-la, sar-ra-par, hey-lo."* They dipped their paddles and held them aloft to the rhythm of the chant in spectacular precision.

I sighed in regret that I might never again see Bangkok's festivities.

On my last evening at Wang Lang, feeling a bit sad, I went out to the landing. "My View" was illuminated by the last rays of the setting sun. How I would miss this sight. When I could see it no more, some misgivings crept to the surface of my consciousness. What had made me take on a responsibility without training and preparation? My usefulness at Wang Lang was in the extracurricular activities with older girls. How had I dared take on a school, however small and primitive – a *boy's* school, of all things? I, who never had a brother or any experience with boys. What would I do alone in the evenings? Would I settle down, an old maid school teacher?

The very idea made me smile and notice what was happening. The darkness was lifted by that strange red glow, the peculiar phenomenon of the tropics known as "afterglow". The sky, river, my view – all nature was illumined by an unearthly radiance.

In a feeling of uplift I stretched my arms toward the sky. This was my farewell to Wang Lang.

16 - Journey to Petchaburi

I left Wang Lang for my new life in Petchaburi as quietly as I had come three years earlier, leaving from the rear gate in the compound wall at noon, instead of the arched entrance on the river at night. Bea and Krern had taken my luggage to the railway station at the mouth of the Bangkok Noi canal by boat, and I walked up the ancient, bricked path with *Maa* Chuen carrying the small packages.

I was trying hard not to feel too keenly the import of the formal good-byes from Miss Cole and the teachers, when running footsteps caught up with us. It was Annie with Muen, asking breathlessly, "*Mem-ja*, may we go with you? Miss Cole say we can return with *Maa* Chuen." Touched more than I cared to admit, I agreed. Then I listened happily as they chattered all the way, saying all the nice, comforting things one likes to hear and wants to believe, when leaving a loved place for the new and unknown. There were tears in their eyes later as the train pulled out.

It was a relief to find I had the small four-seat second class compartment to myself. In fact there was no one in the adjoining first class compartment, so I would have the whole coach to myself for nearly five hours. I relaxed, undisturbed by curious eyes. At last the khaki-uniformed official gave three pulls on the clapper of a large bell hung above the graveled platform. The engine responded with a faint, high-pitched whistle, as incongruous as the plaintive bleat of a huge water buffalo. As the train began to move quietly westward from Bangkok, my thoughts returned to the events immediately preceding my departure.

Throughout luncheon on that day Miss Cole took charge of conversation in her usual manner. *Maa* Puang had a tummy ache and was given some rhubarb and soda. Several girls had been guilty of eating *kanoms* in the dormitory again and would have to be punished. Someone *must* keep an eye on the food-sellers at the kitchen landing. *Maa* Chalaam had coughed a good deal during the night. *Maa* Tong

Dee's father had come to see her about the disappearance of a brooch from his daughter's box. The date for the government examination had been set. She wished there were some other way besides the long boat trip for the girls taking the examination to go, day after day. Being the only girls among several hundred boys taking the examination was an ordeal for them, and she always marveled at their complete self-possession and perfect behavior.

Then looking at the clock, Miss Cole said, "It is about time for you to go to the train. The teachers all have their classes shortly. *Maa Chuen* will go with you. I will say goodbye now." She rose abruptly and left the room, scarcely looking at me.

While Miss Cole had been speaking, I realized the enormity of my offense from her point of view. Although stunned by her apparent coldness and indifference, I had a feeling that she must have steeled herself to deliver this rebuff. I thought I detected a slight falter in her voice and glance, possibly at my look of dismay, as if she did not enjoy the role she had set for herself.

All the preceding days – since I had accepted the offer to teach at Petchaburi – I was wrapped up in my preparations and saw almost nothing of Miss Cole except at meal times when conversation was always impersonal. I might have wondered at the apparent lack of interest in the coming change, especially on the part of the other members of our household, but I had been too absorbed in my own plans to wonder whether they understood and sympathized, or whether they might possibly resent the imposition of the added duties which one less person on the staff would entail.

In accepting the new venture, I felt I was filling a greater need than at my position at Wang Lang. Also, quite possibly there was a greater opportunity for advancement, although I was not conscious of thinking that far ahead. However, having made the decision, it just was not conceivable that I should question it afterwards. I could only throw into it all my energy and enthusiasm– selfish though it might seem – regardless of hurt feelings or criticism.

Now I suddenly saw myself in the eyes of all Wang Lang as the betrayer of Miss Cole's hopes and plans. I remembered someone told me that she had boasted that at last she had someone young enough to train – she had been disappointed in so many new assistants.

And here I was deserting her at the busiest time of the year, when, having completed my three years' preparation in the language, I should be giving my full time to the school.

I had given Miss Cole the loyalty and affection that her personality commanded from all her Siamese associates. I had gladly attempted everything she asked of me – even calisthenics and kindergarten – and did not feel hurt when she told me bluntly that the latter was a failure.

I never expected commendation. I had been sent there by a Board who knew as little about my potentialities as I did myself. They all knew I had no special training. I knew that I could do anything I determined to do, given the opportunity and time to study it out. A little confidence and encouragement would have gone far to bind me to her plans. If she had deliberately set herself to leave all personal feeling out of my training, it was conceivable that she might now regret having been too Spartan in her method.

Now there was no longer an opportunity to talk things over. One thought consoled me, however. Miss Cole was incapable of holding a grudge. I could be sure, judging from what I knew of her, she would at once begin making bigger and better plans.

Bringing myself back to the present, I noticed that we were passing through the fruit gardens that supplied the metropolis with an overabundance of fruit. Towering coconut and *areca* [betel nut] palms lent their shade to mango, guava, *custard apple*, *pumelo* and green-skinned oranges. Here were grown the finest *duriens*, the football-size fruit with heavy spikes and the odor of rotten eggs. Hugging the ground everywhere were pineapples and banana clumps. This entire area between the two canals and the river was a network of small *klongs* and ditches by which fruit-laden *sampans* carried the produce to markets throughout the city.

The pleasant shade of the fruit gardens ended abruptly and we were suddenly in the midst of a sea of green rice fields, dotted with islands of taller and darker green which were village units where a dozen or more families clustered together for safety and assistance. When I saw a sail gliding along in the near distance I was startled for a moment, until I remembered that this was the land of waterways, not highways.

One cannot love Siam without feeling the significance of rice in the lives of the people. From the earliest mention of a Tai tribe in central China, their home more than four thousand years ago, rice has been the very life and sustenance of the Thai people to this very day. Rice is personalized as *Maa Prasop*, a mother who brings life to the world.

The grain in these fields through which I was passing was already beginning to "head" and soon, when the kernels were "in milk", the people would honor her, the Spirit of Rice, as they would a pregnant woman, and enjoin her to take nourishment to produce an abundant harvest. Every owner would soon be building a tiny, temporary shrine in a corner of his rice field, and there spread some fruit and an article of woman's jewelry. He would dress in new or clean clothes with a scarf draped diagonally over one shoulder and caught under the other arm. He would light an uneven number of candles or *joss* sticks (uneven, because only to living priests may an even number be used). Then he would kneel and beseech *Maa Prasop* to accept his offering.

A Siamese farmer does not till his land, plant, reap, thresh or sell his rice on *Wan Phra*, the Buddhist sabbath. Children are taught to revere the five spirits: Mother *Torani* [Earth], Mother *Prasop* [Rice], *Pla Plerng* [Fire], *Pla Plai* [Wind], and *Nam* [Water] as good and kind to mankind. They are warned never to use their names in swearing.

Rice fields.

The train stopped at tiny, bare stations, all alike, built on oblongs of land filled in and raised above the rice fields to be level with the railroad embankment. Adjoining each station was a neat, well-constructed building for the family of the station master, and oftentimes there was no other sign of life around. The railroad was comparatively new, and not enough time had passed for villages to spring up around these outposts.

The first small town touched by the railway was Prapatome, now called Nakon Pathom, where a gigantic, gold-tiled *stupa* [spire], the largest in Siam, was built to enclose two other earlier monuments of different types. They are all that remain of a once great and thriving community. Here, more than 2,000 years ago was a kingdom renowned as far as the Mediterranean, and mentioned by Ptolemy as Syama Rastra, Samarade. Being on a river and close to the Gulf of Siam, the great city traded with many ports of the known world until the Gulf receded and the river became unnavigable. Now all that remains are interesting ruins, concealed in scrub jungle. However, once a year it comes alive with a pilgrimage.

Beyond Prapatome the character of the land changed. There were fewer rice-growing sections and frequent wooded stretches until we reached Rajburi, the most important town in west central Siam. Approached by a splendid steel bridge

Blessing the rice crop

over the second largest river in the country, the railway station was larger and more imposing, in keeping with the size of the town. At this time Rajburi was an army cantonment and military training center, as well as being the seat of the High Commissioner over the governors of several provinces. This is the region of the "River Kwai" and the infamous "Railroad of Death" of World War II, forty years in the future.

Because the station was some distance from the town, there was little of interest to see except the food vendors. Women sold several kinds of bananas, and *kanoms* of glutinous rice and banana steamed in banana leaves. I bought some for my lunch, and looked longingly at a basket of young green coconuts. On school picnics at Wang Lang I had learned to appreciate the sweet, cool, coconut drink, the world's safest, surely.

Seeing my look, the woman held one up and I nodded. Quickly and deftly she made five short incisions at the stem end of the fruit with a heavy blade, making a lid that could be lifted, and handed it to me through the window. Lifting the lid, I drank all the liquid without benefit of a cup, with only a little trickling down my neck. I longed for a spoon to scoop out the soft, satiny coconut but I could find none, and regretfully had to discard it.

Some distance beyond Rajburi, rounding an indentation of the Gulf of Siam, the train took a southerly direction, paralleling the mountain range which separates Siam from Burma and extends from China on the north to the Malayan border and on down the peninsula almost to Singapore. When the scene changed again, I impressed pictures upon my memory as though I might never pass this way again. Occasionally in Bangkok I saw fields beyond the edge of the city where one could look far off into the distance. Now the open spaces gave me a feeling of exhilaration, heightened by a sense of having escaped from the confinement of four walls of an institution.

Here – in contrast to the friendliness of the rice fields, planted and tended, with men and animals threading their way along the dikes – was an expanse of marsh, apparently empty of beasts and human beings, except at the smaller, bleaker railway stations themselves.

These, I knew, must reach out to villages on higher land near the base of the mountains, not visible from the train.

Almost at once the feeling of stimulation vanished, and something like sadness subdued my spirit. The emptiness of the land, the approach of evening, the unknown awaiting me combined to affect me as never before. Those dark, brooding mountains! How often in Bangkok I had longed for a real hill to relieve the monotony of the flat plain. But this great, unexplored range of unbroken, tropical jungle, with its deep midnight blue shadows cast a spell over me. I felt alone.

I was not constituted to know what is meant by homesickness. When told how others suffered, I was unable to comprehend. I was acquainted with loneliness, though. At Wang Lang I had taken that feeling out to the river landing where it subsided into the pure joy of dedication, after reassuring myself that I was where a kind destiny had put me, and was guided and protected, and could ask no greater boon.

But this was different. I told myself that there was not a soul to care what happened to me. Out of sight was out of mind. I had no preparation for the new life I was going to and had been given no instructions. I could sink, drift or swim – it was up to me. The impersonal mission, generous, hopeful, but scarcely helpful, might have a paternal interest in its youngest member, but it was very vague in its guidance.

An uneasiness crept into my thoughts. Would I now, far from social life, lose interest in clothes and pretty things? Would I relax self-discipline and my goal of self-improvement? Would I cease my search for Truth which I had vowed to pursue on seeing the inconsistencies in the lives of Christians and religious teachers? Would I *ever* in such an out of the way place find the man I was to marry?

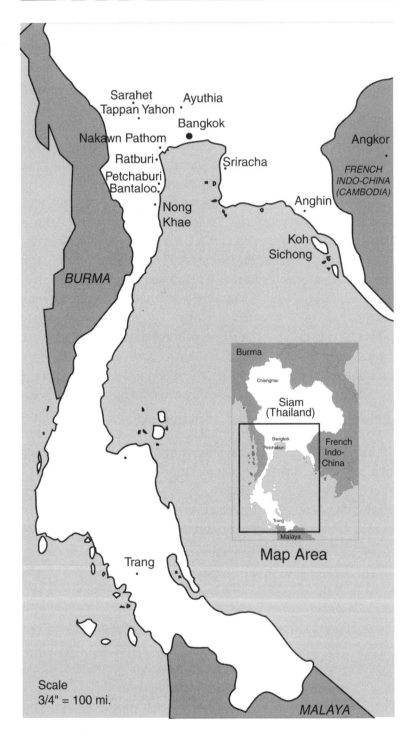

Sarahet
Tappan Yahon
Ayuthia
Bangkok
Nakawn Pathom
Ratburi
Sriracha
Petchaburi
Bantaloo
Anghin
Nong Khae
Angkor
FRENCH INDO-CHINA (CAMBODIA)
Koh Sichong
BURMA

Burma
Chiengmai
Siam (Thailand)
Bangkok
Petchaburi
French Indo-China
Trang
Malaya
Map Area

Trang

Scale
3/4" = 100 mi.

MALAYA

17 - Arrival at Petchaburi

A long drawn-out whistle shrilled over the last mile or two, proclaiming the end of the journey. A quick look out the window as the train rounded a bend revealed hills topped with temples and pagodas. I thrilled instantly to them and hastily resolved to live for adventure, expect it around every corner, gamble on it at every chance. I would make the most of every opportunity, enjoy every experience to the utmost and be ready for anything and everything.

With long drawn-out screeches the train pulled to a stop and as I stepped down on the platform a booming voice greeted me. "Welcome to Diamond City!" (I already knew that *Petch* meant diamond in Siamese). This was Dr. Edwin McDaniel, of Scotch-Irish descent, slight of build, blond and blue-eyed. He had been a cavalry medical officer in the war with Mexico. He was a welcome sight with his outstretched arms. My new mood was firmly established as I thanked him.

"Is this all you have?" And without waiting for an answer, "An ox cart is waiting to take your trunks. Let's go to the baggage car first." That taken care of, I followed to a horse and cart waiting outside in the care of a small boy. The horse was small and black, the cart an English "trap" with seats back to back.

"What do you think of this?" the doctor asked. "It is the gift of Dr. McFarland, sent over from Bangkok a few weeks ago."

"How generous of him, And what a beauty!" I responded.

"Yes. Well, he and Mrs. McFarland have had it for years, and since they are going on an extended leave soon and didn't want to sell the horse to a livery stable, they gave it to me!" He gave the horse an affectionate pat and helped me into the seat, took his seat and we started off. "His father was a missionary here in the early days," he continued, "and he built the house I live in and the school that is to be your home."

Soon we came to a small river and turned to travel the narrow road at its edge, away from the town proper which was farther up on the opposite bank. Here, the length of a short city block, was my new neighborhood. A local official lived on the corner. Next, was a large compound filled with native houses of bamboo and thatch crowded together every which way.

Although I had never seen my Wang Lang neighbors face to face, I would get to know the people here very well.

Beyond was the walled compound of the Mission: a small guest house long unused; the tiny hospital; the school residence whose front along the river was the chapel building; then the doctor's house set back and separated the width of a driveway from an empty house to be occupied by the Reverend and Mrs. Eakin and son six months later.

Next to this, beyond the compound wall was an old abandoned temple smothered in scrub jungle with a mere footpath separating the temple wall from more jungle along the river bank.

Dr. McDaniel identified each building or feature, and now as we turned into the drive he said, "This empty house was the original building on the compound. It belonged to a concubine of King Mongkut. [the father of Chulalongkorn, and the "King" of *Anna and the King of Siam* and *The King and I*.. See p 341] Her father was then the governor of this province as his son is now. When the Mission was invited to start work here and looked for land, the lady offered her house with the purchase of the land."

The young cart driver left us at the door, then led the horse to the back compound. We went upstairs. The lamps were lit and dinner was ready. The doctor did not like Bangkok's late dinner hours.

Mrs. McDaniel's greeting was heartwarming. She said, "I am so happy to have you here at last. We want you to stay with us as long as you can. The room is yours. If you still feel that you must live alone in the school building, we want you to always have meals with us."

Mrs. McDaniel, a Swedish registered nurse, was as self-effacing and calm as the doctor was blustery and excitable – a truly gentle soul. They had two children, Helen, four, and Freddie, two, with another on the way.

At breakfast the next morning, I exclaimed at the sight of thick fresh cream in a tiny pitcher, the first I had seen since leaving the States.

"It's a long story," the doctor began. "Little Freddie here," and he ran a hand affectionately over his head, "wasn't able to stand, much less walk, when he was two. I thought that surely fresh milk and lots of cream would help matters. So I decided to make a special missionary project of training a cow to give milk for humans. Such a thing has never been heard of here. I bought a cow with a new calf, and rigged a harness in a stall so that I could milk it after the calf had had its fill. You can see it worked. Now four months later Freddie's walking!"

He beamed at Freddie as the child wriggled out of his grasp. "I can't promise that much cream every day, but tonight it's all for you. Ellen and I do not want any."

"It's such a treat!" I exclaimed. "I haven't had cream like this since I left Sacramento." The quantity was small, but we were daily informed about how much it increased.

The next morning after breakfast, the doctor went to his hospital, and gave me the keys to explore my domain. A lawn and neat hedge separated the two buildings. Flowers bordered the cement walk, and just inside the picket fence along the road was a gigantic Flame-of-the-Forest, a tree famed for its size and the beauty of its orange-red blossoms. It was as wide and tall as the two-story building.

My new home had been built in the 1870s as a boarding school for girls that never fulfilled expectations because of custom and superstition. The ground floor had storage rooms with a few desks and tables. The main floor had three large rooms (formerly classrooms) in the general mission-style. On the top floor was a dormitory and large room for living and sewing, two large and three small rooms over the chapel – seemingly hanging over the river – for resident living quarters, all long unused.

I thought of Mary Cort who had lived and taught here for ten years, sometimes alone, managing as many as nine primitive day schools for girls scattered around the district. She went to the States, published her book, *The Heart of Farther India,* and never returned. I thought of Dr. McFarland's mother, the first person in the Kingdom to persuade a few brave Siamese girls to come to her for instruction in sewing and household arts, of Mrs. Hays formerly Jennie Neilsen, of Miss Galt and many others of whom I had heard mention while at Wang Lang.

When I chose the suite above the chapel for living quarters, I felt overwhelmed at my good fortune. Suppose I had been unwilling to leave the security and sociability of Bangkok to risk the unknown? I was glad my sense of adventure had not failed me.

From my long veranda, shaded by a tamarind tree at one end and a feathery acacia and "Flame of the Forest" tree at the other end, I could see the old "Elephant Bridge" upriver with its constant stream of people, carts and animals passing to and from the long dense Market Street. I could also see the barrier mountain range on the west and the sea on the east, and a quiet intimate stream as well, its opposite bank an impenetrable thicket never disturbed.

A mile from my house, broad brick-paved walks bordered with exotically perfumed *frangipani* trees led to a hill topped with a palace and *pagodas*. I was told elephants used to carry the King and court ladies up these walks to the palace.

Lastly, I had the simple, friendly association with a sincere couple who were eager to share all they had. And it wasn't long before Dr. McDaniel offered his horse for me to ride, including the use of his McClellan saddle which he had not used since his arrival the year before.

The hum of voices drew me to the school room in the chapel below. An old man, probably in his fifties, sat at a desk and barely looked up as I entered. Standing at the desk facing the teacher, a boy read from a primer. As the doctor's Siamese was limited I thought it likely he had not told the man about my coming to take charge of the school.

I greeted him, smiled, and asked if I might watch a moment. I counted twenty-three boys from around ten to eighteen years of age, and learned they were each paying the equivalent of about twenty cents a month for the privilege of learning at this mission school.

One by one each boy stood before the teacher and recited from where he had left off the last time he had recited, which could have been a week before. I knew this was the manner of teaching in the temple *salas* by priests from time immemorial. I felt the challenge, and hardly knew whether to laugh or cry, until I saw the man's crippled hand. During the dinner hour I asked some questions.

"Oh yes," Dr. McDaniel said, "you noticed *Nai* Kaao's hand, did you? Well, when he was a young man in the priesthood, an enemy from his pre-temple days severed his hand while he was sleeping. Of course he was filled with horror at the thought of entering the next life minus a part of his body. The fame of Dr. Sturgis, the Mission doctor had spread and *Nai* Kaao picked up his severed hand and hurried to the hospital. Although useless, the hand joined successfully and was saved. While staying at the hospital and hearing the gospel preached daily, he accepted Christianity, mostly out of gratitude. His teaching must be pretty old-fashioned, like the free teaching at the monasteries. He lives with relatives and knows his job is only temporary." I decided I would make no change until the end of the term.

Shrewdly guessing my choice of the rooms above the chapel, Dr. McDaniel had foresightedly ordered paint and brushes so I spent most of November scrubbing and painting. A carpenter in the next compound put together a platform of boards to rest on two sawhorses for my bed. A packing case with a petticoat became a dressing table and chairs and a table were brought from the storeroom below. Settled in my new domain, I prepared office space for a desk downstairs and a classroom. Soon I was ready to teach the coveted English to all who would attend regularly.

An ambitious young Siamese mother brought her only child, a five-year-old "to learn." The father was a government official. A servant brought the child in mid-morning, sat on the veranda floor while I took the child on my lap and used the Siamese primer.

An army major brought his only son, complaining distractedly that the boy was too dumb. Perhaps I might succeed where he had failed. He had even hung the boy by his thumbs from the rafter, thinking for some unknown reason it might help. The eight-year-old boy became private pupil number two, and it was good to see him lose his fear and dumbness. About this time, trying out new disciplines, I promised a picnic to the royal caves if the boys would cooperate.

At breakfast one morning early in December the doctor matter-of-factly said, "I have a goiter operation today and Ellen is not able to help. How about you – like to try?"

"Surely," I replied, "if you are that hard up and willing to risk it."

"All you have to do is hold the woman's head," he said. That sounded easy. But it was a new experience to have blood running copiously over my hands. After I had eaten a big dinner, the doctor admitted that he had fully expected me to keel over in the operating room.

Soon afterward their new baby was born, an experience in itself for me, since in my sexual naiveté, I did not know how babies are born. With very little knowledge beyond, perhaps a woman's inborn intuition, I took charge of the infant after delivery, and helped nurse Mrs. McDaniel through her recovery. She was active by Christmas and it was a happy time with a candle-lit tree of fragrant tamarind branches tied together.

18 - Klun

Shortly after Christmas an event occurred of great significance to us all. On my way to dinner at noon I saw a *sampan* at the school landing steps. It held a man, woman and two teenage boys.

When dinner was over, I noticed that the man was waiting on the veranda stairs. When the doctor appeared he crouched at his feet with the *wai* salute accorded a monastery abbot. He was taller than average, lean and lithe. His hair was gray. His eyes had a strange, sad intensity, as of suffering.

"Khun Maw krup (noble doctor, sir) my name is Klun. Long, long ago I lived in your back compound. I did a wrong thing and left the church and lived a bad life." He shook his head and gave a sigh like a groan. "I want to return to a useful life, educate my sons and give my wife the peace she deserves. I am willing to do any kind of work for just enough to support my family."

My heart went out to the man and I looked hopefully at the doctor. I knew he desperately needed help assembling the parts of a huge water tank, recently arrived from Montgomery Ward. Besides, there was the constant need for repairs around the compound.

Dr. McDaniel must have realized that Klun was heaven-sent, for he immediately accepted his service and told him he could live in the empty building behind the hospital, close under the far end of my veranda. I followed him to meet his wife. While he told her and the boys the good news, I welcomed the boys as pupils.

From that day on he and the doctor were practically inseparable, as they worked together on the various projects. There seemed to be nothing Klun could not do and he never tired, or resented long hours, or being called peremptorily from one task to another.

Late one night while I sat on my high veranda in the dark, I was aware of an instant's flash of light up the road, beyond the hospital. A dog barked, then yelped as if hurt. Again the tiny flash appeared, closer. I became curious. It was not the season for fireflies.

Leaning over the railing, I could barely make out a tallish figure pass rapidly and noiselessly below, and disappear at the landing. I settled back in my chair, thinking that the light had come from a dark lantern. Then I heard the clank of a chain. Instantly I was alert, certain that the man could not have been Klun, and that his was the only boat tied up at the landing.

I kneeled down to look through the railing. In the faintest star-light I saw the shadow of a boat move out from the bank and downstream. Obeying an instinct, I ran to the end of my veranda overlooking the hospital.

"Klun!" I called, and again, "Klun! Are you there?"

"Yes, *Mem*. What you want?"

"Go and see if your boat is at the landing!" I urged.

"It is always there, Mem," he replied.

"Look *now*, quickly!" I insisted. A moment later his voice rang out in panic.

"It is gone!"

At the other end of my veranda hung a large bell that had been used for school and chapel in former days. The doctor had told me to use it as a signal if I was ever alarmed at night. I gave it a tap and, at the desecration of the midnight quiet, recoiled almost as if I had been struck. Almost instantly the doctor's voice answered

"Klun's boat was just stolen," I told him. "What should he do?"

"Tell him to go to the police station." There was a pause, "Wait! I'll go with him."

It was about the distance of a long city block and they were soon back with several police. They set off, walking down river with Klun, to try to head off the boat.

The doctor returned to his house but I still stayed outside on my veranda, enjoying the coolness of the night. Presently I was aware of movement. From a narrow lane separating our compound from an abandoned temple grounds beyond I saw a man emerge and walk very rapidly toward me and then disappear beyond the hospital. I would have sworn that it was the man I had seen before. But how? The thief must be far down river by now. Puzzled, I finally decided to forget it and get some sleep.

In the morning the servants talked about a fire that burned fiercely during the night, below the temple grounds. A little before noon I was called out of the classroom. The *Amphur* [mayor] of Petchaburi was waiting in my office to see me about the incident. He apologized for bothering me, and asked me what the man looked like. I explained that it was too dark to see his face, but my impression was of a tall man, in dark clothes, carrying a dark lantern. I felt sure I saw him pass the house again after the police had gone down river.

He agreed, and said that when the man heard the alarm sounded he must have known the *pu yai ban* [village headman] would go to every house to see whether anyone was missing. So he had concealed the boat in the jungle along the river's edge intending to hurry back to his house first and return later. The coming of the police held him up and he ran into the *pu yai ban* who saw his dark lantern and questioned him. After midnight he went to the concealed boat and set it afire with kerosene, knowing he could not get down to the sea before daylight.

"I have come to ask a favor," the *Amphur* said. Will you please come down to the school landing and look over the men in the *pu yai ban's* group and tell me if anyone fits your impression of the man you saw?"

I started to protest, "That is quite a responsibility!"

"Don't worry, *Mem*," he reassured me paternally. "It isn't serious. He will only be in jail a few weeks."

Amused at his casual assurance, I went with the *Amphur* to the landing. All but one I recognized as they smiled their friendly greetings. They were dressed in khaki shorts and white cotton shirts. The stranger in the group kept his eyes sullenly on the ground. He was tall and thin, dressed in long black cotton pants and black jacket. I did not have to say a word – the Amphur seemed to understand and told the police to take him away.

"Thank you, *Mem*," he said. "The man's record is not good. A rest in jail will be good for him."

Klun knew the man and admitted that they had not been on good terms in former days. There was probably some reason for such a long-standing revenge. If so, it remained his secret. Some weeks later, when the doctor's family was away at the beach, I learned that my cook was the wife of the man I had sent to jail and that she also prepared his meals and saw him twice a day. *Maa* Chamrurn, my assistant, heard that he had made some threats against me.

Sometimes on dark nights I would listen to strange sounds and become tense with listening. Because, although the outside stairway to my high apartment as well as the inside one were locked after dark, the great pradu tree barely touched the corner of the veranda, next to my bedroom. But it had no lower branches and I felt certain it could not be scaled without a ladder.

Since his one tie with the old life was now gone, Klun belonged to us and we to him in a peculiar way. Before the theft of his boat I was simply the future school teacher of his children. Now the boys were duly enrolled and I was woven into the pattern of the new life of the family through the shared experience. He was henceforth my guardian angel and devoted friend.

Klun was a versatile man. Among his many capabilities and natural gifts was a love for, and understanding of, horses. Seeing that I had a like passion, he located the most beautiful horse in the entire region and borrowed it for me to try out. It was a two-year-old stallion, full of fire and caprice, the tallest Siamese horse I had yet seen, and the most magnificently formed.

My father had sent me a check from Alaska and I asked Klun to try to buy the horse for me. The owner, a local official, had not intended to sell. It took some time and I never knew how Klun accomplished it – I doubt if anyone else could have wheedled it away so successfully.

The horse had only been ridden bareback two or three times, using only a halter. No one was willing to accept the care of him, so Klun offered, and the doctor consented. Each day when he proudly led his charge, prancing and dancing, out to the river for a bath, people would stop to watch. I too, often found it convenient to be near a veranda door about that time so that I could see the show.

About five o'clock each evening I would go for a ride, never certain what I would encounter or whether I would be equal to the occasion. Perhaps the doctor guessed as much. He often took his family for a drive at that time.

Once the contrary creature – with bit in teeth, head down and all bunched up – played leapfrog on the broad highway to Khao Wang like a mechanical toy. People along the road just gaped, until Klun, running as if driven by the wind, reached the horse's head and put a stop to his fun. The short, sharp jerks had shaken me up badly and I walked home leading my horse, vowing to use a curb bit and spurs from then on.

Sometimes the horse would stand up without warning to look over a high temple wall. Once he backed down the brick-walled moat at the foot of the hill. I stayed on and made him climb up again. He had some scars from that stunt! When he sat down in a pond through which the country lane dipped, only my companions laughed. The final clowning act was when he sat down in the crowded market street, to the amusement of the populace. There was never a dull ride.

Accustomed to horses on my grandfather's ranches, and trained to follow a civilized standard of behavior, I soon learned that the untrained, semi-wild breed of small horse in Petchaburi demanded eternal vigilance. Whereas those I had been used to before would stand quiet long periods by simple devices, it was necessary to have a long, stout rope and remove both saddle and bridle whenever I contemplated leaving my horse alone for even a short time. The Siamese pony has a congenital passion for rolling on the ground.

One afternoon I had ridden to Khao Luang after school and was sitting on a rock holding the horse's bridle, forgetful of time. An old crone, hurrying home after gathering firewood, sat down to keep me company. Looking about nervously, she merely nodded at my greeting, as she said, "It is getting dark. Are you not afraid?"

"What should I fear?" I smiled.

With a shudder she said, "I fear the *Phi* [spirits]. Don't you?"

"No, why should I?"

Ignoring my question she asked, "Why are you here alone?"

"I like to go to lonely places and think about things." I was sure I had not made my meaning intelligible, and of course there was no sign of comprehension.

Returning to the subject of her deepest interest, the old woman asked, "Why don't you fear the *Phi*?"

"Because my religion doesn't teach about spirits, and I can't be afraid of something I don't know about."

There was no reply. She looked at me wonderingly. To people whose life from birth to death for thousands of years has been conditioned by a belief in the power of spirits to rule – and overrule their every simple action – my disavowal would be construed as rashness, another crazy thing about the queer foreigner. I stood up to go and walked with her to the foot of the hill, leading my horse.

Edna with horse.

19 - Epidemic!

Early in January, when I had been in Petchaburi nine weeks, tragedy struck at one of my pupils. It then spread over the city, and caused hundreds to flee in fear until finally I had to close the school long before the hot-season vacation was due.

It began with a day's picnic to the Royal Caves with my twenty or more school boys in fulfillment of a promise made to them soon after I set up new disciplines.

We walked west, out the broad shaded highway to the foot of the Khao Wang hill, then north, along a cart track over the rice fields and across the railway line, three or four miles to Khao Luang. Halfway up the hill was the fence and gate-entrance to a large cave. A hundred steep concrete steps were built into the shady rock wall of the opening on the near side of the deep shaft. The mid-morning sun slanted its full force upon two gigantic stalagmites below on the opposite wall which

In the Royal Caves

formed an arch into the cave. On each side of this grand arch was an opening – one like a window, and the other slightly higher – a natural belfry with a temple bell hanging in it.

Looking through the arch down several broad steps and across a vast circular chamber, I could dimly see a group of images arranged on a raised and decorated dais against the far wall of the cave, lighted by a single small opening at the top of the hill. Oblique rays of sunlight barely touched the damp moss on the floor of the cave causing all the shadows to appear unexpectedly colorful with greens, blues, rust and terra-cotta, blending one into the other. This effect of these colors was always my first impression and on every visit became an increasing delight.

The cave was cool and interesting. The boys followed labyrinths into other parts. Each boy struck the temple bell, ostensibly as an act of merit-making, but I suspected they liked to worry the bats which poured forth from their recesses, darting and screeching like lost souls.

At noon we had lunch at a *sala* where a servant was waiting with rice and curry and banana-leaf bowls ready prepared. While we were eating, a wretched looking man in rags appeared from nowhere and squatted close by.

An older boy asked, "Shall we feed the leper, *Mem?*"

"Certainly," I replied, knowing that it was the custom to give the leftovers to any hangers-on.

So, when the boy himself filled a banana-leaf dish and took it to the beggar, I thought, how nice of him. He must come from an unusual family. That boy was Poom, and three days later, on Sunday morning after church, I went to his home to see why he had not been to school since the picnic.

Instead of going downriver to the mission compound, I crossed Elephant Bridge and walked upriver the long length of the market street with a young boy guide who knew where Poom lived.

I had heard that his father was an orchestra leader. I found his home to be of the better class. When I appeared at the gate, the man with dignified courtesy invited me into the house. "Into the house" is misleading. I climbed some ladder steps to a fairly large open deck, off which on three sides, were rooms on various levels, each room a separate entity with thatched, gabled roof, high and narrow.

I sat on the edge of the raised floor of the only room that had removed the front panels for the day. The floor was highly polished and untouched by any shoe – the Siamese wash their feet at an *ong* outside and leave their sandals at the entrance.

Quite a number of people were sitting around on mats on the deck, and one woman whom I took to be the wife, greeted me with a wan smile. Conscious of my feeble knowledge of the language and customs, and feeling an intruder, I asked their pardon, then bluntly inquired, "Where is Poom?"

"Poom is dead, *Mem*."

"Only three days – how is that possible?" I asked, shocked.

Calmly, without show of emotion, according to custom, the man explained. "On the morning after Poom went to the caves he did not feel well enough to go to school. At night he was very sick. When *Maw* (the local herb doctor) saw the swelling in the armpits he said there was nothing anyone could do. Last night the spirit left the body."

Deploring my meager vocabulary, I tried to express my sympathy in my own American fashion, unfamiliar with the custom which forbade speaking of death with regret, but always with a smile. However, the Siamese being the most tolerant on earth of other races' manners and customs, I had no sense of blundering, from the expressions on their faces.

Still I was puzzled as to what illness could possibly be so violent. I knew that cholera could carry off its victims in a few hours, but cholera was a hot-season disease, and this was January. Besides I did not know the Siamese word for cholera. Finally I asked, "What sickness?"

At the man's reply, "*Ka la roke*," I must have looked blank as it meant nothing to me. After a brief silence a young man with a slight knowledge of English spoke up.

"Pleck, *Mem*, pleck. Do you understand?"

Suddenly realizing what he meant – that most dreaded of all diseases in the Orient – I exclaimed, "Oh no, surely not plague!" Several heads nodded confirmation.

"*Mem,*" the father said, "come and see Poom." Leading the way to the runway, he lifted a covering and I saw the dark, emaciated skeleton that had been my lively pupil just three days before.

The long walk home seemed interminable. It was long past noon when I reached Dr. McDaniel's home. His family was halfway through dinner. I stood in the outer doorway wondering if I could possibly contaminate the children from that distance as I told the news. "I have just seen one of my boys who died of plague. Does it mean bubonic? What do you want me to do?"

Slowly the doctor pushed back his plate and his chair, then challenged skeptically. "How do you know it was plague?"

"The family seemed certain enough," I said.

"How long was he sick and how did he look?"

The doctor looked very serious when I had finished telling the details. He instructed me to take a carbolic solution bath, disinfect the school room and urge the boys to report any and every symptom. He added that the plague carrier was unknown. He was in the dark, along with the whole medical profession, and could only advise me to take every precaution, as he would with his own family. He went at once to Poom's house to see the body and confirm what I had told him. He was very disturbed when he returned, and promptly wrote to the Bangkok health authorities.

It was only after several appeals that the government sent Dr. Carthew to Petchaburi to make a report, and further delays before he returned with helpers to take stringent measures. By then many more were infected. Fear spread and many people had fled to the country side in panic.

When families hid their sick and refused to report their dead, Dr. Carthew had the thatch roofs torn down where there had been a death, and the whole house burned if there had been more than one death. Those home owners, infuriated, threatened the health officer's life. All through February life was grim in the city. With the hot season month of March the epidemic finally died out, but it was some time before things returned to normal.

Years afterward, reading *An American Doctor's Odyssey* by Dr. Victor Heiser, I learned it was during that very winter of 1906-07 that he made his report to the Indian Plague Commission that rats were the conveyors of plague.

20 - Bantaloo

Klun kept telling Dr. McDaniel about a place called Bantaloo where the missionaries used to go in the hot season. It was a beach on the gulf ten miles due east of Petchaburi as the crow flies, he said. It was fringed with a grove of sugar palms, and you could see it from the *pagoda* on Palace Hill.

The Doctor became fired with zeal to blaze a new trail to the seaside so the family could spend a month there. The governor had granted permission for the doctor to use his bungalow, unfurnished and long unused, which was on land owned by the Mission. He had offered to arrange for relays of guides so the doctor could get there. I soon discovered the extent of Dr. McDaniel's determination that I should spend my vacation month with them. I could ride my horse – Klun would take care of it – and the doctor would thus be free to come and go, they said. When I replied I could not possibly go away for a month, they remembered a Mission rule that no one should be left alone in any station.

"You are very kind," I said, "and I do appreciate your concern for me but you know I have big plans for the new school term. *Maa* Chamrurn and I will be very busy all the month. I could not leave her alone, you haven't room for her in your cart, and I can't take her on my horse. I'll be safe in town, you needn't worry."

"Will you go with us for a day's picnic, just to see how far we can get?" the doctor asked.

"Yes, I would like that," I agreed, not rightly interpreting his eagerness and the gleam in his eye.

Little did I know about rice field roads. Less did I know of the tenacity of the Scotch-Irish! If I had known they were up half the night cooking and packing there might have been some awkward questions and answers about "a day's picnic."

We were all in fine spirits as we set off early one morning, I on horseback in my khaki divided skirt and blouse and helmet with chin strap, and Ellen, cool in thin white dress with her three little children in the ox cart, all under a big beach umbrella.

The road was in fair condition the first third of the distance of three miles. Beyond the first village there was a trackless waste of marsh and salt fields. Following the deviations of the cart tracks from village to village doubled the actual distance, and merely getting from field to field trebled the time element.

The Petchaburi rice fields were a crazy-quilt of small patches, different in size and shape. Each field was surrounded by a rough dike of earth, sometimes as high as three feet, to hold in the rain water for the young rice plants. These dikes, patched up after the rice harvest were the only means of communication between villages during monsoon rains.

When family, friends and neighbors gathered to cut the grain, the dikes were opened for the carts to carry it away. For each opening the dike was slashed in two places, the width of the wheel span, just enough for the wheels and the slender legs of a pair of oxen to pass through.

The doctor's cart presented a problem because the body was lower and the wheel span wider than the ox carts'. He knew evidently what he would be up against, for out of the depths of the cart Klun produced an ax and began to slice off the protuberances on the sides of the openings, and shave off the top of the humps between. This meant that from then on, for several hours in the heat of the day, the horse had to be led and coaxed to straddle or sidestep the hump at every dike opening. At first the awkward contortions of the horse appeared ludicrous; then I felt no self-respecting animal should be subjected to such an indignity. It soon ceased to be either amusing or pathetic and was just tiresome and exasperating.

The guide would walk ahead a few fields and then sit on a dike to wait for the doctor to come close enough to get a bearing on his next stretch. I dared not go on ahead of him any distance because of the number of tracks crossing each other in all directions, and the heat dampened any incentive to ride ahead and return just for the pleasure of moving faster.

When I stopped beside the cart and asked, "Do you really expect to get to the beach today?" the doctor answered reassuringly and his

A typical oxcart

wife smiled knowingly. I did not suspect the reason until later. She had a mosquito net for the night and plenty of food, towels and a change of clothes hidden away under the seat. At first I felt sorry for her, compelled to sit inactive, holding the baby, patient and uncomplaining. Then as I wilted more and more I almost envied her cool composure under the big umbrella. My khaki divided skirt felt very heavy, the sun burned through my blouse, and the chin strap of my pith helmet was a nuisance.

But then there was respite and compensation at each village while we stopped to wait until a new guide could be located to take us on to the next village in accordance with the governor's command. Most of the villages were compact. Their little thatched houses, closely grouped together, were so effectively screened by dense thickets, vines and bamboo around the outer edge that from the fields they presented the appearance of green oases. Once inside the village it was dark and cool from the many fruit and shade trees.

The villagers were friendly and offered us green coconuts to drink. The houses were all alike, perched up on stilt-like posts and approached by a single ladder, with pigs, chickens and oxen underneath. Still there was some variety in their size, shape and general appearance. Flowers, clean-swept yards and shade trees reflected the character of the people who lived there.

By mid-morning the rice fields were ringing with the voices of young men singing out from the tops of the tall sugar palms. Petchaburi is famous for its miles and miles of "*toddy*" palms and for the sugar made from the sap. There were thousands of palms growing up from the dikes like giant weeds. Since they are very slow growing, some of them must have been over a hundred years old. Lashed to each sturdy, straight, black trunk was a tiny cane ladder all the way to the top. Villagers were going up and down collecting the long, hollow bamboo containers, filled overnight with sap, and replacing them with empty ones. A strong breeze blowing from the sea carried the surge of waves breaking on shore into the cloudy tips of the palms, and its echo in the stiff fan-fronds above was a lovely sound as it lured us on.

It was two o'clock in the afternoon when, the rice fields now behind us, we reached the *sala* the governor had mentioned – our most important objective. It had a good floor raised about three feet off the ground and a tile roof. Someone had made merit in building the *sala* for wayfarers according to custom in Siam. Someone was also keeping it repaired, contrary to the customary indifference.

At once the doctor's voice boomed out in great satisfaction. "There it is! Bantaloo – just about an hour from here. We'll have lunch first." There, across a barren, windswept salt waste, perhaps two miles away, was a forest-fringe of sugar palms. The March wind came straight toward us across the warm flats carrying with it the roar of breakers pounding the beach.

After a lunch of rice and curry with condiments, brought out from under the broad cart seat and still hot, I said, "I'm ready to go home. Now we've blazed the way it shouldn't take long."

Dr. McDaniel looked at his wife and gave an embarrassed cough. "You wouldn't be a quitter, would you? It's just a little further. We'll spend the night. There is a chicken dinner in the cart and something for breakfast." Not waiting for protest or argument he called Klun to help harness the cart horse.

I turned to Ellen. "You didn't expect to get home tonight?"

"No, Doctor knew it was impossible."

"How about going to the beach some other day?"

"It would be a pity not to see how we like it when we are so near. Besides, Doctor would not give up now."

I decided not to make a fuss, hoping things would be all right at home with *Maa* Chamrurn.

Trustingly we followed our guide as we started out again. However, in taking his habitual shortcut to Bantaloo village he failed to take into consideration the doctor's cart. Instead of taking a roundabout track which skirted the wasteland and reached the beach a mile or so south of the village, he took us in the opposite direction until we came to a slimy sea canal and a narrow foot bridge raised in the middle for boats to pass under.

We gasped at the seeming climax to our day's tribulations. The doctor looked accusingly at the guide and demanded, "Why did you bring us this way?"

"*Mai roo,*" he said with the characteristic shrug, meaning I don't know.

I was sure we would turn back to the sala for the night, but the doctor was already telling Klun to go with the guide to the nearest village and bring back as many men as would be able to lift the cart up over the bridge. As we settled down for a long wait Dr. McDaniel gave vent to his exasperation. "Isn't that the dumbest thing? I know there is another way without a bridge. To think we might have been sitting down to dinner by now. Did that stupid guide expect me to perform a miracle? '*Mai roo!*' He isn't capable of thinking!"

It was beginning to grow dark when nine men appeared with poles and rope and carried the cart across the canal. I led my horse across safely. The horse pulling the cart slipped on the arched bridge and fell into the quicksand. As the doctor shouted and lashed with the long carriage whip the men tugged at the reins. I sent up a frightened prayer. The doctor's wife was very pale but calm and silent, and soon the poor creature was safely landed and again harnessed, all muddy, to the cart.

Now we all walked. Two hours after dark we reached the beach and Klun persuaded the villagers – some twenty men, women and children – to push the cart through the sand to the bungalow.

After putting the children to bed under mosquito netting, and not caring to eat, Ellen and I sank into the warm sea at our doorstep for a relaxing swim in the nearly full moonlight. I declined to share the large family mosquito netting, and chose to sleep on a rush mat in the open doorway, preferring the fresh air and moonlight. As a consequence, the rest of the night was an unrelenting battle with mosquitoes, as I watched the broad path of silver gradually narrow, shorten and disappear, while overhead the sky was nearly as bright as day. At the first streaks of dawn I went out to the water's edge. The tide was out, the sea a pale gray and like glass. Faint undulations broke gently at my feet and snaked along with a soft hissing sound.

How I would have loved even a few days here. If only I were not plagued with a sense of duty. Why couldn't I relax and let others share some of my responsibility? Couldn't someone have stayed with *Maa* Chamrurn?

There were sounds from the bungalow. As I turned toward them the doctor and his wife were watching me. His voice rang out. "How does it look? Think you could enjoy a few weeks here?"

"I'm sure I could. When do we start back?"

"You're staying here with Ellen. I will ride back to town on your horse and get the things we need," he replied.

"Sorry, I can't stay now," I said. "I'd like to come down later if that's possible."

Ellen spoke up. "Be a good girl and stay with me while Doctor goes to town. It will do you good."

"I wish I could but it's really impossible. He wouldn't be able to get my things or arrange for my household. *I* can ride to town and send down what you need."

Dr. McDaniel's eyes blazed as my stubbornness threatened his plans. "You can't go to town alone; you would get lost!"

"I'll manage."

"Suppose your jailbird attempts revenge as he vowed to do?"

"I'm not expecting trouble from him," I countered.

"Well, we can't force you to stay, of course. Klun can go with you on the pony." Accepting my decision now with good grace, they gave me instructions for sending down what they needed by ox cart.

"Remember, we need just about everything for four weeks; we will have to leave before the rains begin."

It was eight o'clock when Klun and I started home. By ten o'clock the heat was intense, prickling the scalp through my helmet. In our haste we missed the way several times and had to retrace our steps. Stopping at a village for a drink of water we were offered instead the boiling sap of the sugar palms from great cauldrons under the shade trees. We drank the syrup out of brass bowls and almost immediately the weariness left, the mist cleared from my eyes and the terrible tension in my head eased. Gratefully we thanked the kind villagers and went on again.

Keeping up a steady pace, we reached the Mission by noon, taking only four hours to return where it had taken us fourteen hours to reach our destination the day before. I plunged my head into an *ong* of cool water on reaching the doctor's house. *Maa* Chamrurn quickly made tea and helped me gather things together all afternoon while Klun arranged for an ox cart to take everything to Bantaloo the next morning. Rice, charcoal and *anglos* for cooking, pots, kettles and frying pans, flour, sugar and tinned provisions, mattresses, clothing, lamp, kerosene and magazines. The doctor's cook bought fresh vegetables and eggs, and his own bundle to go along with the cart.

I found *Maa* Chamrurn none the worse for her night alone in the big building. Often during the following days I thought longingly of the beach and sea bathing. Sometimes at night when I heard a noise in the pradu tree touching my veranda I wished – only for a moment.

Before the next hot season Dr. McDaniel had made several trips to the beach at Bantaloo to improve the accommodations at the bungalow. I was invited to join them and went alone on horseback, following instructions as carefully as possible.

All was well until I reached the salt fields. I could not find the one cart track which led to the beach, and so I allowed my impatient horse to take the lead straight across the salt flats up to the slimy sea canal which separated the salt flats from the grove of palms. I could hear the tantalizing sound of waves breaking on the beach and I sighed that I had to waste an hour or so finding the "road." Before I could turn, and while wistfully looking at the shady grove, my horse gathered himself and jumped! He went down on his knees in the slime and I pitched neatly over his head. He was up first and trotted off just enough ahead so I had to plough through the sand, grass and brush on foot. Stiff from the long ride and provoked at having been caught off guard, conscious of my mud-splattered skirt and tumbled hair, I made a sorry sight as the family greeted me with, "Thought you could stay on a horse!"

As time went on the cart tracks through the rice fields became more-or-less familiar, and I never again got lost or wandered in a growing panic as I had earlier. The return trip could be made in a three-hour hard ride.

On one such occasion, returning home hot and disheveled, whom should I encounter as I entered the compound but the American Charge d'Affaires. He was a highly eligible young bachelor who unfortunately was just leaving to catch the train to return to Bangkok. I never saw him again. How different my life might have been.

21 - Betty and other *Eurasians*

One day Dr. McDaniel returned from a medical call to a distant village in the foothills of the Burma mountains very disturbed. He had gone up the line by the early morning train, then walked westward from a lonely station toward the mountains. Surprisingly, in one of the villages he came across a pretty fair-haired little girl, dressed in a rag of a *sarong*. He heard her called *mah* [dog], by the other children, this half-European child who was like a swan among ducks.

Intent on catching the evening train to return home, he still found time to see the mother and learn the name of the girl's father. First he wrote to the Danish gentleman living in Bangkok to ask him if he would take care of his daughter's education. When it became certain that nothing would be done, the doctor asked me if I would adopt the child. After the doctor made another trip to the village, the grandmother brought her in to me. She told me that the mother now had a Siamese husband and was ashamed of her so-different offspring.

If the coming of Betty was a new experience for me, it must have been momentous for her. To be bathed with soap and shampooed, made to wear clean clothes and sleep on a mattress were equally strange experiences to her. She made no objection to our weird demands. She never resisted our efforts to teach her foreign manners, nor rebelled at the rules for eating, sleeping, and speaking. She was responsive and rarely had to be reproved. She submitted happily like one in a dream. In the classroom she progressed rapidly, and at play with the other children she was mature and gentle. Everyone liked her for her sweet disposition.

Until Betty joined my household I had been having my meals with the doctor's family, except for the month they were at the beach, while *Maa* Chamrurn had hers sent to the house daily in the customary *bintho* [food carrier]. Now it was time to set up a permanent kitchen for the three of us and any others who should wish to be part or full-time boarders. As foreign food and foreign-trained cooks were rather expensive for a single missionary, I began to enjoy living almost entirely on rice and curry and other typical Siamese dishes.

Three years later, before I married and left Petchaburi, I sent Betty to Wang Lang School. Not many months later I received a letter with the sad news that she had died of cholera there. Yet I knew that if Betty had reached marriageable age her mother would probably try to win the girl's sympathy for her own gain. I had seen that the *Eurasian* girls suffered a peculiar loneliness and sore bitterness, so I told myself that she had been mercifully spared more unhappiness in her lifetime.

There were twelve *Eurasian* girls at Wang Lang School while I was there and I became concerned over many of their problems. They were different in feature, voice, manners and dress from their Siamese mothers yet they felt conspicuously apart from their fathers' people. Even those who had a normal home life were seldom received socially unless they were quite outstanding.

Miriam and Beatrice were both daughters of British officials. Miss Cole gave them surnames of American presidents when they were put in her care. Both girls' mothers were the lovely northern Siamese women, but there all similarity in their stories ended.

Beatrice, the younger, was at Wang Lang only a short time after I arrived, but I remember her appealing beauty – her soft, curly brown hair, and sad, sweet eyes. I knew she had a brother who had been sent north when their father left Siam to bring his English wife to Bangkok. The lady was told about the two beautiful children and was urged by her husband's friends to give them a home. Instead, she refused to see them or consent to have them even live in the same city with her. It was then that Beatrice went north and vanished. I heard only that her brother spent years in the Mission school and was a handsome boy.

Many years afterward the English lady returned to Siam, a childless widow. She went to Chieng Mai, where Beatrice's brother was in school. She walked the streets, attended every procession and festival, searching for the face that would remind her of her husband – in vain – too proud to ask for the young man and meet him openly.

Miriam went through all the long school years suffering the loneliness of the castoff, but nursing a secret ambition – to be worthy of her father and be accepted by him. When her *Eurasian* cousin in the north was stricken with leprosy and desperately needed a companion in her long isolation for treatment, Miriam responded to the request from the girl's father and kept house for her cousin in a lonely spot. She was rewarded generously. With a keen business acumen she invested wisely, and entered the University as the first woman law student. She wrote to her father in England and was not only given permission to use his name, but received his proud acknowledgment.

Some seemed to accept their outcast status. One morning I was told that **Lily** had gone away in the middle of the night with all her belongings. When I was told that a strange woman had been hanging around the school for several days, I became worried, because Lily had been put in my care. Knowing she couldn't have left without someone knowing, I questioned the students. Such was their sense of loyalty that no one would divulge any information.

Finally Muen admitted that the strange woman was Lily's aunt. I knew I must find her. Hiring a carriage, I scoured the streets and the shops, hoping for some clue. I visited the homes of other *Eurasians*.

On the third day I finally learned where the aunt lived, found the one-room house in a muddy alley bordering a klong – and Lily. Fortunately her aunt was not there. I scarcely recognized the girl, wearing a *panung*, her long curly hair cut short. In three short days she had been quite transformed. It wasn't necessary to ask any questions, as Miss Cole had warned me that the aunt would probably try to sell her as a mistress to some foreigner. It was also clear that Lily would lose face if she returned to the school.

I persuaded her to let me find her a position where her knowledge of English would be prized, and begged her not to do anything rash in the meantime. She agreed, and with Dr. Hays' help, a position was found for her in a dispensary. There she met a young Siamese doctor and in time was married. His devotion to her and their children through the years left a sweet memory to counterbalance many sad ones.

"German" **Hannah** was starry-eyed, mischievous and merry. She stayed on as an assistant at the school after graduation, because she had had no other home since childhood. A Siamese nobleman in high government position courted her for nearly two years. He agreed to a Christian wedding and made the most solemn promises to have no native women. Hannah yielded at last and they were married. Eventually he reverted to his old ways. We went with her to Bangkok to arrange for a divorce. Hannah went to Singapore shortly afterwards and took up nursing. I was proud of her, when, a few years later, she answered the urgent call for volunteers to help fight a cholera epidemic which broke out in one of the ports.

Milly, one of two children of a violent Dutchman, lived at the school for many years. She learned exactly nothing, but she knew she was pretty, and she wanted her freedom.

One morning the silence of the compound was rudely broken. Most of the teachers and servants were away, taking advantage of the school vacation. *Maa* Cham, who had recently come from Bangkok to work with me, was on duty for Milly. Because her father was often violent, Milly had begged to spend the vacation at the school. Krem, the carpenter was somewhere about, and the cook had not returned from market. I was propped up in bed under strict orders to stay quiet, after my unfortunate fall into the river during the Annual Meeting. I was absorbed in a book, and did not see a man walk up from the landing. Suddenly I was startled by a roar from downstairs, accompanied by loud pounding on the floor. Simultaneously Milly and *Maa* Cham ran over from the school by the connecting bridge, and into my room, thoroughly frightened.

I had heard of this Dutch road-gang foreman, who spoiled the "prestige" of the white man in Siam. Very unwillingly I sent *Maa* Cham to tell him I was sorry I could not see him. If he had come for Milly, to say I was charged to let no one leave the school in the absence of the principal. I could hear his angry reply. "I come for my Milly – I vil not lief vidout her!" He would not sit down as invited, but strode through the lower rooms brandishing his club.

Maa Cham ran upstairs and began to lock the door. The bolt was missing. Milly helped her to move the desk against the double doors which opened inward. None too soon. The Dutchman was tramping noisily up the stairs. While *Maa* Cham and Milly put their weight to the table I tried to urge him to come when the principal could take the responsibility, explaining I would get into trouble – not my reason at all. I felt sorry for the daughter, and besides, I did not like being bullied.

It should have been easy to carry on a conversation through the high, wide, open grille above the door, but the man would not listen. He roared that he would *not* leave without her, and he would not wait. I shouted "Please go downstairs and Milly will get her things."

The minute he clumped down the stairs I sent *Maa* Cham to find Krern and have him go for the police at the gambling den below the school. I hoped I could delay the angry father until they came. *Maa* Cham barely returned to my room before the infuriated man came up the stairs again, swearing he would smash every thing in the house if Milly did not appear.

He put his weight to the door and it yielded in spite of all the girls could do. Immediately Milly, white but determined, whispered, "I must go, he will make too much trouble."

She ran through the dressing room and joined him in the hall, saying calmly as though she had just come from the school building, *"Prom laao Paw."* [I am ready, father.] He cursed until they were out of hearing – I had offended him unforgivably.

I watched the infuriated man take his daughter down to the landing, still cursing, bellow for a boat, then depart. I vainly hoped some stalwart champion might arrive in time to give the man a ducking in the river. An hour later two polite gendarmes sauntered up to the back gate and inquired why they had been sent for.

Milly's father never came to the school again. Not long afterwards he was murdered by the convict laborers working under him on the Tachin railway. Milly's Siamese mother married her to a wealthy Chinese who endured her gambling for several years. Then I lost track of her. Her brother, educated at the Mission boy's school, went through study for the ministry. He married a cultured Parsee Indian girl, a former student at Wang Lang, who had spent several years in the United States, training as a nurse.

22 - Lao Village

School opened the first of May with double the former enrollment. Two new teachers from Bangkok, *Kru* Jarun and *Kru* Puang, had been added and the tuition was raised. *Kru* Jarun, who had been at Wang Lang with me, had a second room on the residence floor, next to mine, and *Kru* Puang, who presided over the chapel, lived with a family in the next compound. Both settled down happily and made friends with parents and neighbors.

During April, with *Kru* Jarun helping me with the language translation, I wrote a prospectus of the new curriculum, the first in this area. This was printed in Bangkok on bright-colored paper and distributed for school boys far and wide over the Petchaburi area.

The Reverend and Mrs. Eakin and their small son soon arrived and occupied the third residence in our compound. Reverend Eakin had come to Siam in Government service and later joined the Mission. He built a large boy's school in Bangkok and spent many years in educational work. Longing to enter the evangelistic field, he volunteered to come to Petchaburi where there was only an old, locally trained Siamese man in charge of the church.

One day after the school had settled into a routine, Reverend Eakin asked me if I would like to start teaching school one morning a week in one of the *Laos* villages. The only cart track was under water in the rainy season, but I could easily reach the village on horseback, he said. Thrilled at the prospect of adventure, I heartily agreed to begin at once.

On Thursday, a school holiday, I rode to Tappan Yahon, the first village, and found the house of the *Kamnun* [head man] in charge of all the *Laos* villages. Both the husband and wife received me cordially, and when I suggested my plan of teaching the children, they begged me to use their house.

I had learned much about the *Laos*. Many years before, a tribe called *Lao Song* had been brought down from an area 400 miles to the northeast as captives and compelled to build on the hilltops of

Petchaburi for a king's pleasure. The people were established in a group of villages to the west of the city, along an old road that followed the base of the mountain range as far as Rajburi. Their descendants had preserved their ancient dress and tribal customs.

The term *Lao*, used until comparatively recent times was misleading. The several million *Lao* in the north and eastern parts of Siam were in reality simply the Thai who did not go south into central Siam. Likewise, the *Shans* who remained in the region of their former empire north of present-day Thailand were pure Thai, arbitrarily called *Shan* by the Burmese.

The *Laos* in this area were also called the *Black Lao*, from the black homespun in their garb – their turbans and their tight-fitting jackets fastened with silver buttons. Their black skirts had vertical white stripes, unlike the *pasins* of the *Lao* in the north who wore bright colors and horizontal pinstripes.

The years I taught at Tappan Yahon were the happiest of all. Soon after dawn, I was frequently told, the children would gather in the road that passed through the center of the village and watch for the first sight of my horse as I rounded the hills. Dashing to their homes for their meal of glutinous rice and dried fish, they would be back in time to escort me to our classroom in the headman's house, above the water buffalo and the pigs which I could see and smell through the slats of the bamboo floor as I taught.

The young women of the village began joining the children, so before long in answer to their plea, I was teaching them to read on Sunday afternoons.

Black Lao woman

The *Lao-Thai* have always been noted for their remarkably sweet voices and for their love of singing. They learned to sing a dozen or more hymns. This singing village was popular when the court visited Petchaburi and the king went out to hear them.

There was an interval of tragedy during the time I taught there. The head man's wife lay dying of lockjaw. My powers of persuasion were not sufficient to induce the woman to go to the hospital for treatment. Whether it was fatalism or superstition, her husband's opposition to breaking with tradition, or whether she feared the foreign place and doctor and the possibility of dying away from home, it was difficult to discover. Simple people do not explain themselves.

The following March, during the hot season, I was invited to witness an annual festival no foreigner had been permitted to share previously. Only because of my friendship with the younger women in the village was I given this coveted privilege.

In every *Lao* village, one night is devoted to courting, a sort of marriage quest. All the unmarried men, supporting each other in a body, go to the different villages in turn.

For the night of fun and feasting the girls wear their mothers' marriage gowns – black homespun with tiny bars of red and yellow raw silk woven on collar and sleeve. It was a custom handed down for generations. Rarely was the dress used again, except as sign or proof of a woman's married status.

As a preliminary to getting acquainted, the young men and the girls lined up facing each other while tossing a bean bag endlessly back and forth, all of them very shy and serious. Gradually during the dances that followed the excitement grew.

Hour after hour, rotating, a man danced to the semicircle of girls while another man played the sweet music of the north on the reed instrument called a *kaan,* the other men and girls swayed and clapped their hands to the rhythm of the song.

The village elders looked on, and when a young man showed his preference and danced to one particular girl, it was accounted courtship. After the round of all the villages with his friends, he returned to claim his bride.

At midnight, when the feasting began, I left for my lonely ride home in the moonlight, musing on this ritual which I had just observed. I felt grateful to have been given this privilege.

23 - River Trip

The lone *pagoda* on one of the Khao Wang hilltops became my refuge in Petchaburi, like the river landing had been to me at Wang Lang. On the days that I did not ride, when I wanted to get away from people for a few hours, I would walk up the hill and sit at the *pagoda's* base until the approach of darkness drove me down again.

Built for elephant travel and steep in spots, the broad brick road that wound up to the old palace and across to the other hilltops was bordered on both sides with frangipani trees growing out of the jagged volcanic rock of the hill. When they bloomed in the dry season one could trace from the city below, the entire course of the winding path by the solid mass of white flowers, the trees then being quite leafless.

One hill had an unfinished temple and another had an observatory. But I liked the large *pagoda* standing solitary on the highest point, where I could see for miles in every direction. Northward was Khao Luang with the royal caves. Looking east one might see the tiny sails of fishing craft out in the Gulf of Siam. To the west, the forbidding barrier range separated Petchaburi province from Lower Burma. Toward the south I could follow the little Petchaburi river on its way to those same mountains by the dense foliage on its banks as it flowed through the rice fields, dotted thickly with sugar palms. Just looking was an endless fascination, and I always returned home refreshed.

Karen woman

In the market place one day I saw some *Karens* [one of the hill tribes of Siam] who had come down from their mountain village near the source of the river. Their strange garb and the mystery of their unknown history set me wishing to see how they lived. The idea of making a river trip gradually grew as I thought about them and all the river villages beyond the familiar areas.

When I spoke to Klun about it, he became an inspired press agent, declaring that the whole region had been his haunt for years and that he loved it and would like to go along as my guide. He said that the little Mission houseboat could be poled easily in the month of December, but not later than January. The river would then be too shallow for so heavy a boat.

The next step was to get permission. When I broached the subject of a river trip to the McDaniels and the Eakins one day I was surprised to find them all sympathetic on one condition – that I find a missionary companion. I was twenty-four, but it was the era of chaperones! I mused that if they were opposed to my doing such a wild thing, they could not have found an easier way of ending the matter. I went to Wang Lang hoping that one of the two new members of the staff would jump at the chance to take such a trip. One of the girls would not go if she were paid. The other, seeing how much it meant to me was willing if someone would offer to take some of her responsibilities. There were no offers.

Dampened but still determined, I remembered Lucy Dunlap. There could be no logical objection to her. She was an older woman, part-time nurse and evangelist, doing sincere Christian work in full sympathy with the Mission. Lucy first saw life in a Bangkok prison where her mother was awaiting sentence for the murder of her husband, an American Negro. The Reverend and Mrs. E. P. Dunlap had adopted the infant and given her their name. On one of their furloughs they took her to the States where Lucy had supplementary schooling. All her life she was a friend to those in need, active and interested in serving others. She became my willing companion.

As plans progressed and the time drew near, everyone on the compound offered helpful suggestions. Mrs. Eakin said she would look after the school and I need not hurry back. Dr. McDaniel said he would manage without Klun, and would lend him his shotgun. Rev. Eakin offered the "magic lantern" and the "baby organ" for use in any village meetings, with Klun explaining the Bible pictures. The doctor declared I must take a medicine chest full of the simple remedies the people would be sure to ask for along the river. I carefully wrote down his instructions.

When the day arrived we began loading the boat. We put our clothes into the drawers under the seats of the six-by-eight-foot cabin. The tiny cupboards held the tins of biscuit, milk, butter, jam, dishes and utensils and the clay jars for the boiled drinking water. Our handyman/cook took a corner of the rear deck outside the cabin window for his charcoal *anglo* [cook stove], and the pots and pans. The all-important rice – to be shared by all – was stored in large kerosene tins under the deck along with the vegetables, dried fish and chilies brought by the men, to be pooled. The only fresh meat would be what Klun shot along the way. With two men to pole the boat, we were off at daybreak.

The first night was spent near a village where Klun's wife had lived. I was taken to meet her great-grandfather. He remembered the last battle with the Burmese a hundred years before when he was twelve years old. Whenever I mentioned the old man's age afterwards, people said, "Oh, he must have added a cycle or two. It's easy to make a mistake when you are counting chickens or snakes by twelves!" The old man was uncommunicative. I doubt if he was aware of his times and surroundings.

I never checked up on the date of the cannon hole in the temple I passed frequently. There seemed to be no one in the city who was interested, nor anyone who knew the story of a village outside the city, called *Sai Kundan*, "Sands of Starvation," other than it had been a battlefield.

After three days of steady poling, the fruit trees and coconut palms began to give way more and more to tall jungle and dense undergrowth, and the villages became farther apart. By now we were used to a certain routine. Toward evening the boat was drawn up to a sand bank for the night, sometimes near a village but never too close to jungle. The men pounded stakes into the sand, laid a crosspiece on which to hang their *kachang* or shelter against the heavy dew. One man started a fire and put the kettle of rice on to cook while the other foraged for logs to keep the fire burning all night.

After eating and clearing away the day's accumulations, our cabin had to be readied for the night. Before unrolling the mattresses and hanging the nets, Lucy and I had to struggle with the floor to raise it to seat level. This and reversing the process each morning was our particular chore.

There was a mysterious something – impossible to describe – about those lonesome nights in the wilds upriver that yielded a source of happiness not found in cities bent on material pursuits. With all the others in my rosary of nights spent in far, strange places – sleeping on sand or stony ground, out under the stars, in the deserts and scenic canyons of America, by waterfalls, in jungles, on hilltops or a black beach in Siam – these were pleasant to recall and relive in times of illness or sleeplessness.

Lucy was a restful companion. People called her quaint because she dressed in a long outmoded fashion, and was nebulous like a fluttering moth. When she smiled politely her thin face screwed up betraying many little wrinkles, that vaguely showed her age, at some twenty years more than I had believed.

She was quiet and self effacing and when she was not studying her Bible, her dark-skinned bony hands kept busy tatting lace for her undergarments. She was not a conversationalist but then neither did she "talk shop" nor gossip, and I never heard her speak disparagingly of any human being. She was tolerant of the faults of others, knowing her own limitations.

Unless we were too far from a village, Klun's old friends turned up to listen to his story about his new life. Far and wide the news spread. Men, women and children came with their resin torches to light the way and keep them safe. Then we got out the stereopticon and the harmonium for an impromptu meeting on the sand bank.

And wherever we stopped, night or day, the people were pathetically eager for the medicines the doctor had provided – peppermint for indigestion, quinine for fever, and zinc ointment for their eternally present syphilitic sores.

Late one afternoon we drew up to a bank where people were bathing. As usual, I went out to see what the village was like. A pretty young woman was on her way to carry water. I smiled and was surprised when she backed away and disappeared. Klun saw my bewilderment and told me the women here had never seen a foreigner before. She had asked him if I was a man or a woman. I felt as if I had suddenly been projected into another world.

Once the unmistakable call of a tiger broke the night silence. We woke instantly and the word *"sua"* was voiced by each of the men. More wood was thrown on the fire until it burst into high flames and for the remainder of the night the men took turns keeping watch.

The talk veered to the subject of tigers almost daily. Klun told us the villagers took their dogs up into the house at night and pulled the steps up too, and that a child lagging behind his father had recently been seized and carried off.

The last river village was now behind us. They said we would see no more such signs of life until we reached Sarahet. Late in the afternoon we saw a water buffalo standing in the river, its back horribly lacerated by a tiger's claws. Plucky animal. Man's friend. "What a fight that must have been!" we commented, and wondered what happened to its enemy. Yet Lucy and I had no thought of fear, and often wandered away from the boat following faint trails.

Next morning our boat stopped at the base of a steep bank in a deep bend of the river. We climbed to the top to wait while the men cooked and ate their breakfast. Crossing a narrow promontory we looked down upon a strange boat moored in the middle of the stream. There was no sign of the owner and we wondered where he might be and what sort of a person he was.

I sat on a log in the shade of a large tree to enjoy the faint breeze. Lucy decided to take a stroll. No sound came up from the boat. It was infinitely peaceful. Suddenly a wild shriek broke the stillness. I ran toward the bush calling, "Lucy, where are you?" There was no answer.

Just as I got to the edge of the clearing looking for an opening into the cane thicket, Klun reached the top of the bluff and met me.

At that very moment Lucy came flying out of the scrub, eyes staring, hair tumbled, and fell at our feet, gasping "Tiger!" The boatmen following in Klun's wake now joined us and began asking whether it was a *sua lai* [striped tiger], or *sua dao* [spotted], as if that were important!

As soon as she could breathe normally she insisted she had met a striped tiger. "I turned a bend in the path and there it was, looking at me!" What could she do but scream. She shuddered at the thought of her terror and put her hands to her face to shut out the memory of the sight.

While I lifted her to her feet and the men discussed the proximity of the prowler, a strange man came out of the clearing farther off. By the time he approached a few steps, six other lean Siamese woodsmen had left their cane-cutting and run all the way on hearing Lucy's scream. Their astonishment at the sight of our party with two strange women in foreign dress would be difficult for an artist to paint, blended as it was with incredulity, awe and disapproval.

The boat we had seen upriver was their home for the months of cane-cutting, and they supposed they were the sole inhabitants of this bleak section of the earth's surface. They admitted they had seen the tiger's tracks that morning and quickly dismissed the subject, showing little interest in our excitement now that there was nothing to do about it. There was but one question of importance to them – who were we and why had we come into this wilderness?

I then saw another side of Klun as he became an inspired emissary, fulfilling his destiny. His reply had a strange effect upon the men. They squatted in the shade of the single large tree overlooking the river and asked to hear more. I sat on a fallen log for three hours while he told Bible stories and explained the Christian message as he had absorbed it since being with us at the school.

One of the men said, "I've done too many evil things."

Another asked, "Do you really believe that a man is not doomed to a miserable rebirth on account of sin or lack of merit?"

"Is it possible for a man to lose the fear of consequences of past wrongs? To make a clean start?"

"We never heard there was any other religion. Our Buddha is not accessible like your Christ."

"You cannot leave us yet!"

Their urgency touched me, and I consented to spend the night there. Lucy too was reconciled to this unforeseen climax to her adventure. However, we both had to promise Klun that we would not stray from the boat again.

Our new friends helped make a campsite near their boat where there was a broad sandy stretch of clearing on low ground. After the men had eaten rice together, Lucy and I sang hymns and showed the lantern pictures, then retired. Long after midnight, I woke and saw the men sitting around the blazing fire, still talking, so deep was their conviction that they had found new incentive for living. In the years that followed Reverend Eakin visited their homes and saw their families formed into a Christian group.

Next morning when we came to the shallow rapids all four men walked in the water to pull and guide the boat. Beyond, there were long stretches of forest on one side or the other, and at one place where they met, the narrow river running between was deep and dark.

Klun pointed to a smooth, flat rock just above water level saying, "The people believe it is sacred, *Mem,* because it is never submerged. They say it rises and falls with the river, and that death will overtake anyone who stands on it. Many years ago an American doctor came this way and jumped on the rock in spite of warning, to show that he was not afraid. He died a few months later and the people believe it was because he defied the spirits."

The story that had circulated around the Mission was that the good doctor died from eating too many overripe mangoes in the hot season, but I said nothing.

On arrival at Sarahet we saw that only a canoe could go further to the *Karen* country. I looked at the small stream longingly, but decided that walking would probably be quicker anyway. So I took Klun with me to the *Kamnun's* house to secure a guide. When the astonished official realized that I wanted to go by land to a *Karen* village he was as shocked as if I had asked to go to the moon.

"Impossible, impossible, *Mem!*" he kept reiterating. "There is every kind of fierce animal and deadly reptile, besides boar and wild buffalo, leopard and tiger. There is the terrible *sladang* (I don't know what fierce creature he referred to), the most dangerous of all, because it attacks on sight and is very swift and persistent. You would not be safe even with many men with powerful guns!"

That seemed to settle it! As I rose to leave, the official added, "It is too bad you did not come a week earlier, you might have gone by canoe with the governor, who is just returning from an inspection trip. His boat is across the stream from yours." And I had supposed that my arrival was unheralded!

Back at the boat we could see activity across the river, and sensed an air of expectancy among our men. Soon a fine large fish was delivered by the governor's servant with the message that the *Chaokhun* would call in the evening. After dark a crowd gathered and Klun and Lucy got out the stereopticon and the governor watched the pictures. Before he left I had accepted two invitations from him. Things were looking up and I almost forgot about the *Karen*s.

Soon after daybreak I joined the governor on an inspection drill that he had set up in every village, and which he was very keen about. When we reached the *pu yai ban's* house, the owner began to tap a slow beat on a hollow bamboo. At once all the male villagers began to assemble from all directions. The governor addressed them and they returned to their homes.

Then, at a succession of double taps on the bamboo, the men ran stealthily with knives, staves, spears or fishing prongs, bending low, on guard as if against bandits.

The third signal was a rapid tattoo for fire fighting. The men formed a bucket line to the nearest well or source of running water. This exercise was particularly important, because when a native house of flimsy bamboo and thatch starts burning, it is soon an inferno, exploding like firecrackers. The sight and sound is terrifying but it is soon over. The most that can be done is to protect the other houses clustered about.

The governor had invited us to stay over a few more days and follow his houseboat on a leisurely trip to Khau Chang. When I told him that I had overstayed my time and must leave the next day for a quick return, he convinced me to change my plans. I had heard only rumors of an unusual topography for which there was no explanation, somewhere in the north. The place had been buried in jungle for a very long time. Now it had been rediscovered, he told me, and men had cleared a path in from the river. The governor promised there would be a guide waiting, and I would be the first woman ever to see it. How could I resist such an opportunity?

Gliding swiftly down river for an hour or so, we found the freshly cut opening in scrub jungle. A guide was waiting, with a horse for me to ride. Riding through the beautiful parklike jungle, we suddenly came to the "Elephant Rocks" in a clearing like a giant's playground – gigantic, odd-shaped granite boulders piled every which way. One, high as a house, rested on a pivot point.

We climbed bamboo ladders, and I saw the footprint of Buddha on top of one rock. The guide announced it had once been visited by a king. What made the whole scene uncanny was that there was not a hill or boulder for miles in any direction on this east bank of the river. The eeriness about the landscape could lend itself to legends, I mused.

Our guide took charge of the canoe and I rode back to Sarahet on the pony through forest that was like a beautiful park, while Klun led the way, walking. As I rode, retracing our steps to return finally to the familiar life of school and "civilization," I remembered what an old-timer in Siam had told me about Miss Cole's tragic first journey to the far north before 1880. During the many weeks traveling upriver in a native Laos boat, under far more primitive conditions than my present trip, her companion, Mary Campbell, drowned. I tried to imagine her courage, alone after that occurrence, in this vast region of impenetrable mountain jungle, with its dark, silent gorges and roaring cataracts – a stranger to the country, knowing no word of the language. How fortunate I was by comparison.

24 - Marriage

I was now 25 and in my fifth year in Siam, fully established and dedicated in the Mission. I had come to Siam in the naive faith that should my destiny include marriage – there must be one man in the world meant for me – he would appear at the right time and place. I would recognize him by some miraculous instinct and the matter would take its natural course. Somehow I knew that the romance promised by the island *pagoda* my first day in Siam would claim a place in my personal life.

That when I went to Petchaburi I was still heart-whole and fancy-free, was surely because of Miss Cole's watchful eye at all times. Bangkok was full of bachelors because the Siamese government, the diplomatic services and the business firms would not employ married men except for the highest posts. And dismissal could be expected to follow if a man married before completing a certain number of years' service. For that reason most young men fought shy of foreign girls and spent all their spare time at the clubs and drinking. The system being what it was, there were few opportunities to develop serious relationships for any of us unattached women. Only at Wang Lang was I safe from heart entanglement.

Constantly chaperoned, I could still catch the gleam in many an eye, but the inviolate barrier of the British social atmosphere was formidable. One time a young Englishman called, but just once. Miss Cole sent me on an errand to the school dormitory and on my return the young man was gone, walking my dog at Miss Cole's earnest entreaty.

In the fall of 1905 ending my second year, two new missionaries were appointed to Bangkok. Margaret McCord arrived first for Wang Lang. I then had companionship and the beginning of a lifelong friendship. She looked eagerly for the arrival of the other appointee whom she had met at the annual Board Conference in New York. She told me about this medical doctor, but also implied that I should keep hands off. She had designs on him.

Since travel times were always uncertain, no one knew when Dr. Lucius Constant Bulkley would arrive.

One day, while shopping downtown, I stopped at the Snyder's as we generally did. When I reached the top of the stairs, both Mr. and Mrs. Snyder gave a shout, rushed forward and grabbed my arms on both sides and propelled me up to Dr. Bulkley who

Lucius Constant Bulkley, 1904, 27 years old.

had just arrived. The introduction was amusing, but I was not particularly impressed with the man. Year after year subsequently he would be away on long tours with the Dunlaps, and I rarely saw him except at Mission Meetings.

Two years later, in 1907, I went to Bangkok for the Annual Meeting and stayed with the Snyders in their home where Dr. Bulkley happened also to be staying. A committee was elected to leave immediately after the Meeting to sail down the coast before the monsoon struck to explore possibilities for a mission vacation place at Koh Lak, a beautiful bay on the west shore of the Gulf.

For reasons known only to themselves, the Dunlaps and Miss Cole requested that I accompany them, along with Dr. Bulkley and Dr. Walker, who had lost his lovely young wife from illness the year before. The six of us were to go by a steamer up the coast, and wait at a government bungalow at Koh Lak bay for its return. It would be a ten- or twelve-day outing. I was anticipating the trip with mingled and somewhat mischievous feelings, for Dr. Walker had become more and more attentive recently, and I was also becoming attracted to Dr. Bulkley, although I had heard that he was engaged to someone in the States who was reluctant to leave her home.

However, shortly before we were to sail, Dr. Bulkley came down with typhoid fever and could not go. I thought better of going if Dr. Walker was the only single man, because I was not really drawn to him. I told them, despite their arguments and appeals, that I had changed my mind about going.

In 1908 Manning, the Britisher with the Royal Survey with whom I'd been in touch for three years, came to Petchaburi at Mrs. Eakin's invitation. An extra horse was borrowed from a Colonel friend so we could ride together. Dismounting at the end of a long ride, Manning proposed marriage, but I refused him because I didn't love him enough to leave the missionary work. He said he would wait.

The following year I made the long voyage from Bangkok to the States for my furlough year, stopping off in London. Manning had tried to arrange passage on the same boat and fortunately for me did not succeed, or I feel sure I might not only have changed my "Miss" status but also my nationality. As it was, his brother, taking consular examinations in London, took me around the city, the law courts and cathedrals, and I spent a day with his mother and sister in Surrey. All that year I received letters from Manning. He was planning to cross the Pacific and see me in my home in Sacramento. In panic I begged the Board to change my return sailing by a month, which meant that our ships passed close by each other not far from Japan.

Soon after this the High Commissioner of the six southernmost provinces on the west side of the peninsula made a proposal. He would build a hospital and doctor's residence if the Mission would undertake educational work and supply personnel for both. He wanted a mission station down in his isolated district. Because of its isolation government officials were given a "jungle bonus" as inducement to be stationed there. When it was agreed that there might also be a church and evangelistic work, the little village of Taptieng in Trang province, halfway down the Malay peninsula, was chosen, and Mr. and Mrs. E. P. Dunlap and Dr. Bulkley were appointed to pioneer the project.

Late fall, before leaving, Dr. Bulkley came to Petchaburi to say goodbye. The next morning instead of seeing him off at the railroad station, I found myself walking up Palace Mountain to a spot overlooking the plain. Why am I doing this? I asked myself, as I sadly watched the train snake out of sight. My reason told me that this was probably the last I would see of him. I had virtually closed the door to a relationship with Manning, and anyone else. Why was Dr. Bulkley so unresponsive? During any times we had been together he had never shown any sign of affection for me. Was it simply shyness? Had I been too forward? Maybe I hadn't let him know I was attracted to him. I was sad, for I now could acknowledge that I did have strong feelings for him. Did he care anything about me? It would probably be a year before I saw him again because of the physical distance now between us. A feeling of despondency stayed with me.

However, soon after Christmas I received a letter from Dr. Bulkley inviting me to join him at the new station as his wife! That was his proposal of marriage. He wrote that he had been released from his engagement to a nurse in the States who was not willing to join him in Siam.

Accepting his proposal by mail, I acknowledged to myself this was hardly the romantic way I would have chosen, but realized it was probably more characteristic of him.

The wedding was set for the twentieth of March when my school term was over. Life took on a new turn as I began making preparations for the transfer of my duties. Mrs. Eakin was willing to take over the school again after my move south.

I made my wedding dress of *pont d'esprit* [a fine French fabric], over white satin. Con, short for Constant, the middle name he went by, gave me definite orders when I prepared to pack for the move that no furniture or "doo-dads", as he described nonessential belongings, could go to the new home! I began to resent the phrase in the marriage vows about obeying.

The wedding had to be at night in order to accommodate out-of-town guests arriving on the evening train and leaving the next morning.

It was held in the church so that all the officials and school patrons might witness a foreign marriage ceremony.

To conform in part to Siamese custom, and at Klun's special request, the evening before we feasted on rice and curry on the lawn with about fifty of our Siamese friends.

There was no carriage in the city except the governor's so I drove with my maid of honor, Margaret McCord, to the church in the doctor's two-wheel trap for the wedding ceremony. That is, I held the reins, for Klun – after presenting his gift, an heirloom ruby ring – refused to drive or sit with us in the cart, but insisted on walking at the horse's head all the way to the church. Returning to the compound after the ceremony with my new husband Con, Klun again refused to ride, and this time ran all the way to keep up with the spirited horse.

In the bright light of an over-full March moon the wedding reception was held on the lawn. After changing into riding clothes we mounted our horses, decorated with old shoes, and set out for Bantaloo. Lotus blossoms that had been carried up the church aisle pelted us as we rode out of the compound.

Muen, my cook, who had accompanied me during the river trip, went ahead early in the morning with an ox cart loaded for a week's outing. Instead of going through the rice fields as usual, Con and I decided to try the new embankment road, built straight to the sea which King Chulalongkorn had ordered during his visit to Petchaburi. No one knew much about it except that work had recently stopped when news was received of the King's death.

We found the going rough, the road broken wherever there was a ditch or stream of water. This meant we had to continually urge our horses to climb up and down the frequent detours. Finally the embankment ended miles from nowhere and we wandered in the moonlight, lost, hunting for the only cart track across the swamp. We could hear the incessant surge of the sea breaking along the shore for hours so near, yet so far. It was nearly three o'clock in the morning before we finally reached the bungalow! What an inauspicious beginning of our honeymoon!

Edna and Con

25 -Arrival in Trang

"You've not been listening!"

"Oh, yes I have," I exclaimed eagerly, "but the countryside is so beautiful, so different from the Siam I've known. I was too busy taking it all in to comment or ask questions."

For about twenty minutes – ever since we left the mountain pass where we spent the night – the man beside me, my new husband, had been trying to prepare me for some of the things I would need to adjust to in my new life.

I had listened respectfully, too absorbed in the scenery to wish to break in on the discourse, which had surprised me very much, being more of a speech than I had heard in the three weeks since our marriage.

The raised road on which we were traveling in the governor's car was the vermilion of laterite clay. It was edged with neatly trimmed grass mile after mile. Jagged hills dotted the land. Here and there villages stood out green in contrast to the yellow of the rice fields, which stretched away on either side, golden with the long stalks of cut rice lying on the ground. Here in this province the ripened grain was cut close to the head with small blades held in the palm of the hand.

The people we passed seemed a different type from the Siamese I had been familiar with in central Siam. The women dressed in a strange fashion – long flowered cotton coats over *sarongs* [a skirt-like garment] – long hair worn in a high knot with gold pins or flowers as ornaments. Barefoot, they carried themselves with the free swing and grace of those who bear burdens on their heads. Several men had prostrated themselves at the approach of the car, thinking it carried the governor, then gazed incredulously at the strange occupants.

Now I attempted to enumerate the last few remarks I had been conscious of. "We are sharing our home with Mr. and Mrs.

Dunlap until their home is finished. Most of the furniture is theirs and as the servants belong to them, I will just be a guest in my own home. Really I won't mind at all. You are wedded to your hospital. Your gun and mandolin have shared your solitude quite some time and I am to find my place somehow, somewhere, in relation to all three. I am sure I can fit in all right."

Con seemed to stiffen at my bold statement of his tactful tactics, and looked sternly ahead. Afterwards when I teased him about my being his *mia-noi* or secondary wife, he was amused, but for a moment I wondered if I had gone too far with this older man I did not know very well, who was my husband.

Just then we cut a swath down a busy market street and I cried out, "Oh Con, is this our village?" shocked at what I saw. At once he was stricken with the realization he had not prepared me, as he had intended, for my first sight of my new home.

Now he started to say, "I forgot to tell you . . ." but it was too late. Perhaps it was just as well, for he had no flair for describing places satisfactorily, anyway.

We were crossing a bridge beyond the village crossroads and the hospital burst into view. Huge and bare and barn-like, at

Village Street

least it was set back impressively from the road in a goodly space of ground. Beyond the hospital was a small thatched cubicle perched on stilts, which instantly reminded me of the tiny spirit shrines all over the kingdom.

Feebly Con spoke, "There is your home!"

Taken completely by surprise by its primitive appearance, I barely restrained a laugh.

As the car drove through a gap in the scraggly tea hedge, Mrs. Dunlap appeared on the veranda to welcome us. "This is a surprise! We did not expect you until evening, knowing the pony cart takes all day. What happened?"

"The cart is on the way," Con answered. "The car is reward for being up most of the night nursing the High Commissioner."

"That explains it then. How fortunate for you, Edna," Mrs. Dunlap said. "It would have been a long tiresome ride. Oh by the way, doctor, Mr. Mathieu left a message for you. He is waiting for you to join him on a deer hunt."

What the alarm bells are to the fire brigade, mention of hunting was to my husband. Now he dashed inside for his old clothes, hanging in readiness for any emergency, and was soon off on his bicycle with a fond apology, "You don't mind, do you dear? Mrs. Dunlap will show you around."

What was a bride supposed to do? Standing on the veranda, I called after him, "Bring home some venison!"

I should have seen the handwriting on the wall. I had been warned that being a doctor's wife would be a lonely life, and I was ready to give him up to every call of duty but I could not have foreseen the import of being passed up for a buck. If I had wept and protested that I couldn't bear to be left so unceremoniously, might I have become a clinging vine? One thing is certain. I soon realized I must be the oak tree.

My husband should have been an explorer, pure and simple. Instead, he tried to combine his explorations with medicine, surgery, big game hunting, skinning and stuffing birds and family life, and the urge to travel new paths.

The journey from Bangkok to Trang after our wedding actually had begun to prepare me. In the past Con had made this journey by various routes, including crossing the peninsula on foot, bicycle and elephant, and by the northern pass from Sritamarat. On this, my first trip to Trang, we left the East Asiatic Steamship Company's vessel at Singora in order to go up the inland sea to Patalung, then west overland fifty miles, a three-day walk over the southern mountain pass.

We had been guests of the British Consul and his wife while waiting for the next scheduled passage, with no premonition of what it would be like. The twelve-hour launch trip up the inland sea was not a day of honeymoon bliss or carefree ease. No sight-seeing, no meals, no cool drinks. The decrepit old craft had forgotten it was ever painted and clean. It was just a poor battered hulk, skulking in this backwater like a mangy alley cat, picking up a living among the flotsam and jetsam of a most out-of-the-way spot in the Orient. However, it had one bench, center-forward, long enough on which to stretch out, and I was the favored occupant, an ameliorating circumstance in an otherwise nightmare experience.

It happened to be that time of month when I experienced pain, hours on end, wave upon wave. I was constantly breaking into perspiration from the heat and the effort to let no moaning sound escape my lips, ever mindful of the natives sitting all over the deck, crowding every inch of space. As if that were not enough, because of faulty loading and overcrowding, the launch rode on an uneven keel so the deck had a precipitous slant. I was terrified every time the boat suddenly lurched from one side to the other and the cargo shifted. I would find my head lower than my feet, and would be compelled to rise and change position.

The medicine kit was my pillow but held no comfort. Con was not going to give morphine to this young person he scarcely knew – it might start a precedent. No softy should his wife be – the times needed fortitude, stoicism.

When we were deposited at the governor's landing in Patalung that night, late as it was, our Siamese host and fatherly friend was waiting up to escort us to the guest bungalow. He told us the welcome news that our pony and ox cart had arrived from Trang.

The next day we were off before noon. Con walked ahead with his gun while the ox cart with all the camp equipment lagged farther and farther behind. Our new cook from Bangkok stayed with it. I sat alone in the tiny springless Malay cart, pulled by our wild-looking *syce* practically straddling the small horse. Trying to curb my restless spirit, my mind pictured an Indian princess in her *howdah* [canopied seat] on an elephant, a Chinese lady in her curtained sedan chair, the pioneer woman crossing plain and mountain in one of the covered wagons, or a desert nomad going to her new home on a shaggy steed.

We spent the second night in one of several bungalows on the western slope of the mountain range at Chong. About midnight I heard the call that was to haunt my married years in Siam: the word *Maw*, spoken in the dead of night under our bedroom window. It always contained a world of pathos, whether spoken by the hospital night watchman announcing the relapse of an inpatient, one of a group carrying a wounded stretcher patient, or a lone man walking in from an outlying village seeking help for a loved one.

It was always I who heard it and woke the doctor. I would listen to the voice beneath the flickering light of the resin torch, politely answering questions and marvel that there was never a

The hospital at Trang

hint of urgency while the man waited to be the doctor's guide. I would worry that someone might die in the interminable process of his getting away. On this occasion it was a messenger begging the doctor to hasten to the High Commissioner – just arrived by car with his nephew, the governor of Trang – who had the symptoms of cholera.

Con stayed at the man's bedside until all danger was past. For that, we finished the third day of the peninsula crossing in a motor car, taking only thirty minutes instead of the five or six hours it would have taken by pony cart, thus our early arrival in my new home.

Con relaxing

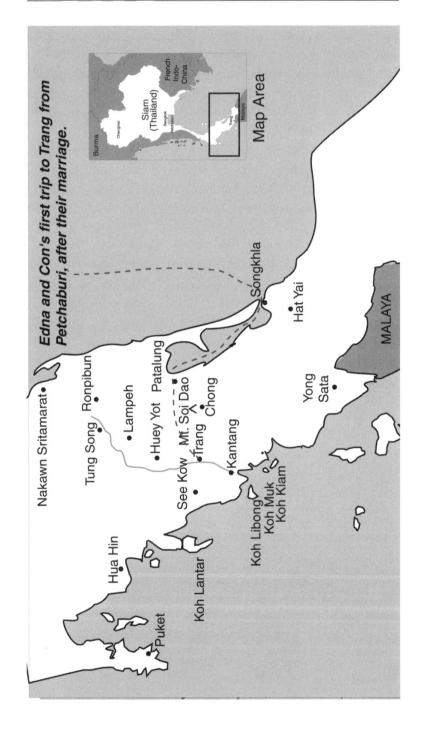

Edna and Con's first trip to Trang from Petchaburi, after their marriage.

26 - The First Few Years

Looking down from the sky, facing north, picture with me the center of the Malay Peninsula. On the right the deep blue Gulf of Siam; on the left more blue of the Andaman Sea near where it begins to run into the Straits of Malacca. This is dotted with hundreds of silver-rimmed spots of green – islands. Many are jagged and uninhabitable except for the birds whose edible nests are so prized by Orientals. The water is deep so ships can pass very close. Many islands have fantastic shapes – one like a tea kettle. On others are found the nomad Water Gypsy tribes. Several of the larger islands have a village and a harbor. Between the two seas is "home" as I knew it, and I explored its radius of forty miles for nearly twenty years. In my opinion Trang is the most beautiful province in Siam, endowed as it is with red earth, hills, streams, lakes, rivers, waterfalls. In later years all became accessible by a masterful road-building plan.

Trang province is approximately halfway between Bangkok and Singapore, on the west side of the long Malay peninsula, which at this point is only eighty miles wide. An almost impenetrably dense tropical mountain range runs the length of the peninsula. Halfway down this range, a lonely peak dominates the two provinces which it separates – Patalung on the east, touching the Gulf of Siam, and Trang on the west, along the Andaman Sea. The peak is called *Soi Dao*, meaning Pluck the Stars.

The home I came to with my new husband was about ten miles west of *Soi Dao* as the crow flies, in a village then called Taptieng, meaning noonday rest. And its name was no idle one. Near the crossroads, under a great shade tree on the bank of a stream fed by Mount *Soi Dao* was a monumental bench with a receptacle for burning *joss* sticks. Built by the Chinese, it had been kept whitewashed and repaired through many decades.

People said it had been dedicated to the truce enacted after a battle between rival Chinese clans at the crossroads. Another story was that it had been the scene of the settling of a serious difference between the governors of Sritamarat and Trang. It may have been both. Whatever its history, wayfarers could find shade, water and relaxation during their noontime stop in Taptieng.

Taptieng was at the intersection of the fifty-mile east-west highway across the peninsula – 20 miles to a little river-bank town on the west, and 50 miles over the 1,000 foot Southern Pass to the ancient town of Patalung on the Inland Sea to the west – and the main north-south road. This is a stretch of 100 miles, from the little port town of Kantang, 16 miles south of Taptieng to the railroad junction at Tungsong in the north. From there it was said to be a three day journey by elephant west to a port on the coast. A road winds east from Tungsong over the Northern Pass, then northeast to another ancient city, Nakawn Sritamarat near the Gulf. Radiating

Atop an elelphant

Women walking to market.

from the center of Taptieng like spokes of a wheel were roads going northeast to a tin mine at Lampeh in the foothills of the mountain range, and southeast to the little town of Yong Sata.

Since it was the hub of the area it was only natural for it to be the marketing center, and from olden times the public market was held here every third day. It was an institution. People walked to and from their towns with their produce; some even from Patalung, a three days walk each way.

The region had been known around the world for its Trang pepper, but when the market dropped, the growers allowed their vines to die out. The High Commissioner of the six southern provinces gifted one of these abandoned pepper gardens to the Mission of the Presbyterian board. The hospital and a small house for a bachelor doctor had been completed only five months before my arrival on the scene.

At first I supposed the region was newly opened up – there were no ancient ruins, only old tin diggings and stories of a battle between rival Chinese tongs at the Taptieng crossroads. Later a cave was discovered with quantities of clay plaques with the *Siva* [Hindu deity] image, and the people said, "Many centuries ago

Indians swept over our land, and we still keep some of their customs."

Through the years we learned something of the history of the peninsula. Just as Englishmen crossed the Atlantic a few hundred years ago to escape religious intolerance and found a new homeland in America, so the Hindu Dravidians of South India crossed the Bay of Bengal to this peninsula to escape the militant evangelism of the Buddhist King Asoka of North India, more than 2000 years ago. They, like the English Pilgrims were colonizers bringing their traditions with them, and ensuing centuries brought both Hindus and Buddhists from north and south India, traders, and warriors and priests.

At the same time, before the Christian era, the Tai of Northwest Szechuan province in China, migrated south as far as Java to escape the aggression of the Chinese. In the fusion of the meeting here, the Tai became dominant, and adopted many Indian customs. The present-day native Siamese of this area are descended from that Tai migration, and they still speak in their strange, quaint singsong dialect from the far north. They keep to their compact village life – with flimsy bamboo houses usually on stilts – and their rice planting.

Over the centuries generations of Chinese settled in this region as well and made it prosperous. They planted the immaculately kept pepper and nutmeg gardens, the coconut groves, and later the rubber for export. They raised the finest pork in the orient from hogs fed on cooked mash and bathed daily. The hogs were often better housed and cared for than their owners' children. On their scattered estates the Chinese lived in barn-like structures with earthen floors solidly built to withstand robbers.

The prosperity was still evident at the present time, undoubtedly due to the fact that the High Commissioner was a Chinese of advanced ideas who had a passion for order – a man with vision and ambition. He was a self-made man, unable to read or write in any language, but with a phenomenal memory for faces, facts and figures. The Siamese government had given him the title of *Phya Ratsada* (High Commissioner) and made no attempt to interfere with his little kingdom during his lifetime.

A sketch of a native house on stilts

We saw the little village of Taptieng, without even postal service, become Trang, the capital of the province and a good-sized town of considerable importance. In the early days all our mail was sent from Bangkok, first by ship to Nakawn Sritamarat, thence by carriers walking six days to the port of Patalung for distribution. After that, unless we sent for it by messenger, it came any which way, but generally by someone coming upriver in the steam launch.

The break of the monsoon that first year in Taptieng was long delayed. All the month of April was exceedingly hot. The grass was yellow and the withering tea hedges were gray with dust. The unseasoned lumber used in building our house had shrunk, letting the sunlight through chinks in the wall of our eleven-by-eleven foot bedroom in the mornings and in the west bedroom occupied by the Dunlaps in the afternoon. The small middle room held a crude table and bentwood chairs for dining. It was a tiny room with four double doors opening on to front and back verandas and to the two bedrooms. It had no windows.

The house had been built for a bachelor, and we were two couples occupying it. Usually I preferred to spend the forenoons in the open ground space under the house. Mrs. Dunlap never complained. Years afterward I learned from her friend in Bangkok that she had spent the long hot afternoons lying on the floor under their bed!

Most of the rainy season was a succession of downpours at twenty or thirty minute intervals, with hot sunshine in between. The minute it cleared I would dash out on errands, or hang bedding and clothing out to dry, ever alert for the roar of the swiftly approaching deluge as it raced towards us over miles of jungle without any darkening cloud's shadow to herald it.

When we had days of almost incessant rain and everything was damp, we put a charcoal brazier under the beds and draped our clothes around it. Much of my time would be spent helping the Boy combat mold on the floors and walls, books and shoes. When a capricious wind accompanied the rain, even with doors and windows shuttered, it was difficult to find a sheltered spot in the tiny house because of the lattice between the top of the wall and the ceiling, and from the ground to the roof on the outer side of the stair well. Often the rain would find a weak spot in the wind-ruffled thatch and then come down from the ceiling as well.

I enjoyed occasional jaunts with Con to explore my new surroundings. One of our excursions down the river took us on an adventure through a *mangrove* swamp in an attempt to shorten our return trip. At the mouth of the river the right bank was bordered by low jungle. The left bank ended abruptly then curved in to make a tiny cove bounded by four gigantic cliff rocks – all four in a row jutting straight out into the sea. Any boat going south would have to go out to sea and around the last cliff.

The boatmen were talking together as we reached the cove.

"*Mem*, there is a short cut to the beach through *mangrove* swamps that are flooded at high tide. The tide is high now – it will save much time." It was about eight o'clock and as dark as the river Styx.

"Do you know the way?"

"Someone took me once."

"Well, if you are sure you can take us safely – "

Our house in Trang

We inched our way toward the cliff. It was impossible to imagine any opening between the towering rock cliffs.

The Englishman in our party had a five-cell flashlight without which we could not have succeeded. As it was we spent a great deal of time weaving back and forth, searching for the elusive opening. We had not eaten since tea at the Rest House in See Kow, and I for one was longing to get at the rice and curry. But this was no time to search through our fully loaded sampans for something to eat in the pitch darkness, and besides, we were far too intent on keeping our boats together and locating the shortcut that might save us a few hours.

The flashlight showed an impenetrable tangle of trees in the narrow space between the two walls of rock. We nosed nearer and then back and forth for a while quite baffled. The Siamese insisted the opening must be there.

When at last we found the narrow, shallow channel just wide enough for our boats with no room to spare, we spent the weirdest hour and a half that any of us had ever experienced. A *mangrove* tree even in day time is interesting. It has a smooth whitish trunk and many forms of limbs and every limb with manifold tentacles reaching down, down, as if just about to coil around man or beast.

But on a black night with thousands of them all around us and towering overhead, ghastly and ghostly in the light of the roving searchlight, the snakelike roots seemingly writhing only inches from us, it was a surreal world.

The slightest whisper echoed uncannily. Then, as we twisted and turned through the narrow channel opening, our boat snapped a branch and it was like a revolver shot, reverberating through endless corridors. No one talked except once when I couldn't help saying "how absolutely uncanny!" and even the words seemed to press in on us. The boatmen believed it was the abode of evil spirits, and were most anxious to get along as quickly and quietly as possible to avoid attracting the attention of the spirits of the place, the *Phi*. After what seemed an interminable period of time the channel widened and we were again on the river and on our way to our destination. The boatmen were noticeably relieved. I was reluctant to question them about their previous passage through the mangrove swamp, thankful we weren't stranded there through the long night.

For our first few years, until the government moved up from the river port and displaced the facility, we lived with the sour smell of a winery, gently wafted to us by the prevailing winds for nine months of the year.

Later, when we had a fine girls' boarding school northeast of us, there was a *kapi* factory [fermented shrimp paste used in making curries] built between the school and our house. The monsoon then had an even more pronounced effect on our lives. One morning I greeted the American principal with the remark, "The monsoon must have changed overnight, judging from the smell of things at our home."

"Yes, I enjoyed my breakfast for the first time in nine months," she replied. "You are lucky to have the *kapi* smell for only three months." Such are the joys of the tropics.

27 - Guests and Neighbors

After the Dunlaps' new home was completed and they had moved out, it became necessary to go to Penang to buy house furnishings. We had been sleeping on the packing case in which some mattresses had been shipped from the States. Besides the crude dining table and wretched chairs, Con owned a roller-top desk and two teak bookcases. We definitely lacked the feminine things.

We drove the sixteen miles to the river port of Kantang, then boarded a small steam vessel captained by a Malay. Its cargo was a deck-load of hogs in rattan slings packed so close together that to cross the deck, we walked across their backs. There was no passenger cabin, so we spent the next twenty-two hours in lawn chairs on the tiny upper deck.

We were scarcely settled back at home with our new purchases when the Danish chief of provincial gendarmerie, a Colonel Kolz, arrived in our village on an inspection tour, suffering from his twenty-third attack of dysentery – he seemed to feel that it was his last. Con brought him to our house for better care but it was too late. He was the first to be buried in the new Mission cemetery.

At that time there was no room in the hospital equipped to accommodate a foreigner. I asked and was given permission to spend a small sum of money to fix up a special room for those who wanted the luxury of first-class. Up to that time I had never been inside an American hospital and did not know the white sterile simplicity that ruled. Here was an unpainted room without a ceiling and devoid of any means for cheering a sick person. I bought an iron bedstead and scoured the village for a gay print to make a flounce around the top of the four posts to hide the sagging of the mosquito net. I confess I squirmed every time I thought of the hideous pink of that ruffle, yet Con didn't seem to mind. The first patient to use the bed was a Hindu who, to show off his English, wrote a letter when he left praising the "beautiful, fancy, flowery rosy scene that met my gaze while I was recovering from the tender, merciful, loving treatment of the kind doctor." I kept the letter for many years as my first and only testimonial in connection with the hospital.

Our next house guest, also a Dane by the name of Steiner, was taking his English bride overland to a new post. He took mischievous delight in telling his wife and my husband about the manner in which I had made a call upon him when we were both very new in Siam. It had happened when I was making my first visit to Rajburi from Wang Lang, and he was gendarmerie captain, training the local police force. My hostess had sent him an invitation to dinner, and in the note asked if it would be convenient to send a horse over for me to ride. Led by a Siamese policeman, a horse promptly appeared which must have been a woman-hater or most certainly antiforeigner. As soon as I mounted, there was not another dull moment. It brushed under low-hanging trees, broke a garden fence, backed to the very river's edge, and jumped a ditch. Finally, with the bit in its teeth it raced down the narrow river road, scattering market women to right and left; dashed into the police compound and stopped short under the open window where the captain was shaving, so startling him that the blade gashed his face. Such had been our introduction!

After the Steiners left, they telegraphed that a jewel case had been left under a pillow. A search of the room failed to turn it up. At the time we had a new cook and a young house-boy, both being trained. Con explained to them that we would "lose much face" if the jewelry were not returned. Con's first thought was to offer a reward. His second thought was to pay a man to worm the information out of the thief. In the meantime, he brought all the hospital staff over to the house to help in the search. He led them in the weirdest search I could have imagined – up into the attic, into every corner of every room, even using a mirror to check under the flooring. I wondered if he had gone berserk.

When they stopped at noon and the staff returned to the hospital, Con again searched around the bed, lifted the mattress, reached his hand deep into the pillowcase and there was the flat jewelry case he had not felt in his initial search. In it were Mrs. Steiner's earrings and pendants, ring and chain, aquamarines and diamonds. Greatly relieved, we immediately wired the Steiners, who meanwhile had already wired the Bangkok, Penang and Singapore police to watch the pawnshops. Con had given the young culprit a chance to enter the room alone to return the stolen article while the party was looking elsewhere, knowing no questions would be asked. The *Boy* developed into a good, responsible servant.

Soon after we returned from the shopping trip to Penang, Mr. and Mrs. Dunlap went to Burma to attend the Judson centennial and we were alone for several months. On Saturday nights our cook put forth his best effort and we dressed in our wedding clothes and played innocent games after dinner, with the idea that we needed to keep up our morale.

At this time there were few "foreigners" in peninsular Siam. In Nakawn Sritamarat, five days' journey from us, lived two missionary families. Two Swiss brothers and a German were building the branch railway to join the future main line there. Ronpibun on the eastern slope of the northern pass, which later became an important tin mining center with more "foreigners," was then just a night's stop overland. Singora, a difficult four-day trip away, had one or two "white men" besides the British consulate.

At Huey Yot and Lampeh, twelve and fifteen miles from our village, the tin that later would bring both English and Australians to be our neighbors had not as yet been discovered. At Kantang, the river port south of us lived a German businessman, and an Englishman building our branch railway line north to meet the main line. Both had native women managing their establishments, but we saw no sign of them when we were invited to dinner. One other Britisher on the railway construction, and a genial *Eurasian* managing the first rubber plantation five miles north of us, completed the roster of *farangs* within five days journey from us.

One by one in the course of time we met them, those nearer coming to tea or dinner. Other strangers, passing through, spent the night or a few days. Because there were no hotels, hospitality was obligatory, and through the years we entertained almost every European nationality including Russian and Latvian. There was a Siamese prince, an Oxford graduate, who, with his wife and sister vacationed with us as paying guests, and became lifelong friends.

Then there was the Chinese doctor who was a friend of Dr. Sun Yat Sen; and the wealthy Moslem who spent several days with us and in an aside in charming English said, when all the Mohammedans in the region were prostrating themselves at his feet, "They've all been thieves or murderers in their own land and can't return, probably."

A German Baron – formerly a Prussian general – apparently was in the same predicament, for it was said that he could not return to his country. Rumor had it that he had come to life in his coffin, which explained his snow-white hair.

An Arab on his way north by train from Penang had asked at each stop for the American doctor he had met in the Persian Gulf and whose name he had forgotten. He finally connected with my husband.

One of our Siamese friends, a nobleman, had three wives. I was on friendly, calling terms with all of them. The two lesser wives both had children, the First had none and felt the humiliation bitterly. "Oh Mem," she would wail, "I would bear illness or poverty or ill-treatment gratefully if I could but bear one child!" The nobleman's daughter by his deceased first wife took precedence over all the household. She had been educated in the large Methodist mission boarding school in Penang, and I loved her as a younger sister. Then the daughter learned that wife Number One was spending large sums of money to buy charms and potions from a *Maw-du* [native doctor] to win her husband's sole affection. My heart was wrung at the tales of intrigue in the home. When the gentleman was in his last illness, there was utter confusion. Con was called at all hours by the daughter. He tried desperately to save his life, but each of the wives had her favorite old-school doctor or remedy and the combination was fatal.

An American millionaire and his wife one time wired from Penang, "We have heard of your hospitality. Could you accept two lonely Americans?"

These and a host of others enriched our lives. I'll never forget a Danish adventurer who came to the hospital completely exhausted after walking for three days across the peninsula with his *Boy*. After lunching with us and being supplied with medicines he returned to the guest bungalow where he had left his *Boy* to cook and serve him. In the middle of the night the *Boy* came running to the hospital in tears. The *Nai*, his master, was dying, he wailed. Con rushed to the bungalow to discover the man had drunk the liniment meant for his sore muscles, instead of the laxative! He refused to be put in the hospital or to stay where he was. We had no choice but to bring him into our home.

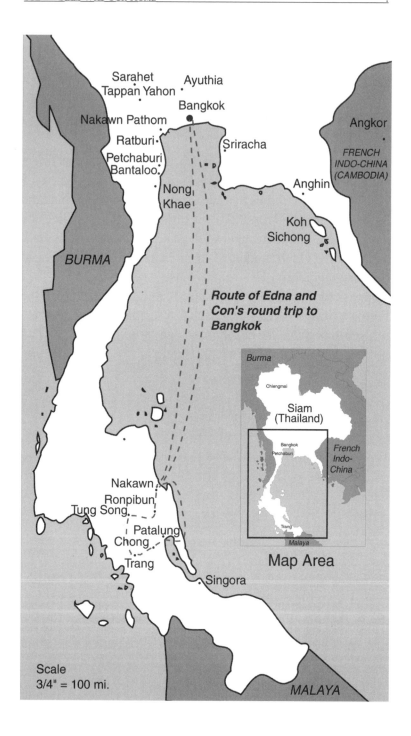

28 - To Bangkok and Back (1911)

In early August of 1911, five months before our first child was expected, Con received permission to enlarge the house. We had decided to add six-foot verandas on two sides for bath and dressing rooms, and to enclose the front stairs and veranda. While the lumber was being brought to the compound to be cut, hewn and planed and all the doors and windows made by hand on the spot, we decided to make the 600 mile Bangkok trip to attend the annual get-together of the Mission. I was having an uncomplicated pregnancy, was feeling well, and was still able to wear my clothes – it was the year of the high-waisted empire fashion. Otherwise I doubt I would have attempted it. The days preceding were very full: planning for the trip, taking care of the hospital, our house and compound, and arranging for the dogs, cats and monkeys to be left behind.

The day we left on our trip, near the end of August, we were up early for the final packing. Our young Chinese cook filled a small box with cooking utensils, potatoes, onions, squash, limes, etc. I filled the market basket with sugar, canned milk, butter, tea, salt, jam, all in small tins or jars, sardines, sausages, tin cups, enamel plates, cutlery. I filled the canteen with water and the thermos bottle with hot cocoa mix. By seven o'clock we finished our packing and everything was put in the ox cart, along with a sack of rice, a lantern, Con's medicine case, a Chinese sleeping mat with mosquito net and rain coats.

After breakfast the house was shut up, using hammer and nails freely. About half past ten we piled our bedding, an army blanket, two steamer rugs and couch cushions into our pony cart. By the time we got ourselves in, plus the gun and dinner pail as well, we were wedged so tightly that we could scarcely move. The *shandrydan* we were riding in was a two-wheeled, closed cart with a door in the back, side seats and a half-door, half-window in front opening onto a narrow platform for the driver. Out of consideration for the pony and the heavy load it was pulling, we often walked. The loaded ox cart followed behind.

A short distance out of town a strange noise behind us caused the pony to run. Finally it was controlled enough to pull to one side and allow several automobiles to pass us. We discovered that our slow pace was holding up a cavalcade of the High Commissioner, the Governor and their party, who were all escorting a Prince on a tour of the province.

The day was dark and cool. The drive was delightful. The fine, smooth, red road, bordered on either side with grass as fine as any park boulevard, stretched through miles of rice fields and rubber plantations. Then we reached the jungle and foothills, with the mountain looming up ahead.

We had our rice and curry lunch at a small village, sitting on a shady river bank beside the road. As usual, some children gathered, followed soon by a few men and women. Con played on his mandolin to entertain them.

About five o'clock in the evening we reached Chong, the beautiful park at the entrance to the mountain pass. It is surrounded on three sides by mountains, beautiful drives, lawns, flowers and terraces where once was dense forest. Shaded paths lead in different directions to the cascade where two mountain streams from the slopes of *Soi Dao* (the principal mountain peak in the region), converge almost in sight of the houses. There were five houses in all: the royal guest house, two picturesque smaller ones for women, and two other pretty rest houses, all available for us to use when not occupied by royalty or guests of the High Commissioner or other officials.

All this was only nine miles from our home in Taptieng. Over the years it became one of our favorite getaways, whether by cart or by car with the children, or alone by horseback. Here in fact I was later privileged to watch the filming of a sequence of *Chang,* the epic film of the silent movies with its elephants, tigers, boa constrictor and gibbons as actors. The directors, Merion Cooper and Ernest B. Schoedsack, stayed at our home.

The casade and sala at Chong

It was nearly dark when the cook arrived with the ox cart and while it was being unloaded I noticed that my trunk was missing. "Didn't you see to its being carried downstairs?" Con asked. "No, I supposed you had told the servants what to do."What excuse did I have? I was learning that in this life I had to jolly well look after myself.

The next morning we sent the ox cart driver back to Taptieng to hire a man to help bring the trunk in the customary manner, slung from a pole carried on their shoulders. By the following evening they were back. Although I was much chagrined at my carelessness, I was not really sorry because this was the only day on our trip that I didn't feel well. I was grateful for the beautiful, restful place in which to spend the day.

The men arrived with the trunk just before dark. On the third morning we were up very early, had a little breakfast and started out walking to enjoy the early morning air. Then for a couple of hours we climbed steadily. The road was as fine as the one we had come on, perpetually winding and crossing the mountain stream. We could scarcely see the road ahead because of the dense forest – giant trees, covered with many kinds of orchids, palms, and ferns – rose high on one side and fell steeply away on the other.

Con shot a huge black monkey – *kang*, it is called. They are weird looking creatures with the deep white circles around the eyes. The fur is very soft and pretty but does not compare with the beautiful white monkey or *cha-nee*, which is tailless and has black circles around the eyes. The Siamese believe that there are no male *cha-nee*, and that the cry of the females is *pua* which means husband. However, at the Governor's we saw a whole family of *cha-nee* – father, mother and several young ones. The call of the white monkey is as sweet as a siren's call. The voice has a wonderful range which can be heard for a long distance. In the early morning the forests resound with their music.

At the summit of the pass an arch marks the boundary of the two provinces. From that point on to the end of the road at the town of Patalung on the Inland Sea, there are 62 small bridges, all numbered.

About an hour after noon we reached a rest house where we had lunch and waited for the ox cart, a much slower traveler, to catch up. After supper, about seven o'clock, we started out for the next rest house where we were to spend the night. The road was a lonely one, going by moonlight, often through dark, shadowy jungle stretches.

Con walked ahead with his gun the entire distance, while I rode, or had the man lead the horse. It was much farther than we had expected. By eleven p.m., as we neared the village, the moon had set. This guest house was a very fine large house. The man in charge received us royally, and we spent a comfortable night.

Right after breakfast the next morning, Con left for Patalung on foot. He hoped to be early enough to find a boat so we could leave the same day for Nakawn Sritamarat. Our intention was to stop off there on our way to Bangkok because Con had been asked to help with a surgical case there. I left several hours later with our cart and provisions. The road now was through rice fields, without shade, the sun's glare frightful. It was the hottest day since we left home.

The Governor entertained us when we reached Patalung. When he learned of our plans, which included taking a launch down the inland sea to Singora — a 12 hour trip — then back up the coast for our stop at Nakawn Sri before resuming the voyage to Bangkok, he mentioned that there was a shortcut to Nakawn by a series of canals and rivers.

Con was intrigued by the possibility of a route that might save time. He decided to take it, in spite of the fact that there was a perfectly good road from Nakawn to a river village if we had kept on. As a result we ended up spending an exasperating week of delays and discomforts. First we had to send the cook back to Taptieng with the *shandrydan*, pony and ox cart and most of the cooking utensils. We kept only a little brass tea kettle, a pan for cooking rice, a small frying pan and our personal things.

Then Con hired a large *sampan*, one with a sail. We draped the low rounded shelter under which we were to live, with a crocodile skin and a tiger skin. These the governor gave us in exchange for taking a cage with five little *ling-loms* to Bangkok – three of them for his daughter. These curious creatures appeared to be half-monkey and half-squirrel

With sail set, we skimmed over the northern tip of the inland sea in a nice breeze when suddenly Con gave a violent start and said, "Keep perfectly calm. Don't say a word. I am going to order the boat back to Patalung. I left my money belt hanging in the bathroom with four hundred *ticals* [approx. $150] – all the money I brought with me."

The boatmen complied, asking no questions, but in a manner that seemed to say, "These unpredictable *farangs*!" Arriving at the landing Con jumped ashore, made a dash to the bungalow and returned looking happy. Not a word was spoken. The men looked mystified as we resumed our sail. As for me, my conscience felt quite a bit lighter about my trunk episode.

The "cabin" of the boat was so small there was barely room to lie down, and so low that we could not sit up straight. We had to be content to eat and read lying down or propped on an elbow. For four long nights and five days, this is how we lived. We crossed a neck of the inland sea and spent the first night at the mouth of a canal. It was lots of fun cooking breakfast at the little *sala* there. Whenever it was possible in the canals we got out and walked. We cooked our meals on a bank twice a day. I was the "camp cook," and our simple fare was soft-boiled rice, scrambled eggs and cocoa made with water from the canal (boiled, of course).

It was fun watching the dear, furry little *ling-loms* in their cage, and I begged to have one out to tame. They had such beautiful golden brown, innocent eyes. Con warned me, when he took one out, that it could bite if not properly held. I tried to do as he suggested, holding it tight around the neck but it still managed to give me a nasty bite. Back in the cage it went and thereafter I was content to just look at them. The boatmen assured us that the animals could whistle up a wind if properly coaxed. Ours refused to cooperate, and we wasted half a day while we were becalmed where the canal emptied into the gulf. That night while we were sleeping, both of our pith hats were stolen. Thereafter, when we were in the sun, our heads were swathed in wet towels.

Out on the sea again the boatmen had trouble finding the entrance to the river leading to Nakawn Sritamarat. After sailing back and forth we finally found it, only to learn that there was a long mud bar and the tide would not be high enough to cross until three o'clock that afternoon. The boatmen were very hungry and there was no way to cook on the boat, so they got out into the water and soft mud, tied a rope to the boat, and with a great deal of grunting and laughter while Con helped with an oar, managed to drag the boat inch by inch over the bar. As soon as we got over it, about ten a.m., we stopped on the shore and had breakfast.

There was a skeleton of a huge crocodile there. Con had shot at one the day before, while we were going through the canal. Later we heard that a few weeks previously the father-in-law of the hospital assistant in Nakawn had been dragged out of his little boat by a crocodile and never seen again.

That afternoon we turned from the river into a narrow canal controlled by water gates, which led to the city of Nakawn. We had to transfer everything into smaller boats and walk along the path most of the distance. We reached Nakawn about 8 o'clock that evening and proceeded to Dr. Swart's home. All that day we had eaten only a few crackers and a little drinking water. After a good hot bath and dinner we had a welcome rest.

Two days later we left for Bangkok. We got up about three a.m., had breakfast, got into the doctor's pony cart and drove five miles along a lovely country road in the cool early morning to a river landing where the little mail boat was waiting. This river was very windy and tropically beautiful. We reached the steamer about 9 o'clock and continued uneventfully until the night that we anchored on the bar of the river to Bangkok four days later.

It was exceptionally hot, and the ship was invaded by a swarm of mosquitoes so the walls of our cabin were literally black with them. That experience was the worst of our whole trip. Those on the ship without a mosquito net were unable to sleep. We sat up reading out loud, drank lemonade, our faces and hands reeking with eucalyptus oil, until about midnight and we could stand it no longer. I thought of a brilliant scheme. We pulled our two steamer trunks out in the center of the cabin, put the bunk mattresses over them as best we could, tied up our mosquito net and finally sesttled down inside despite the bumps and ridges and cramped quarters. We somehow survived the rest of the night.

We were in Bangkok two and a half weeks for the Mission meetings, and most of that time we debated on what route to take on our return to Taptieng. I was extremely unwilling to go back by the same tedious canals. We finally decided to return to Nakawn by steamer, rest a few days, then go south to Ronpibun, then west across the mountians by the northern pass to Tungsong, then south by river to Taptieng. Thus we would have made the four sides of a square and I would see the other mountain pass.

Our four-day steamer trip from Bangkok to Nakawn was perfect in every way. We were just able to stretch out, and were fairly comfortable with our pillows and rugs, except for a few mosquitoes. It was a lovely moonlight night. On our fourth night we reached the landing stage at two a.m. Dr. Swart's pony cart was waiting for us. An hour's drive brought us to the home of Mr.

and Mrs. Eckels who were expecting us and we went in to bed and had a few hours sleep before breakfast.

Since I was nearing term for Katharine's birth, Con was forced to consider how on earth he was going to take his "handicapped wife" on the rest of the journey home the hard way in her "delicate" condition. No pony cart was available. Ox cart and elephant were both out of the question. Someone suggested, and we hired, the town's only rubber-tired *ricksha* and an ox cart for our baggage. The ox cart was loaded up and started on its way in the afternoon. Early the next morning we were taken a couple of miles to where the *ricksha* was waiting for us. We transferred rugs, pillows, umbrella, lunch pail etc. into it and started on our way with Con walking ahead with his gun as usual.

The owner-driver of the *ricksha* was a kindhearted, friendly, talkative old man with a turn for the unusual. He was as solicitous for me as I was for him. He was much amused when I let a little Siamese kitten I had been given ride in state in the *ricksha* while I walked up the hills and over rough places.

We had lunch at a pretty rest house on the bank of a river. During the afternoon we were caught in a heavy rain storm while going through a bit of jungle. The umbrella leaked so badly and the little bit of oilcloth apron-front to my *ricksha* had seen its day, so both Con and I became drenched. We just laughed like two silly children and made the best of it.

We reached the next rest house at Ronpibun in the late afternoon. Our ox cart was there waiting. We managed to sleep until about four a.m. when we packed up again and started out with a pale moon over a wet and muddy road. We stopped at a *sala* for breakfast about nine o'clock and then went on until we got into the mountain pass. Con found it much changed because they were building a railroad through at this point. The road was very poor through this shorter pass.

I walked all the way. Con pointed out the place where he had encountered a tiger when he was riding his bicycle over this pass years before.

The second night was spent in the jungle pass in a dreary guest bungalow. The jungle pressed close on three sides of the house. We were told a tiger had made a kill there the night before. The old caretaker and our oxcart driver kept a fire burning all night. I tried to sleep, but their droning voices, and the chewing and stamping of the oxen made it difficult.

On reaching Tung Song we stayed an extra day. The *Amphur* was very cordial and I felt safe and comfortable. From there we could have gone by oxcart over a good road, a three-day journey south to Trang, but we were bent on exploring new ways. At this point the Trang River was a small jungly stream, not far from its source. We stowed our things in the bottom of a *sampan* and had to lie flat for the first few miles while the boatman dragged it along until the stream broadened and left the jungle. Then we put up our "house top" of skins and began housekeeping as on the canal trip. The rest of the trip was uneventful. The kitten was a joy, and the scenery was grand.

On arriving home, we found the house was wide open – not one of the 14 pairs of half-shutter doors had been hung. The smaller west bedroom on the hospital side, with its new bath and dressing room was rushed to completion. It was quite sumptuous.

On January 5th I had worked hard all day and counted on a luxurious long night's sleep, but Katharine decided to make a night of it for her debut. Before dinner was over, the doctor at Nakawn Sritamarat arrived by pony, elephant and hand car – a strenuous trip, alone. Some time before he had lost his wife in childbirth. When complications developed there was not a soul within a hundred miles to aid or advise him. The Mission then ruled that a doctor should not deliver his own wife unless, in the event of an emergency, there was no other medical help within reach. Now Con's friend had come to help. Fortunately for us he came early.

Born prematurely, Katharine weighed only about five and a half pounds by the kitchen scale. Because she was so frail, no one expected her to live. I fully believe she survived because of a special preparation called Mellin's Food which I procured from Bangkok, and also because of the cold baths I gave her.

29 - Home Life (1915-1916)
Reconstructed from Edna's letters to Con's family.

Less than two years after Katharine was born in Taptieng, Constance was born on November 12, 1913. The next year Con and I and the two girls left for our furlough in the United States. On January 26th, 1915, Dorothy was born at 531 Madison Avenue in New York City – Grandpa Bulkley's home. In May Grandma Bulkley accompanied us by train to California where we showed off our three little girls to my relatives in Sacramento and San Francisco.

After Dorothy's birth I had severe misgivings about my mothering role. How would I be able to cope with three children under three in my missionary role in Siam? I felt so inadequate. All the time I was with my family and relatives I could barely stand to talk about it and was very unhappy. While we were in the East Con's sister Yula had sensed how overwhelmed I was, and offered to keep Katharine and raise her, for which I was profoundly thankful. I prayed harder than ever before, and finally felt an inward change and realized I could keep her and do my best. What a tremendous relief that was! Perhaps some day I would have to give up Katharine – and I hoped that Yula would still want her - but for now I felt secure and happy.

In July Con and I and the three girls boarded a Japanese vessel, the *S.S. Chiyo Maru* for the long voyage across the Pacific with stops in Hawaii, three weeks in Manila, and brief stops at Yokohama and Hong Kong. It was a very pleasant trip. Six of us fifteen women on board played jolly games of baseball. The ship's crew entertained us with games of various sorts, and there was wrestling and dancing and moving pictures. The children were so good and absolutely regular in everything so that I was free and nothing was burdensome, nothing hard. Con helped with the girls, and the days were all joy.

We reached Bangkok in September and finally arrived back home in Taptieng near the end of October. After a year and a half

Con, Katharine, Edna and Constamce

away the house was in a deplorable condition. Fortunately a friend volunteered to keep the children for ten days while we unpacked and cleaned out the scorpions and poisonous centipedes.

During this time there was a severe epidemic of fever. I knew real fear, and was so nervous at night. Again I did a lot of praying, and I told God I could not watch over the children every minute of the day. I could not prevent sickness. Wouldn't He just keep them Himself from all these dangers? Every morning I committed them to His care and thanked Him each night and felt blessedly free from worry, and was happy because we were all well.

Before long our home was more settled and attractive. Katharine was such a beautiful child, simply overflowing with life and mischief and fun. She and Constance had glorious times – racing over the house, singing at the top of their lungs, dancing to the phonograph music. What with two monkeys, two pups, two swings, walks, rides, their days were full of interest and fun. They all woke about 5:30 a.m., my rising time too.

After dressing and having warm milk and bread and butter the children were outdoors with the *Amah* [nursemaid or servant] until eight o'clock.

We were very pleased with the *Amah*. The only fault I could find with her was that she spoke pidgin English fluently rather than Chinese which we wanted the girls to learn. Thankfully Katharine kept the *Amah*'s English and ours quite separate and distinct. The *Amah* knew nothing about our religion, and her vocabulary was so limited that it was impossible to explain it.

Con would be over at the hospital before eight o'clock, take his rounds, then come back for prayers with all the servants about 8:20, have breakfast and return to the hospital at 9 o'clock for prayers with the staff there. At 10:30 the two older children had cold baths (a la Siam – they loved it!), then napped until noon. Bedtime was at 6 p.m. after another cold splash. By then it was dark and the mosquitoes bad. With the *Amah* watching Katharine and Constance most of the time it was easy to care for Dorothy and I found I could manage very well.

As time went on there was more and more work for Con at the hospital. Though there was no cholera, hookworm was very prevalent and he was doing a lot of investigation into it. He had to take on another man as anesthetist and dispensary clerk.

That year we had extraordinarily heavy rains and flooding – the water rising higher than it had in 20 to 30 years, with bridges washed out and some track as well. Some people experienced real distress as walls caved in. Some of the houses near the river were entirely under water, and people were living on boards placed across rafters just under the roof. The mold that came with the rain really troubled us. Soiled clothes were mildewed before you knew it, and an occasional centipede found within them. Even our new books were powdery with mold. Con had to wait for a warm dry day, to dry them out thoroughly and varnish them. Shoes left for a few days needed to have the mold wiped from the inside and the outside.

Our church dedication and two days of Conference, scheduled for the week before Thanksgiving, came at the time of

The growing family: Con, Constance, Katharine, Edna, Dorothy.

highest water and was held in spite of the floods, although athletic activities had to be curtailed. There was a lake between the hospital and the church. One man came through water up to his armpits, and had to call to a boat and pay 8 cents to get himself out. We had expected four missionaries and about ten Siamese to come from Nakawn Sritamarat by train, but when a bridge went under water, no train ran for days and Nakawn was totally cut off. In spite of the difficulties, the Conference was good. We opened our house for about a hundred people both nights. First we had a prayer meeting upstairs, conducted by different Siamese in turn. Then we had games downstairs and entertainment by a dozen men who were clever actors and singers, until about eleven o'clock.

Because the delegation from Nakawn couldn't get there, our Thanksgiving dinner suffered. However, the five of us had plenty to eat, the *pièce de résistance* being a small roast pig. What an extravagance! Actually it cost us just 40 *satangs* – 270 *satangs* being equal to U.S. $1.00 – about the same as for two chickens. That is a quarter or fifth the price a few years before.

But money was scarce and I economized as never before in my life. I knew the price of nearly everything in the market and could make a little go a long way. Our entire food supply for one month, as well as the wages of Cook, *Boy*, and laundress came to a little less than $63. I couldn't imagine any family living for as little as that in New York City.

After the conference, we emphasized the social side of our missionary activities strongly. Every Friday night we lit up the house and got out the games. First, for half an hour, Con was in charge of preparing the Sunday School teacher. Then I taught do-re-mi and drilling on the scales following which Miss Eakin had a choir practice. After that we had the games. The Siamese were very fond of *crokinole* [sic] and jackstraws. They also enjoyed our stereoscopic pictures and Con's collection of puzzles.

Finally in one week the weather became hot and dry. It still took a while for the railroad and the bridge to be repaired.

On Christmas Eve we took Katharine to see the main tree at the Church, a thick-leaved, symmetrical *jackfruit*. Three dozen candles lit it up well and popped rice, paper chains and various gilt ornaments made it pretty. She was overwhelmed by her presents from the Siamese – quaint things they had made. The biggest present was a little mongoose in a wire cage which she carried home all by herself. Going out in the dark with a lantern was great excitement for her.

About half-past five Christmas morning we gathered around our own little tree. We had cut off two lower branches of our little pine tree in the garden and put the main stems together in a flower pot. The branches went out in the four directions and it made a very respectable tree especially when all a-sparkle with candles, tinsel ornaments, presents, etc. Con and I were probably more impressed with it than the children. In the afternoon we indulged in the very exciting and typically Christmas sport of croquet.

Right after that Con had to go on a call again. Just as we were sitting down to dinner, he had to rush off to catch the train with only a few sandwiches in his pocket. Oh how we wished we had the car! We expected its arrival imminently, but its availability and the price and freight charges kept changing. In spite of the uncertainty, we planned to take little medical-evangelistic trips

The people here are gathered at our home for a prayer meeting.
Part of the living room can be seen above.

together since we knew we could leave the children with our good
Amah and *Boy*. I was really getting heart and soul into evangelistic
work, and had visited seventeen homes, sometimes with one of
the Siamese women helpers. I always took the Bible, and it was
easy and natural to teach and talk about the Sunday School lessons
they might have missed. Eventually I planned to go a little further
in my pony cart to visit some women who had expressed some
interest. My three Siamese women leaders in our church came to
me each week for instruction and preparation to teach their own
classes.

Con's family in the States was always supportive of our work.
Whatever we needed that we couldn't get here we simply had to
ask, and it was sent. Because of the continual warfare with rats,
Con asked for several varieties of rat poison and any traps that
might be available. We were always careful to keep our food
covered, but the rats nibbled at all sorts of impossible things –
even the nose of a 20-year-old well-tanned coyote skin Con had
brought back from the States and an old pistol holster. Besides
the damage and annoyance of having them around, there was the
danger of plague if that showed up.

Children's shoes was something else we often asked for, and
the size didn't matter because they would always fit someone.

The girls went barefoot most of the time, although we made sure they dressed up and wore shoes on Sundays so they wouldn't forget how to walk in them, even if they were a trifle clumsy.

An Austrian who was in charge of a rubber estate five miles away often came to dine with us after church. We were rather sorry for him. He came from Trieste and so was an Austrian politically, although his speech, sympathies and friends were all Italian. He was sixty-two years old and had been in Sumatra on tea, rubber and tobacco estates for decades without going home. He gave up that work and was living with a son-in-law in Singapore when the war [WW I] broke out. They interned him as a possible spy in spite of his age and his real nationality and sympathies. Finally they relented, but decreed that he must leave the British possessions. So here was this old man, banished from friends and relatives, at work again in the jungle, and faced, as his predecessors had been, with little money to do the work required of him.

One time, all alone with a fever, he nearly died when the long grass surrounding his house caught fire, destroying many trees. Another night a tiger walked twice around his house. Although he was a Roman Catholic, he came to our church nearly every Sunday, and generally one of us invited him to dinner. Because he had no money for transportation, he walked the five miles to Taptieng and back.

One time a Siamese Prince, the younger brother of King Vajiravudh [Rama VI] came on an inspection trip to our hospital. After the inspection he and his mother, an aunt and a sister, his children and seven or eight other women came over to our house for tea. They were all captivated by our children. Katharine was four, Constance three and Dorothy almost a year and a half. Afterwards Con and I wondered how many mistakes we had made, as democratic Americans. However, with their generosity of spirit they gave no indication that we had said or done anything amiss, and the visit was very pleasant.

30 - The Islands Trip – Water Gypsies
Reconstructed from Edna's notes
and letters she and Con wrote to his family.

Edna: Con had been working steadily in the daily grind of hospital routine, night and day with no letup. Banditry brought a heavy toll of broken bodies. There were the usual filthy ulcers, consumptives and other complaints. It was a nerve-wracking time and we both felt the need for a change – something to do entirely different, away from the hospital. The Mission encouraged missionaries to make tours into the outlying areas, so this seemed a good time to do so, and possibly do some missionary work.

We decided on a trip by *junk* to some islands off the west coast of Siam. Although they were only about thirty miles away, we had never visited them. Con hoped to make contact with some of the natives to encourage them to use the facilities of his hospital. We started off on our two-week tour on our fifth anniversary, with two wagon-loads of supplies.

At the village on the river, a mile and a half from our house, we hired three *junks* and a boatman for each of them, all glad to go on a pleasure trip. Our party also included the chief boatman's wife, Con's first Hospital Assistant *Nai* Chuang, another assistant/ evangelist *Nai* Joon and our cook as a general servant. This was luxurious in comparison with our earlier *sampan* trips.

We took four-year-old Katharine with us, and left Constance and Dorothy, ages three and one in the *Amah*'s capable charge. This was an experiment. If anything happened, of course I would never leave the children again. The house was left in the care of our splendid *Boy* who'd also cook for the children. He was to keep the house open and protect it from mildew and white ants.

We are fairly comfortable in the boat. The part that is floored and roofed for us is about 9 feet wide at one end and 7 feet at the other end, and 12 feet in length. We can not stand up, but Katharine can very nicely. The roof is several layers of palm leaves. Katharine has her doll and doll trunk along and has quantities of shells to play with and amuses herself and is as happy as the day is long. Yesterday morning we were becalmed in the middle of the sea and she was sick for the first time, but got over it quickly. We all felt miserable.

Con: The first hitch occurred when we found the tide would not let us go for three hours, so we had our lunch first instead of on the way. Down the river we had a little surprise, in the shape of a furious wind storm. The water insisted on getting through and around the roof, and in the front and back. In spite of all we could do, things were pretty well soaked, including some of our bedding. Not more than a sprinkle, and very rarely that, is normally expected at this season.

We had to anchor when the tide turned again, as the boat is too heavy to row against it. We went on again by moonlight, and anchored before daybreak the next morning. We had some buying to do – some extra thatching for the roof, etc. Also I had to declare our errand when the Customs Office opened at nine o'clock.

Then as the tide would hold us further, I decided to visit some hot springs across the river I had heard of for years but never had seen. It was quite a row, and a very hot two hours trip into the mountains, but I was glad to see them and taste the water. I want to get an analysis made some time – it might be of medicinal value. I would also like to develop the country, give somebody a chance to make something out of it. There is a strong mineral element, though the water is beautifully clear. A hole four feet in diameter and seven feet deep, it has a good body of water flowing through. Steam was rising, but I was able to dip my hand in and take a drink. Further down we still could not bathe except by having the water thrown a little to cool it, while at the same time we rubbed down vigorously. Then it was hard to leave and take the hot walk back. That evening we showed the pictures [of Biblical stories] in Kantang, in the Chinese Chapel there, to an appreciative audience of about forty. The radiopticon went very well. It is a fine addition to a trip like this.

Little Katharine and her doll

At daybreak we were on our way down the river, and soon had a pleasant sail along the shore of Koh Libong, a large island in the bay. We stopped to explore a little cove near the seaward end that we think would be a good place for the station to come in the hot season, perhaps build a rest house there.

Edna: We have been looking for a suitable place for a summer resort for the Mission. Con and I are now *very* enthusiastic over Koh Libong, an island just across from the mouth of the Trang River. We went ashore on our way out. It seems to be ideal except it is far from any people and we would get nothing to eat except what we would take with us. The eastern end of the island is very flat and on the south there is a village of Malays where Con went when he shot a wild buffalo several years ago. But on the extreme western shore is a range of mountains. One big beautiful rocky mountain falls straight to the water's edge on the northwestern point. Just inside the little bay is a wonderful beach with a long gentle slope and it stretches unbroken around to the east and south of the island. We went ashore about three in the afternoon and there was perfect shade for bathing as the sun was behind the mountain.

The edge of the shore has a grove of pine trees. A little house among them would be the loveliest place in the world to brace up the children once a year. It would be about a day's trip from Trang in a little boat. Captivated by it, we dreamed of a bungalow there for a vacation getaway. Oh, how we hoped it would be. [The dream never materialized because the Government saw the possibilities for a Naval base there.]

Con: That night we reached Koh Muk, another island about the same size as Koh Libong. There is a village here of people called Chow Nam, which means literally water people, for they live along the sea. They were sometimes called Water Gypsies, as they were originally wild sea folk. Now they are more civilized. They are neither Siamese nor Malay, though their language seems similar or at least much intermingled with the latter. They live in tiny low huts on the ground.

Some of their habits are peculiar to themselves; they only learned to use fishnets from their neighbors. Their own method is spearing, in which they are very proficient. They are not Mohammedans but a kind of spirit worshippers. We were able to treat a few, and talked with some who understood Siamese. There was an old man with cataracts who promised to come to the hospital at Taptieng, but I hardly think he will. He is one hundred and six years old, so it may be almost as well if he does not come.

Next day we had a good run from there, almost too good a wind when we were lying over on our side and Edna was saying to the men "Look out! Look out!" We were not really in any danger but we could have been more comfortable if we had picked up some stones for ballast, as we had planned to do. See Kow [or Sikao] which is on the coast due west from Taptieng was our next objective, but our helmsman was afraid to try to tack it with such a wind. The only thing we could do was to run before it far past and get behind a promontory. It seemed best to give up See Kow for the time and go first to our next point, Koh Lantar.

Our stay in Koh Lantar was pleasant. We went ashore and stayed in a comfortable rest house near the landing (except it was full of fleas). The dense shade around it and a strong sea breeze most of the time made us wish for warmer clothes.

Edna: Our house is right on the shore and much of the time the breeze has been a regular tempest straight from the sea rather too cool for comfort. For about the first time in Siam we are sleeping on land without mosquito net. For days now we have been eating, sleeping, reading, writing, in other words, *living* on the floor. I am beginning to get used to it. Haven't seen a table and will hardly know how to behave in a civilized house.

Con: Every day we had plenty to do with patients, preaching and teaching, and selling books. The *Amphur* (the highest official there) bought my personal Siamese Testament. They were interested in the pictures I showed with the radiopticon too, and we sold some of the small Sunday School pictures, three for a cent, as is our custom on tours.

Edna: Poor Con – the word quickly spread that he was a doctor. Alas, there was no rest. I wish you could have seen the scene out under the wonderfully dense shade of many mango trees. There is a broad platform around one huge tree and the medicines are spread out there early each morning. Also the scriptures and tracts. A great crowd of people buying medicines, being examined or treated and others listening to Nai Joon as he talks with a picture roll. Con pulled dozens of teeth. We are besieged with visitors from morning until night. Many women have come. Katharine enjoys her role immensely.

On the third or fourth day we had visitors. The Water Gypsies! A long, strange, cork craft beached in front of us. It was riding so low in the water, that it looked as though the Water Gypsies and their Chief, were sitting in the sea.

Con: The Chief told me his son had jumped on some coral under water three or four months before, and although he had drawn it out, the wound had not healed and the foot was swollen. He asked if I could help him. I explained I would do what I could if he did not object to an operation. He didn't, and the next day the emaciated young man was brought in. I operated on the spot and took out a piece of coral a half inch long that was buried deep in the foot. The people watching were full of ah's and oh's. His wife especially was relieved. She had first been very unwilling to have him come into my hands. The wound healed cleanly and rapidly. The Chief was most grateful and gave me a large model of a sailing vessel beautifully executed in the native palm cork, the same material used for their own boats.

We have had no hospital patients from this island or See Kow opposite, though they are only about fifteen miles from Kantang. That was one of the reasons for our choosing this trip – to get acquainted here. So I was glad of this case and hope it will help the hospital.

We were sorry to have to leave Koh Lantar in spite of the disappointment in food. With no food supply nearby, on a future trip we would have to bring plenty with us, or occasionally send a boat back to Trang. But the food supply is apt to disappoint anywhere, so it is better to prepare and not count on it. For instance on this trip whether sailing or stopping at various places, we have been able to buy almost nothing. Of course no vegetables at all – that is to be expected – but we did hope to get some kind of sea food every day.

Instead of that we have had to depend on canned food. (Imagine having sardines, canned oyster soup, etc. while living on an island.) It has been an event when we could get fish. Oysters we had twice and crabs once. The men were sometimes hard put to it when the dried fish brought from home was gone, and nothing else was in sight, and this with quite a population around us. Part of the time the wind was bad for fishing, but later there seemed no reason at all for the scarcity.

Then after another short stop at the island of Koh Muk, we reached Koh Kiam Saturday afternoon, a place we had never visited. There are several hundred people on this island, mostly Malays, but speaking Siamese. We are glad to have come here, though disappointed in a way. They did not seem to trust me medically. I could do almost nothing. There are two cataract patients who promised to come to the hospital, and one or two others, so there may be some gain from our visit. And some heard the Gospel who might not have otherwise. Also we sold a number of books, in Chinese, Malay and Siamese. We will hope for some result from it.

This is only a couple of hours from Kantang by small boat. It was too much for Edna to resist, so she and Katharine went at half-past-five Sunday morning and caught the morning train to Taptieng.

Kantang, Sunday morning eight-thirty. The tide turned about six o'clock and there was a favorable breeze though light, so we have had a pleasant sail in the twilight and night. The men are glad, for now one or two or more of them may go to Taptieng on the morning train. I will stay with the boat to push them along and to look after the things, and get there before night, I hope.

Goodnight, Mother Dear, much love to all,

from your devoted son, Con.

Edna: The one thing that stood out on this trip happened the last night at Koh Kiam. I had a strange premonition of danger at home that would not let me sleep, and all the next day it tortured me. Con laughed at my fears. The next night, the storm having abated, we crossed the bar after dark and the men refused to go any further. I was so agitated that Con hired a rowboat and a native along the shore to take Katharine and me up river at daybreak so we could catch the six o'clock train to Trang. Con thought I was being rather silly. He had no choice but to stay with all our belongings.

When we reached Taptieng there was scarcely a soul on the streets. The house was shut up – most unusual. Constance and Dorothy were all right, but the *Amah* and *Boy* were white-faced and frightened – they had scarcely slept or eaten. In fact the whole town was in much the same state. Then I heard the story from Miss Carter, the trained nurse who carried on at the hospital in our absence.

Two nights before, the exiled Austrian from Singapore who worked on a rubber plantation five miles from us, and his Chinese cook, had both been brutally murdered. They were hacked into pieces by a band of robbers who expected to find in his iron safe a great deal of silver money for paying laborers on the plantation. The robbers found eighty ticals – less that $30.

All the rest of the Station were away on vacation. It was Miss Carter who had gathered the fragments of the bodies and attended to the burial. The Siamese officials had begged the "*Mem*" to take charge.

Con did not get home for another thirty hours.

31 - Mountain Jungle Vacation

Reconstructed from Edna's notes

A few months after our trip by *junk* through the islands, a young *Eurasian* couple, the Mathieus, offered us the use of one of their two bamboo shelters for a month's vacation in the mountains about 8 miles north of Tung Song and we decided to take them up on their offer. Con had hunted with him when they had lived on a rubber plantation near where we lived.

A French Concession had begun construction of a hydraulic tin mine there and Mathieu was now the caretaker. In six months time only a small patch had been cleared out of primeval forest at the base of the 4000 foot mountain, for two tiny primitive, bamboo shelters. There was also a narrow clearing straight up the slope of the mountain for the huge pipe which was to tap the stream above the high waterfall.

Con and I, with our three children, our cook, *coolie* and *Amah* started out early Tuesday morning. We went north to Tung Song by train about three hours. From there it was only a short distance. Since there was no train until the following morning, we spent the night in a newly built Railroad Rest House. Mr. Dunbleten the Division Engineer invited us to dinner. We had an enjoyable visit, also meeting an interesting Australian, a mining engineer by the name of Horton. He had never seen a white woman in these regions evidently and expressed great surprise that I was coming up here "where there are tigers and things!"

Wednesday morning we had a half-hour train ride and were let off by special permission of the railway at the edge of the jungle. From there it was a four mile walk over a root-entangled path to the clearing at the mountain's base. Fortunately Mathieu had provided *coolies* and a chair to carry the children. How I wished for our camera when the three children were being carried in a chair through the virgin forest by four men! Dorothy got tired and cramped and the *Amah* insisted on carrying her piggy-back the last twenty minutes. I couldn't possibly have attempted this trip with the children if it were not for my wonderful Chinese *Amah*. She endured discomfort like a soldier and was equal to anything. She came on an hour's notice. I had hired her after only a half day's acquaintance!

I walked the hour without fatigue. Constance and Katharine sang and furnished much amusement for everyone. Our cook and coolie carried an unbelievable amount of stuff suspended from a bamboo pole resting on their shoulders. Keeping it down to the minimum of what we needed for a month, we still had to have pots and pans, bedding, rice and canned foods-stuffs, etc. On the way we saw tracks of a wild pig, and were told that a pack of them had been seen the day before on the path.

When we reached the clearing, by the bend of a tumbling, bubbling stream, we found the primitive bamboo and thatch cottage we were to occupy, surrounded by towering trees, a wild profusion of all kinds of plants, ferns, orchids, and the majestic silence.

Never in my wildest dreams had I imagined such an isolated spot, seemingly out of this world and any communication with it. It was most inspiring – a perfectly ideal and restful change, several hundred feet higher than Taptieng and perceptibly cooler. The Mathieus were in another cottage a little distance away, and we often got together for meals. And such a surprise – we had tomatoes Mrs. Matthieu had grown in her little garden there.

The children had the time of their lives. There were big ducks and six tiny ones, which came and ate out of the children's hands. Chickens unnumbered, ponies and colts and the Mathieu's four fluffy little white dogs. From the cottage we could watch the huge long-tailed black monkeys jumping from tree to tree. Morning and evening the air rang with the siren calls of the white monkeys. They were all around us but we never saw them.

A clear cold mountain steam flowed in front of the house and was a source of great delight to the children. Con, however, worried about them and would only allow them to splash in it a little. After a heavy rain the stream would rise several feet and be dangerous for them. Constance had come with a cough which

Constance, Dorothy and Katharine with their Amah, Ah Sam.

wouldn't go away in spite of trying to keep her in dry clothes and shoes and doctoring with cod liver oil. Dorothy survived the trip well, but then after getting wet in the rain had ear trouble which gave her some bad nights. Fortunately Katharine stayed well.

Con kept insisting this wasn't the best place for a vacation with the children. He believed they were much safer at the seashore, and the salt water, sea air and sand were healthier. Here he worried about the danger of hookworm if they went barefoot.

The most wonderful thing to me (and to Con, too) was that I was able to walk across streams and gullies on a single little log, even carrying a gun or a child. For years I had not been able to walk on such things without holding onto someone. I felt very proud to be carrying a shotgun, dressed, as Con was, in khaki trousers, coat, leggings and soft hat. I followed him, with his rifle as we explored the forest day after day. One night we started out to find an old blind near a grass clearing. After crossing the stream four times we got lost in dense jungle. It was getting dark. Our *coolie* climbed a tree but he couldn't see anything. Finally we found a stream, and followed it back to our cottage.

For me the crowning experience was the time we sat up all night on a rough platform of saplings in a tree waiting for a tiger to come for our monkey bait. No tiger came to the kill. The mosquitoes were so thick I never had a camphor bottle far out of reach for five days after that. Con went without me on every subsequent tiger hunt.

There were two waterfalls within a mile or so. One day Con and I were picnicking above a waterfall at three thousand feet in a surpassingly lovely spot with a view of the entire plain below. A sudden rain cloud enveloped us and we were literally washed down the cleared slope, falling, sliding, and convulsed with laughter.

This was one of the most interesting, memorable and altogether delightful vacations I ever had in Siam.

32 - Letters to Home (1917-1919)
Excerpts from Edna's and Con's Letters

Editor's note (Mary): After a year in Trang, Con was transferred to head the hospital at Petchaburi, southwest of Bangkok on the gulf. After three daughters – Katharine, Constance and Dorothy – Con wrote to his mother that Lucius Daniel's arrival on May 5th, 1917 in Bangkok, was "just what I wanted for my birthday," which was a few days later. Edna's letter two weeks later described Danny as "a darling little fellow, looks rather like Katharine did as a baby, so I think he will be like Con." Con quoted Edna as describing him "very strong, has a beautiful head, and is nice and fat." Later he wrote "I take it back about his head. Edna wrote again from Bangkok that his head 'is developing bumps, and the hair is thin on top, and he has the funniest eyebrows I ever saw on a baby. They stick out like the bushy eyebrows of some old men! Please make up some particularly sticky kind of Vaseline or cream so I can massage them smooth when I get home.'"

The group at Petchaburi. Edna and Con, holding Dan, are far left.

Edna: [May 1917]: I was very happy at the Nursing Home until the tenth day when they were determined I should get up and walk out to the long chair at the end of the veranda – just imagine! That is their English way, but I was absolutely firm and resolved not to do it. The two nurses who took turns with me, were rather nasty for about three days. Then they were lovely and I left with pleasant memories and invited all three to visit me in Petchaburi.

Excerped from letters (Mary): The name Lucius was chosen to carry on the Bulkley tradition – Lucius Constant, (Con) and Lucius Duncan (Con's father). As for choosing Daniel, there had been several Daniels in the Bulkley line, and Edna's grandfather was Daniel Sivarsey Flint. Con especially liked it for it's biblical meaning, "God my judge" with hopes that he would be a power for good.

The war, seldom mentioned – although Con often reminded his parents about the censorship – became more real when they learned that a railroad bridge nearby was guarded by soldiers. Some Chinese had come under suspicion for making bombs. In mid-July Siam abandoned her position of neutrality and declared war, took over German shipping, and began interning German subjects, all in remarkably short order. Censorship of mail and packages caused much frustration and meant long delays. The letters speculated about the whereabouts of long awaited boxes – particularly one from Montgomery Ward – whether it was held up in Hong Kong or Bangkok. It finally reached them after thirteen months. However, the arrival of Ah See, a new Chinese *Amah* from Macao, was the event which provided the most important news. They had high expectations for her: she spoke English after a fashion, had done nursing, traveled widely with her employers, and was highly recommended. A few months later Danny had diarrhea because the *Amah* wouldn't boil his bottles. She was also causing trouble in other ways, so they had to let her go. Being the first boy, both Edna and Con doted on Danny.

Edna [July, 1917]: He is a very fine boy, I assure you, and a better baby than even the three girls, so it is not always true that boy babies are harder to train. He is no trouble at all, and such a jolly smiling youngster. His sisters love him devotedly and it is "Isn't Danny sweet, Mother?" "I love Danny," "Can I kiss Danny, Mother?" all day long and every day. He is showered with attention and seems to love them quite as much in return. The Colonel lent me an old goat of his which gives just a small quantity of milk, and now I am negotiating to buy another.

Note (Mary): In November, during a vacation at Nong Khae by the shore, Edna had an abscess on her back and had to return to Petchaburi for treatment, leaving the four children with the servants and three school girls. She left on the morning train, expecting to return on the afternoon train, and invited Miss Mercer and her guest Miss Worthington to return with her.

Edna [November 1917]: A good Providence made them come on without me when Con found it would be necessary for me to stay in Pet. The day following I was given chloroform and Con dug quite deep and had to scrape out a little cyst which was the cause of the trouble. Con had thought he could take me on the train that afternoon but again it was not possible. I was so worried about Danny.

The next day (the third of leaving the children) I was all ready to go to the train when word came that the line was under water and there were no trains. I was so distressed. I went up to see the Division Superintendent as soon as he returned from the washout and he promised to take me just as soon as he could get permission and a hand-car could go through.

All day Sunday I waited for news, and it was dreary weather too, everything flooded! Sunday night a note came saying I could go with him, early Monday morning. Mr. Crum (the District Superintendent) had wired to Bangkok for permission and himself asked the Prince that very day, but he could only take me. He was very kind.

I was three hours on the hand-car. Rain for most of that time but Con had made a 'poncho' for me so I kept perfectly dry. It was very interesting to see twenty-five [railroad] ties suspended in the air with a torrent of water rushing through what had been a solid embankment. I stayed on the car while it was pushed across inch by inch. I had a comfortable three hours, waiting in the train on the other side of the break. An hour's ride then brought me to Nong Khae.

There was great surprise when I appeared at the house. The children were well, (Danny had not had a bath those five days) and everything was all right but there was not much to eat. The train was not running for a week, and oh, I was so thankful to be with my children. . . .

Con came down as my back still needs to be dressed. It is so disagreeable in Pet. with roads and lawn under water and the house damp and dark that I persuaded Con to stay over Sunday. We return tomorrow.

The Christmas box arrived and words cannot express our appreciation of the love and thought which must have gone into it. There is enough for several Christmases. Please do not think of sending anything more until the war is over. I quite believe that will not be for several years. We will put things away carefully and choose wisely. There is such a wonderful collection. You asked in one of your letters if we would rather have a sum of money to order from Montgomery Ward ourselves. No, indeed!!! There could not be a quarter of the joy there is in a box from 'Home'. I am so glad to have the jams, preserves and especially candy. One stick of candy after the noon meal is the children's keenest enjoyment and is their reward for taking naps and going to bed quietly. . . .

Danny has been very fretful [cutting his first teeth], but no trouble. He calls "Mama" incessantly, when he wants to be taken up. That has been frequently of late, and I am sorry to add that I generally run to comply with his request more often than is good for his discipline. . . .

You ask if I do anything at the hospital. I gave it up when I found I could not trust my women servants. You know the Chinese *Amah* turned out very badly. I will not try again [sending for one], and I will never have another Siamese nurse unless I am desperate. The present nurse is about four-fifths Chinese, was a pupil-teacher in the market school for three years. She is of good family and related to both my cook and *Boy*. So we have a very happy household at present, all satisfied and doing well. . . .

Katharine did not go to [Siamese] school more than a month. It seemed to have a very harmful influence on her. I spend a little time each day. She loves to learn and it is a pleasure to teach her. I cannot seem to make any impression upon Constance in the matter of lessons.

She shows no sign of wanting to learn and I think it is well to wait until she does.

Con: We are now in the throes of Chinese New Year. They buy things then for *Wai Chow* which is one of their chief deities at this time. Really making offerings to the devil.... Paying up all their debts is one of the good features of the occasion, also giving presents around. The cook and *Boy* each gave us a chicken, and some fruit etc. The man painting the hospital gave us a big slab of pork.

But a feature we do deplore is the very free drinking and the universal gambling, with the fighting and stealing resulting from both. As a counter attraction we collected as many of our people as we could and had singing, and some Bible charades at the school this afternoon. If it were a week day we would have had a more elaborate jollification. I wish I were out there where things are happening. Here the world rumbles along same as ever. It reminds me of the Siamese railroads which are said to repeat as they go: *"Tung, ke chang, mye tung ke chang."*... It means "Get there, no matter; don't get there, no matter." And sometimes here when you are not sure just when or where you will arrive, it is a very useful piece of philosophy to have dinned into your ears.

Every picture so far of Daniel has been good – he seems to have the knack. Looks rather intelligent, I think, and Constance a little blasé. Daniel has six teeth now. He is not fat but very strong and active. He creeps around the room like a flash and is always wanting to stand up. Can't stand alone except a few seconds.

Edna: I was miserable all week and then caught the Spanish Influenza which seems to be going around the globe. The Sunday I was sick with it all three hospital assistants had it. Incidentally 18 regular and prominent members of the congregation were absent with it that day. And Con was away for four days! First I worried because I couldn't do anything for the fever. Then the terrible, racking cough that accompanies the disease worried me. I did not understand and thought I must be in the grip of consumption. By the time Con finally appeared, my nerves were in a dreadful state. I could scarcely endure the least noise of the children. And Mission Meetings one week off!

I suddenly made up my mind to go down to Nong Khae, and rest with the Clarks who are down there. I was quite weak, and the cough so bad. I went down Thursday afternoon, lying down most of the trip, and returned Monday morning. Then I had to improvise three bedrooms and be ready for guests by Wednesday. The rest had done me wonders – it was the first time in seven years that I had been away from every member of my family. Even on Tuesday the nervous pain in my neck and shoulders was terrible at times, and I wondered if I would be able to sit at the table with our guests, or get to any of the meetings. Well, I did, and got better every day. I went to bed early and rested and took things easy and enjoyed entertaining. . . .

Note (Mary): There often was competition among the different missions for where to hold the Annual Meeting, with sometimes a tug of war between meeting at Bangkok, or at Nong Khae, which was closer for Edna and Con, and less hectic. There was also competition for replacements as older members retired.

Con: Each side will make the most of every advantage possible. We had a great shock reading in a religious paper lately of seven new missionaries coming to Siam. Then another paper or a later issue said they were going to Chosen [China]. A careless mistake and really unkind to us when we are so keen for reinforcements. We get two, both going to Wang Lang.

It seems the Siamese are able to distinguish whether a handkerchief or anything belongs to a man or woman by merely smelling it. Edna is not quite so clever but she is suspicious when a letter in a woman's handwriting comes to me. You'd better tell your Brick Church Secretary to use her typewriter. Or if she is over sixty it will be all right if she sends her picture . . .

Circus

Con (October): We have been having a little diversion of a different kind lately – a circus. It has been in town for three days, with elephants, ladies riding horses, trapezes, clowns and all, in a big tent. One ring only, and very crude compared with what we are used to at home. But quite an event, the first circus which has ever toured here.

The house at Nong Khae where we vacationed.

No easy thing in this country with its lack of accommodations, since there is no hotel here. The Governor found places for some, but could not for all. The Girls School took in an Italian couple and their three children, all performers. I had to treat the father for dysentery and he could not perform. The last night a Malay employee was bitten by a snake and was brought to me. Also the fire eater brought his wife, a Ceylonese, for a consultation. They all have gone on towards Bangkok now. Poor people – I don't envy them the life. In Nakawn they had a robbery of one night's receipts – five hundred ticals. We all went and enjoyed it too. As prominent people here, I felt we ought to be willing to help a legitimate enterprise.

Victory Celebration, December, 1918

We are still rejoicing in the recent Allied victory. Neither your letters nor the Outlook [magazine] speak of it,. We have been waiting for some official action before celebrating, and now the King of Siam [Rama VI] has appointed the day, tomorrow, December 2nd. His proclamation is interesting. I am sending an English copy of it to the church. As a loyal Buddhist he "holds the belief that the Holy Buddhist Trinity which we revere and daily worship, and the virtues of the departed monarchs who have been the Protectors of the Siamese nation in the past have also aided in the achievement of the victory, which has brought about this happy result. So on this day there will be a great celebration in Bangkok, and all are ordered to attend and offer up a thanksgiving prayer to the image of Buddha, and pay reverence to the royal statues of the five reigns." . . .

I hear they have singlets or undershirts, (also called athletic shirts) at the ten cent store for forty or fifty cents. Perhaps 'seconds' would be quite good enough – only neck holes and arm holes – no buttons or seams. If you should run across a couple I wish you would mail them out quick; I am in rags. . . .

My teeth now make eating a pleasure again. I had three filled and a fourth gold crowned, and what do you suppose my bill was? Twenty-five ticals – $9 gold! . . . done by a Chinese. An American dentist would have been several times that. . . .

Still in Bangkok, harder to get servants than I expected. Edna will not think my visit here had accomplished anything if I do not succeed in getting a cook and a nurse girl. That has been my reason for waiting longer here. . . .

[from the shore]: Here we are having the usual kind of a vacation time, though all four children have a cough. The three older have had it longest and have shown the typical whoop. Now we are sorry to hear Danny beginning. A larger crowd than ever before. One more house has been built. We have a beautiful beach for bathing, and go in twice a day. The women loaf around and gossip and read a good deal. The men also go out after rabbits, jungle fowl, etc. . . .

Still the hot season continues with us, and with the cholera plague etc., there is enough to make life interesting. The temperature on the veranda the other day was ninety-six, the hottest I have ever yet seen. But no one dies of the heat. . . .

You may have heard by this time of Miss Cooper's death, and now more recently of Dr. Shellman's. This last was the greater shock, it came so suddenly. He was well Friday evening, sick with cholera at nine o'clock, and dead by nine the next morning. Just imagine his poor wife, and two small boys. They were planning to go home in another month or two. . . .

Con [to his brother Kenneth]: An important event in Bangkok just now is the arrival of the first returning contingent of the S.E.F. [Siam Expeditionary Force] from France. The city was decorated .. . and they were received with a good deal of ceremony. They say they look very fine and fit. The King has given each a medal. So far only the aviators have returned. . . .

[May 16, 1919]: A longer wait than we expected but last night at 11:10 the boy arrived rather easily, only four hours from the first to the last. Only two hours in the Nursing Home. Seems like a strong child at 8-1/2 pounds. We will call him Dwight Hatfield. . . .

You may wonder about the name. It is Edna's choice, after Dwight Potter, through whom she came to the Mission field. . . . Well Danny now has a brother to punch, and the family is nicely rounded out. 'We are seven,' the girls slightly in the majority but they need that, to hold up their end.

[June 15th, from Petchaburi]: Cholera is about over here in town. It was rather bad while it lasted. We lost our washer-woman, a good steady middle-aged woman whom we prized. . . .

We hear there is still a good deal of cholera in some of the outlying villages. Of course many, if not the majority of people, still believe in the spirit agency in the matter. They do not take the precautions advised.

You heard of course of the death from cholera of Nai Joon, your *colporteur* [a peddler of religious books]. He had come up from Trang to help in the hospital here. He had been ill off and on for some days, seemed to be recovering; but was warned to be very careful of his diet. He got bad again one evening, and died next morning. . . .

Cholera has been very virulent, taking a large proportion of those attacked. . . . We are glad so many of us have taken the cholera prophylactic serum I brought from Bangkok. . . . We have given it to about a hundred [people]. . . . Yet much as we fear cholera and plague, the influenza has taken very many more [lives] than the other two. But it is not so awfully sudden.

I wish you could see the baby [Dwight]. Thursday I laid him on the table in the operating room. He naturally squealed somewhat, but came back to the house sleeping as peacefully as you could want. Taking it well himself, does that mean that he will make a good surgeon? One of them will have to be I suppose, to keep up the tradition. Today he seemed to really give intentional smiles.

Danny is pushed up now into being a boy rather than a baby. He has developed a great deal in the last couple of months. He and Dorothy are too near of an age, and have it in for each other. Squabble a great deal, and tease each other. It is not possible always to discover which is the offender. The other day she had a ball or something of his, and he politely asked for it. "Say please again," she said. "Say it a third time" – the rascal, just to tease him, and because we sometimes make them repeat that way when they forget to say "please". It won't be long now before he gets on top, though. . .

The Siamese are fond of spelling their names exactly as written in Siamese, not omitting the silent letters, and transliterating the rest according to rules long ago established by Sanskrit and Pali scholars in India. So don't assume you know the probable sound of any word until we have explained it to you. For instance this town please pronounce "Petchabooree," and Trang to rhyme with "hung."

The other day on the train I met an aviator just back from France. He came up and wanted to shake hands with me just because I was an American. He said the Americans were so kind to them in France, so different from English, French, etc. They helped them in various ways, gave them tobacco and things. And elsewhere I have heard the English were too distant and ignored them, while the French laughed at them. . . .

Dwight is getting to be quite a boy now – three months old, and beating the other children I think. . . . They have their little tiffs often enough. Danny has learned the effectiveness (with the nurse) of a good hard bellow. I imagine he must have found it effective, or he would not try it so often, like whenever he does not want to take a bath or get dressed or something. Also when he and Dorothy want something the same time. But he quiets down quick enough and listens to reason from me. The nurse isn't much good that way. We are disappointed in her another way too. She has not taught them a word of Chinese, it is a shame. They ought to know a lot. But she is too quiet and meek. Still with nurses so hard to get, we had better be satisfied.

[October 5th]: The Siamese Expeditionary Force returned [to Bangkok during the Annual mission meeting] about fifteen hundred of them, so the town was *en fete.* In the U.S. that is getting to be an old story by now but we are behind in everything. To think most here have not even seen a flying machine of any kind. I myself saw an aeroplane just once in San Francisco, and a tiny little one-man dirigible in New York. But perhaps in a few months we will see more airplanes when the army makes a landing field near our house here – one of the stops on the projected Bangkok-Singapore route. . . .

[November 19th]: I was disappointed in not completing a recent surgical case that would have been rather noteworthy, a record for this hospital anyway. The patient had an ovarian cyst; her girth was 55 inches. To relieve tension and lessen shock I tapped it first. We got 60 pounds of fluid out . . . there may have been 20 pounds or so of it left there. At operation I was disappointed to find it very densely adherent to the abdominal wall, and worse and worse as I went around, about 6 inches on either side, so I never got into the abdominal cavity. It seemed her best interests demanded a halt. . . . Would have been

Ah Sam, Constance, Katharine, Dorothy, Dan, Edna, Dwight

quite a tumor and quite a case to report. But no jar could have held the specimen. . . .

Siam is slow in taking our religion, but accepts other things. The latest I heard today, an equivalent for our Good Morning i.e. "Morning Happy" . . . And nowadays you often see a notice in the paper of a wedding in the Palace where the bride is spoken of as Miss, family names are given at length (an innovation) and there is a question and answer with mutual promises, and the couple sign a register, and there are witnesses as well. For important persons the King is described as performing the ceremony.

33 - Tiger! Tiger!

Life in Trang was often rugged. Con's small hospital, one of only three between Bangkok and Singapore, was built for him by the High Commissioner in the days before any railway existed. Although exceedingly primitive, it met the needs of a large area which had no other doctor trained in Western medicine and surgery.

He had frequent emergency cases – from the depredations of tigers and wild elephants to the menace of outlaw bands who swooped down from the jungle mountain range less than a dozen miles from our village. At first, for ordinary illnesses, confidence in our "foreign" medicine made slow progress against the centuries-old native custom. But even from the start of Con's practice, the American way had little competition for the healing of wounds.

Guns were scarce for the natives, as owning a modern rifle was prohibitively expensive. But in many an isolated village there would be an ancient gun of sorts, carefully guarded. The very knowledge of its possession might be invitation enough for *dacoits* [gangs of bandits or thieves].

Con's brother, who worked on the New York Stock Exchange, sent him a powerful new rifle. Word soon spread all over the province that the *Maw* had an "elephant gun." Until he had the new gun and royal permission to shoot an elephant – since elephants belonged to the King – Con had used various devices when an elephant was destroying property. Once he threw a torch on to the back of an elephant. The burning resin sticking to its hide made it run off.

Tigers were always with us, and were fair game. Singly, or in pairs, taking several months, they would slowly circle an area of many villages. The people would guess at the approximate time of their return, but could do little until their cattle began to disappear. After the arrival of his new gun, Con's chief extra activity was cut out for him. He settled with his conscience as to the loss of time from his hospital work by giving up the customary month's hot-season vacation.

I came to know what to expect whenever I saw a couple of lean, bronzed Siamese – rarely one alone – walk into the hospital compound with word that a tiger was endangering lives and property. As long as there was no urgent case requiring his attention, Con never refused to drop everything and go back with the men who had come with the request. Nothing else had as much importance.

Late one afternoon as I was giving orders to the house-boy in the dining room I saw two men walk up the hospital driveway. I knew they were countrymen by their swift, purposeful walk and the long curved jungle knives they carried. I wondered, but not for long. Soon Con came dashing down his office stairs and crossed to his study in the house. I met him as he entered the door.

"They want me to get the tiger that took a bullock from under a house last night," he said, already untying a shoelace with his foot on a chair. "The villagers located the kill and sent two men to tell me. They've been walking five hours. If we catch the five o'clock train down a few stations we can just about reach the place before dark. Will you get the 'usual' ready, dear, while I change?"

Con went upstairs to the bedrooms and I went to the pantry. The 'usual' consisted of: a small loaf of the market bread, cut in half to fit easily in the pockets of his hunting coat, unwrapped; a chocolate bar kept on hand for these trips; a handful of whole roasted coffee beans to go loose into one pocket for keeping awake in the long dark hours. All were ready as Con came down the stairs. With a kiss and a "Goodbye, don't worry," he was off on his bicycle which he would leave in the Station Master's office.

Minutes later I heard the shrill whistle of the daily local as it rumbled past on its last fifteen miles down to the river port. I began to wait for the children's return from a walk with the *Amah,* and to plan their early supper. I didn't worry ever, for I had a deep conviction that God honors faith – that those who trust Him are protected according to the degree and quality of their commitment. I felt certain that Con had the same assurance.

The next morning, shortly after the train passed on its way north, I saw Con, on his bicycle, heading a procession up the hospital drive, followed by two men carrying a third on a stretcher. Safely back, I thought, but I wondered where he found the new patient. I told the *Boy* to get breakfast ready for my husband, and waited for Con to finish giving orders for the new patient's care. As soon as he reached the dining room he answered my unasked questions, more seriously than I had ever heard him speak before. "Yes, I got the tiger, but it almost got me! We brought its victim back with us."

Shocked because all previous tiger hunts had been without serious consequences, I begged him to tell me every detail, and this is how he told the story:

We were about thirty minutes on the train. It took fully as long to walk to the village. By the time a half dozen men were ready to join us it was beginning to get dark. When we reached the "kill," they quickly chose a tree and worked fast to lash together a *hang* [platform in tree] and get back to the village as soon as possible.

The place was scrub-jungle, the trees low and scraggly. The hang was the tightest fit I've ever been in. I couldn't even change position. After the men left, I settled down at once with the bread, chocolate and coffee spread out on my handkerchief. While it was still light enough to distinguish the carcass, I got my gun sight on the part of it nearest a clump of bamboo. I hoped the tiger would come early for a leisurely meal; but I knew that if it had heard the men working or picked up their scent, it might creep up and drag what was left of the carcass to a safer place.

The hours dragged by, and it was so dark I could distinguish nothing. I almost gave up, thinking the tiger must have been too suspicious.

Then just before dawn I sensed movement in the direction of the bamboo. Rather than wait and risk having the tiger snatch the carcass away where I couldn't follow in the dark, I shot at the spot I had fixed earlier where I had heard the noise. I heard a crash as the tiger bounded away. I felt I had hit it, but it was impossible to know where or how seriously I had wounded it. I could only wait for daylight.

The villagers came as soon as there was light enough to see. I met them on the ground. The village Headman said, "We heard the shot, *Maw*. Did you hit it?"

"I don't know. Let's look around." The men examined the ground near the carcass.

One of the men exclaimed with satisfaction, "Yes, you did, *Maw*, there is fresh blood here!"

Their leader asked, "Will you follow it, *Maw*?"

I told him we must not leave it wounded. As you know, a tiger in this region seldom attacks a human being, but it is dangerous and unpredictable as long as it lives, once it has been wounded. They said, "Let's go then."

I walked ahead, ready for instant action. Six men with jungle knives and one old muzzle loader followed in single file in silence, keeping step – as you've seen them do – each stepping in the footprint ahead.

After a bit we came to an open space of *lalang* – the razor-sharp grass higher than a man, where tigers like to rest in the day time. We walked along the edge of this a little distance, knowing the danger. Suddenly the Headman, who was halfway down the line, called urgently, "Stop, *Maw*! We must go back for more men and guns."

You know how I have trained the older children when we're out walking, to stop instantly on command because of snakes, making a game of it? I did just that myself, automatically! Stopped, lowered my gun, and was about to turn around.

The man behind me stepped ahead, probably carried by his momentum, unthinking, unhearing. Just two steps! The tiger sprang from the tall grass upon him – the first man in line – the poor villager who had not heeded the warning and had stepped up ahead of me.

With lightning speed the tiger dragged the man along the ground, facing me as it backed off. What would have been an easy shot at such close range was dangerous to the man underneath. I would have to aim for the tiger's brain. Any moment the tiger might get the man's body in its jaws and leap into the grass.

The shot went true. The impact threw the tiger backwards into the air and it released its hold on the man, who dropped to the ground. Instantly regaining its balance, the tiger disappeared into the *lalang*, seemingly all in one motion and moment of time.

The man was carried to the village where a crude stretcher was made. Fortunately we were in time for the train. The village will organize a hunt for the tiger's body in time, as a prize. The man will recover, but he'll be disfigured.

When Con told of the tiger's spring, I had gasped. I was limp at the thought of the close call. "To think that with one more step, you might have been in the place of that poor mangled man, waiting for the surgery, with no other doctor here to perform! That is, if you were lucky enough to be rescued. The alternative is too dreadful to contemplate!"

Before we were married Con had had another close encounter with a tiger. He had bicycled for five days from the northern pass south and west to Trang. While crossing the mountains over the northern pass he saw a tiger in the road ahead. As he had already started down a considerable slope with gathering momentum, it was impossible for him to stop. There was nothing to do but pedal furiously, ring the bell and yell at the top of his lungs for the right of way as he headed straight for the tiger. Possibly the faces he made helped also, for after a startled look the tiger turned and slipped silently into the jungle, acceding him the road.

34 - Furlough (1921-1923)

On our next furlough in the late Spring of 1921 an Italian freighter took our whole family back to New York. A near catastrophe on board the vessel involved Dwight who was only 2 years old. Somehow during a storm he managed to get away from me on deck. A huge wave sweeping over the deck nearly sent him overboard until a quick-thinking Belgian sailor managed to catch him in the nick of time. Dwight carried that memory with him for decades.

We spent the summer of 1921 at Grandpa Bulkley's new home in Riverdale-on-Hudson, at the Bulkley family farm in Norfolk, Connecticut, and at the family cottage on Lake Doolittle. That winter we stayed in Ventnor, New Jersey, near Atlantic City where the three oldest girls attended school for a few months.

Christmas was spent at the family home where Con's five brothers and sisters and their families all gathered for a large reunion and a family portrait. Dorothy had tried to cut her own hair the night before and I had to even it up a bit.

Our sixth child was born on February 8th, 1922, at the Bulkley family home. We named her Mary Daggett after Con's maiden aunt, Mary, and his Grandfather Henry Daggett Bulkley, who was the first physician in this country to lecture and practice dermatology. I think Con was hoping for another boy – he didn't make any fuss over her.

I was so thankful that Yula and Ned, Con's brother and sister-in-law offered to keep Katharine and Constance until our next furlough. The girls are of school age and need proper schooling, which they can't get in Siam. We left them in Plainfield, New Jersey where they seemed happy to stay with their aunt, uncle and cousins.

Our return to Siam in 1923, this time by way of the Atlantic, was uneventful until we reached Brindisi, Italy. There we boarded a small Austrian freighter which was to take us to Singapore by way of the Mediterranean and the Red Sea.

As long as I live I shall never forget my misgivings at the sight of the tiny vessel which was to carry us for a whole month. Nor when we

1. Grandpa Bulkley, 2. Grandma Bulkley, 3. Con, 4. Edna,
5. Katharine, 6. Constance, 7. Dorothy, 8. Dan, 9. Dwight.

embarked were all its dread secrets known. Day by day, little by little we learned it was a war-built boat. It had not been outside the Mediterranean. There was not one single item of comfort except the food!

The bunks had life preservers as pillows. There was no stewardess, no lounge, no library, no music, not a light on deck. There were two tiny dining rooms, two captains and two sets of officers, whose status I never understood. The vague explanation was it was a holdover from the war.

We were a cosmopolitan lot and I imagine we were all stunned and suspicious at the trick played on us. The seven French nuns were absorbed in themselves and their mission. Con had long talks with two priests, Swiss and Brazilian. We also had a Chinese Secretary of Legation, a Portuguese Consul General, an Italian Naval officer, a Swedish lady returning to her husband in Singapore, a lady escaped from Russia on her way to Ceylon to teach and begin life anew and a young Italian doctor. An American Army captain and his wife returning to the Philippines were very exclusive in the upper dining room until the Indian Ocean literally threw us all together.

A week in the Red Sea in June! You may believe all they say about the heat. We got through three days at Port Said and wondered why our boat signaled every boat in the Canal and as far as Aden to know whether the Monsoon had broken. We existed for three days at Port Sudan. Massawa was worse.

By this time every passenger but our family and the nuns had commandeered deck space to sleep in the open. On the first night that Con followed suit, I heard a crash down the corridor. Grabbing my kimono I ran barefoot to our other stateroom and saw Danny lying on the floor with a long gash in his forehead, bleeding profusely, his face covered with blood. He had fallen from the upper berth. I rang bells frantically. Eventually the Chief Steward appeared and went for the ship's doctor, telling every one he met to find my husband. A German war surgeon sewed up the wound while the ship's captain and stewards and several passengers kept up the hunt for Con.

While I held Danny's head, sitting on the floor, I remembered stories of passengers going overboard in the Red Sea from heat and despondency and wondered if heat could actually upset a perfectly sane man. When the last stitch had been taken the Captain roared with laughter as he came to announce the lost was found, "asleep in the hay". It was a rather sheepish husband and father who confessed that the only unoccupied clean spot on the deck happened to be at the very stern. Being a surgeon he felt the irony of fate because his son would now have to bear an unnecessary scar. The ship's doctor had a huge scar across one cheek. Con removed the dressing, and told Danny if he saw the ship's doctor again, he'd better "run like a deer."

Nothing on earth could have prepared us for what we met when our ship rounded the point of Aden. A heavy double-cross seas tested it – and us – for three days. Then the Captain mercifully turned about and drifted. Some $40,000 worth of acetic acid and carbide were thrown overboard since fumes from broken jugs had penetrated below.

For three days and nights there was little sleep. One did not care to lie down because as often as not the head was lower than the feet. The icebox turned over and pans would not stay on the cook stove. We were lucky to get cold meat and bread and preserves to eat. When we finally crossed the Indian Ocean, the sight of our destination – Singapore – was never more welcome.

35 - Motor Trips

In 1923, after years of negotiations and correspondence, and contributions from family members and friends in the States, the family was finally the proud owner of a Model T Ford coupe. Our cars were fondly called Isabel when they were good, and Jezebel when they behaved badly. I learned to drive and loved it, but it took courage. Siamese truck drivers resented a woman driver, and a foreigner at that, and would try to run me off the road. I wasn't one to give up easily, and eventually they gave up harassing me.

One year we were presented with a gift from the Government of ten *rai* [about four acres] of land on a black sand beach. It was fenced and had a caretaker, but was difficult to get to because of the badly neglected roads. I said to Con in April that the monsoon might break any time, and if we were going to go to our beach we had better go soon. The trip had been postponed several times because of emergency cases at the hospital. At last we were off in the coupe, with our cook in the rumble seat surrounded with everything for camping out a few days – bedding, food, fuel, clothes, cooking utensils, etc.

We took the road southeasterly from Trang to reach the beautiful beach property. When we reached a river we found the bridge had been washed away. In order to ford the river we decided that two sampans could be lashed together to act as a ferry to get the car across. I love tricky driving as much as dealing with a tricky horse,

The touring car all packed up, ready for an excursion.

and fortunately Con humored this indulgence of mine and allowed me to drive this time.

Starting off, the weight of the car bogged it down in the small stream which separated the steep bank from a sand bar. We quickly hired some men who happened to be nearby. They uprooted some bamboo and using some limbs as crowbars, they got the bamboo under the tires, which kept the car from sinking further. Then, with planks laid down from the sand bar to two sampans lashed together and two more planks fastened across the sampans, we were able to proceed. I concentrated intently on Con's quiet signals, to guide the car up the incline and across the sampans. There was but an inch or two to spare at each end when finally the brakes were set and I could relax. Fortunately the river was so low that the men waded across, pushing the sampan raft while holding onto the car. The landing was easy, with no steep incline.

From where we left the main road and turned west to the ocean we made such poor time that it was long after dark when we pulled up at the rough shelter on the beach. We had taken all day to travel forty miles, and almost three hours to go the last twelve miles.

The beach extends for many miles in a broad gentle curve. The sand is black and so fine and hard that when the tide is out cars can race on it. Con told me that some years before when he visited the beach for the first time as the guest of the Viceroy and the Governor, their two cars did race along this unparalleled stretch of beach. On that same visit when all three were having a swim, Con encountered a stingray and suffered agonies all night.

A peculiarity of this beach was the incoming tide over the almost half mile of flat sand. In the twinkling of an eye, the flat which had seemed to stretch half-way to the little cliff islands that thickly dotted the horizon would bristle with an army of invading waves, glinting in the sun's rays. They came with the speed and roar of a sudden great wind similar to the roar of approaching monsoon rains over miles of jungle and rubber groves such as we were familiar with in Trang over the years.

We ate our supper that night under a tree by the light of the car's headlights. There was a full moon with a total eclipse. As we watched it on the beach, we could hear the faint din from a distant village where every man, woman and child was out beating gongs and setting off fire crackers to drive off the monster which had swallowed the moon. How pleased they must have been when their noise made it disgorge. That was our signal for a warm moonlight swim, the water at body temperature. It was after midnight when we went to bed in the little shelter.

To return home we went through the same experience to cross the river, only this time we knew what to do. With the sand bar more firm so that the car didn't sink in, and with the sampan raft and bamboo in place, there was no delay, and we made it back in good time.

Another year after driving my children down to Penang to take the ship to return to their school in India, an English lady accompanied me on the return trip. My car broke down toward evening a few miles out of Haad Yai, the Railway Junction, where we were to spend the night. Ahead stretched the lonely motor road, hemmed in by trees, with no sign of life except a *sala* for wayfarers to rest from sun or rain, with its tile roof and floor raised three feet off the ground. I hoped for a passerby to take a message into town to get help, but although I dared not tell my companion, I knew that we might have to spend the night there.

The jungle pressed close on three sides, as we sat on the *sala* floor. My friend was new to the country and very nervous. Suddenly she screamed. A man, wearing only a loincloth and carrying a long jungle knife, stepped silently from the thick screen of jungle a few feet from where we sat. Then another and another joined him until there were five in a row, close enough to touch. They stood silently rigid and motionless as statues for a few moments, before they moved on across the road and disappeared again into the jungle. I would have greeted them, but my companion had grabbed my arm and was trying to get me to run away, sobbing, "They will murder us."

The men were probably respectable villagers who had been away all day working, and must have thought we were strange *farangs* indeed, to be fearful of them. A few minutes later a boy appeared on a bicycle and took a message to the hotel proprietor to send out a tow-car. Then dark night descended while we had a long wait, followed by a hair-raising drive. We were towed to town through midnight jungle without headlights!

It was good to reach the railway hotel with its three or four guest rooms, and to be greeted, late as it was, by the Chinese manager who had sent help on receiving my message. How grateful we were for the mattress and sheet and mosquito curtain provided. I remembered how primitive travel had been in my early years in Siam, when the government bungalows of early days, spaced at intervals of a day's walk, furnished only the mere frame of an iron bed. As I dozed off to sleep, visions of arriving late at night and leaving before daylight floated before me.

We followed the road north to Huey Yot and then said goodbye to speed and comfort. Northwest we bumped and lunged and straddled here half a road, there a whole puddle, here a detour and there a gully. The earth had been washed away from several bridge approaches and we found that the planks were loose or missing.

The river banks were very high and steep. We crossed in a canoe as the sun was setting, with an extra man to help Cook carry the bedding and provisions. Our hands were full with small personal needs. A two hours brisk walk in the light of a full moon brought us to a giant tree. The Siamese guide pointed out the mud marks of a wild elephant on it. The second half of the walk was among big forest trees and very lovely. Eternal silence broken only by the jungle insects. In such lonely spots there is no need for conversation. Any talk would be idle, insipid and as bad manners as talking when a musician is performing. Just the thrill that some one else is sharing it is satisfaction.

36 - Pets and Other Creatures

From our earliest days on the peninsula, the word got around that my husband would take – actully pay cash for – all sorts of animals. So all through the years every kind of wild animal or bird, killed or trapped was brought to the hospital compound, and if he had no use for it, he'd pay the people a few *satangs* for their trouble. The years brought an endless succession of jungle denizens.

Snakes

Con started out from the beginning of his career in Siam to believe nothing and prove everything. I think it was his experience that every native he ever questioned about various snakes invariably labelled them "pit" meaning poisonous.

He learned to pin them by the neck with a forked stick before they knew what he was up to, and looked for fangs with his pocket knife. The first time he tried it on a python in the kitchen, he was not quick enough and it stuck its fangs into the fleshy part of his palm and a tooth broke off and had to be cut out. Con preserved the head. I never had a fear of snakes but did not ever enjoy seeing him hold them, and he usually insisted on my being an observer and witness.

When the hospital was being built in Trang, a *hama dryad* (king cobra) was killed on the grounds and the townspeople were not at all surprised when a few days later a windstorm blew down all the scaffolding. The king cobra is considered sacred, and killing one is inviting catastrophe. Within the year another was caught – possibly the mate? – and brought to the compound. One man held a pole attached to a noose around the neck, and another man had a noose around the body at poles length apart. I was called out to photograph it with hood spread front view, quite confident with the men and their poles. Con did get it by the neck in spite of my remonstrances. There was a whole dispensary of medicines and a surgery behind him, he said.

We learned never to kill a harmless snake, although they sometimes came into the house. A green "coconut" snake was on my desk one morning. With the house open night and day as it was all year around, it is a wonder we did not have more. One night I was alone in the house lying on a couch, reading. I heard something drop. I saw a picture lying on the floor, and looked up to see a four-foot black snake with yellow bars fumbling along a ledge on the wall above me. My first thought was of the deadly "banded *krait*." I scrambled up. A closer look revealed it was a harmless variety, though it did give me a start for several moments.

Hornbills

Sometimes I had to make decisions, and once I paid a stiff price for a large hornbill and its young one. They were walled up in a mud nest built with only space enough for the male to feed them. A giant forest tree had to be cut down in order to obtain them. The mother continually hammered at the box cage and broke through, so it was necessary to make a new cage. We finally tired of the nuisance, and gave them away.

A most exasperating pet was one of a smaller species of hornbill presented to us. At first it was tied by a cord to one leg, which got broken. My husband put a splint on the leg and turned the bird loose. It stayed in a dense, high tree near the kitchen until the leg was healed.

That hornbill was the family favorite for many months with everyone but

Dwight and Dan with hornbill

the cook and myself. It would sometimes swoop through the kitchen window and steal eggs, cucumbers, string beans. Or it would swoop from the roof of the house, and land gently on the shoulder of anyone walking in the garden, or swoop from a tree and catch the shuttlecocks in midair during a game of badminton.

It would perch very coyly on the window sill of Con's office, and the minute his back was turned, it would fly off with a medicine dropper, pencils or whatever was out. It would snatch toothbrushes from the bathroom. Nothing was safe. When food was thrown to it on its high perch, it caught it with a high crescendo whistle. Our guests were much entertained, but when it ate the tops of all my precious young tomato plants, which I so jealously guarded on my bedroom veranda, that was the last straw. I gave the hornbill to a friend, to the children's grief.

Over the years we have given a home to a pair of dancing cranes, peacocks and Argus pheasants. These pheasants resemble peacocks in size and plumage, but in shades of brown rather than blue-green. Once we had two mynah birds in adjacent cages. Both were the deepest black velvet: one with a bright yellow crest and beak, the other with a crest of kingfisher blue. I was not successful in teaching the mynahs to talk, unfortunately.

The Otter

The *Amah* always had the children out of doors soon after daylight. One morning I was awakened by screams. The children were up in their favorite tree-house. As I looked out the window, a full-grown otter was flopping around the base of the tree, looking up at them hungrily. The *Amah* was as frightened as the children. By the time my husband could dress and get downstairs, a crowd had gathered on the road. Soon the otter's owner, a *Baba* woman (Chinese-Malay) appeared. She ran to the otter, gathered it in her arms and went off reproving it affectionately. Con learned later that she treated it as a child. It slept with her inside her mosquito curtain, and on this particular morning, when she'd left it to go out to the stream for a bath, it had ventured away in search of fun.

The Fish Tiger

We had a few chickens in a chicken coop which had a high fence of chicken wire around it with a gate which was securely fastened each night. In spite of that, the chicken coop was occasionally raided. One beautiful moonlight night we jumped up at the sound of distress from the coop, and reached it just in time to see a catlike animal, larger than any dog in our neighborhood, bounding away. The next day we set a trap, and that night caught a fine specimen of *sua-pla* or fish-tiger, black with striking white stripes. At another time, a fourteen-foot python was killed in the chicken yard.

The Honey Bears

At one time we had a pair of baby Malayan honey bears. We had read that they made good pets, but our Toofy and Woofy were little demons. Con was bitten once by one of them, and I by the other.

I wooed Woofy with tidbits daily and thought I was safe in letting him lick my hand after giving him some sticky taffy. He cleaned all the sweet from my hand, then deliberately sucked the inside of my palm, gave me a dirty look, and slunk away.

The two were chained so they could play together. Toofy got loose once and climbed up a high tree by the tennis court. The whole neighborhood had a holiday bringing Toofy down. I think the indignities of that day and the sense of futility shortened his life.

Edna with tiger cub, monkey and dog.

Tiger Cubs

Our biggest investment was a pair of unweaned tiger cubs which were brought in late one afternoon. We agreed to pay five *ticals* for them if they survived a week. The odds were against it. I set to work with feeding bottles and nipples and had both *Amahs* helping. Nursing time began to be exciting about the second week. They were strong enough

Ah Sam and Con with tiger cubs. Dog and cat between them.

to assert themselves and protested strenuously all the time they sucked greedily. I was thankful we were not nearer the jungle where their parents roamed free.

Our tiger cubs grew and grew, had their pictures taken, and were becoming a real problem when along came a young Englishman from a tin mine up-country who had visions of transporting them to England on his coming leave. He offered sixty ticals. We were delighted. He fed them on expensive imported powdered milk until he got panicky about the expense and sold them to two Swiss brothers who had a menagerie in Nakawn and collected animals for a German Zoo. I saw the tigers later in their pen on the veranda of the brothers' home.

Monkeys

We were never without a monkey or two in all our years in Trang. Sometimes we would have as many as four or five. The common gray monkey had a long tail and blue belly. The *chanee*, was a tailless white gibbon with black face and palms. The unusual and appealing *kang* long-tailed black monkey had white rings around the eyes, Last

but not least, the grubby brown monkey with its finger-length tail, had a red face that blazed when it was angry.

They all had paperweight chains and good runs, and the grays and browns were arranged so they could play or fight without getting tangled. The roofed-over space of some twenty feet between the house and the kitchen was alive with pets. The cook and Boy endured them with miraculous patience.

The gibbons had the highest perch and walked back and forth on two feet, holding the chain daintily in one hand. They were usually named Aunt Dinah or Black Sambo. They were not allowed on the ground but had access to some windows. Our "grays" were called Funny Face and were quite mischievous. The browns, named "Dinky," were taught to salute us and our friends by presenting a reddish posterior, then peeking out from underneath with its face upside down and shaking our hand or its left leg with its right hand.

When they were not away at school, the children fed and cared for the pets.

Moosang

We had many *moosang* during the years, an animal similar to a civit cat, or perhaps like a cross between an opossum and a mongoose. We often had two at a time, and called them Moosie and Frisky. When young, they made adorable pets. They have a long body and short legs, long tail and fox-like face with small ears, a little button nose, and inquisitive, beady black eyes. Some were black with white stripes, and some were white with a smoky black tail, feet, ears and nose. It was fun to watch one walk

White moosang

a taut wire. Its long tail had great strength and served to preserve its remarkable balance.

We discussed daily whether Moosie should be loose for awhile. The dining room was screened and we generally allowed it the run of the large room at meal time. I often held my breath expecting to see some choice bit of glass or china broken, as it raced back and forth on the pantry shelves, but that never happened. It climbed straight up the walls and cabinets, scampered around the room, and loved to climb up on Con's shoulder.

I was adamant that they be chained every night because they could get into the most impossible places. Our house was loosely constructed and for years I feared that a snake, would possibly wriggle through the ceiling boards and land on my bed.

One night I was awakened from sleep by a soft plop and I did what any normal woman would do when she meets danger in the dark. I screamed. Con jumped up from his bed calling, "Moosie, Moosie" in his usual endearing falsetto call. I thought he was having a nightmare and shouted, "There's a snake on my bed. Quick, get the flashlight!" He kept on feeling about and still calling "Moosie, Moosie. Ah, I've got you now. Why do you go around scaring the *Mem*?" He had noticed when he returned late from the hospital that one of the *moosang* had escaped its chain. We never did figure out how it got into the screened room.

The Poodle, the Kitten and Pang Pang

Early in the fall of 1928 a governor in one of the Southern provinces made me a gift of a Chinese poodle, which I named Spot. A day or two before her first puppies were due, I was brought a Siamese kitten, not yet weaned. I fed it milk from a medicine dropper until it became so bloated that I feared I would lose it. Seeing Spot's concern when the kitten was needing help, and hoping I could work on Spot's maternal instinct, I sat on the floor for about an hour, talking to her and asking her to cooperate with the helpless kitten. She began licking it tenderly. Then I made a bed for the kitten and told Spot to guard it. Then I watched. She was all quivering eagerness and concern.

Spot had the freedom of the downstairs room but had never been upstairs to the drawing room and bedrooms. Late the following night she came upstairs to where I was reading and looked at me with such pleading that I knew what she wanted. I went downstairs and showed her the large packing case I had prepared for her puppies. Next morning, when Spot got into her box to feed her offspring, I put the kitten down among the litter and it began to suck ravenously. I held my hand on Spot's head and talked to her. She made one nervous movement and looked at me reproachfully, then seemed to relax and accept the kitten.

After that first meal, the kitten would climb up a beach umbrella and jump down into the box, always getting the best place among the puppies. It became a "seven-days wonder" and people came from far and near to see the two.

Each year before Dorothy, Dan and Dwight arrived back home from school in India [see chapter 46], we would collect some new interesting pets. One year we had an animal neither Con nor I had seen before or since. We called it Pang Pang. It seemed to be part *moosang* and part mongoose. I raised it from a mere baby at the same time I was playing nursemaid to the Siamese kitten and Spot. Thus the three were brought up in complete harmony. Pang Pang was the leader.

Of all our pets, little Pang Pang most endeared itself to us. It won our hearts completely. Even a staid English guest visiting us admitted a secret fondness for Pang Pang. Mealtimes were inclined to be uproarious when the kitten, the poodle and Pang Pang played around the room together. The kitten and Spot, so unsophisticated in comparison, were no match for Pang Pang's wit. They tumbled around and looked foolish when Pang Pang tricked them. They were a lively trio and an endless delight. Unlike the kitten and the poodle, Pang Pang loved to be held and petted. It had a peculiar purr quite different from a cat. Sadly, it did not live very long.

The puppies were given away, one by one, and the kitten developed into a beautiful Siamese cat. Spot and the cat were inseparable, and always slept side by side.

37 - *Gambusia* and the Walking Fish

During my first months in Bangkok I met a charming older woman. She had come to the capital from Burma as a young bride fifteen or twenty years earlier. Both her father and her husband were British and had come to Siam in government service. Because her mother was Burmese, most of the ladies in the capital had left her strictly alone, as if she had committed an unpardonable offense. When I left Siam, she was probably the most loved and highly respected woman in the land, the friend of princes, diplomats and people of many races and creeds.

Through her hobby of collecting plants, many rare tropical specimens were named after her in Kew Gardens in England. When in her seventies she spent a month with me, hard at work every day drying some specimens, classifying others and preparing them for transportation.

Returning from a trip to England, she stopped off in Syria to get some tiny fish called *Gambusia* that lived on mosquito larvae. After the long voyage and a two-day railway journey to her home in Bangkok, only seven of the 26 *Gambusia* she got in Syria had survived. These, she promptly delivered to the Siam government's Director of Fisheries. They multiplied to such an extent that many were constantly being sent to the other Asian countries.

On one of my infrequent trips to Bangkok I met the Director at a dinner party and asked if I might have some of the little fish to take back to Trang to propagate. Perhaps the *Gambusia* would help control the malarial mosquitoes at Chong, our favorite vacation place.

The *Gambusia* were brought to me at the railway station in a five-gallon kerosine tin. The journey took 25 hours. It was at the height of the hot season in April and all were dead on arrival. The Director sent another lot some months later by his Siamese assistant, who was making a field trip.

As soon as they came, I told the gardener to clean out the lotus pool in the front garden and to make sure there were no fish left which could interfere with the propagation of my *Gambusia*. In digging out the mud, the gardener discovered a fish six or seven inches long and put it in a bucket of water behind the kitchen, unknown to me, intending to take it to his home in the evening. This is an unusual species of fish which "walks" upright on its fins and so is popularly called a walking fish. Then he returned the mud, replanted the lotus and filled the pool with water.

It happened that my British botanist friend was spending the month in our home collecting jungle plants and we were having tea when a commotion outside interrupted us.

On the driveway, about thirty or forty feet from the back of the kitchen where it had jumped out of the bucket, the walking fish was inching along steadily and purposefully. Passersby along the highway were coming into the compound to join my husband, the hospital staff, patients and servants who stood watching. No cock or bull was ever more sportingly cheered on by a crowd of spectators than that walking fish at our home in the Malay Peninsula. In the crowd, as we approached, we saw Siamese, Chinese, Malay and the *Baba* mixture (Chinese-Malay), Afghans and a Hindu cloth merchant, all watching the progress of the walking fish.

"Baba" or Malay-Siamese woman

My Siamese cat had followed us outside and ran on ahead to investigate. This added to the excitement as the conglomeration of Orientals speculated as to where the fish had come from and where it was going. I caught Con's eye. We both realized that it must have come from the pool and some powerful instinctive drive was drawing it back to its home.

The cat gave the fish a poke with her paw, knocking it flat, sniffed it thoroughly, then walked away defying anyone to laugh at her for showing curiosity. I gave a sigh of relief, wondering if the onlookers, suddenly still, had been holding their breath like myself.

After a moment the fish got upright on its fins and started moving again, in short, zigzag jerks, seemingly with a new urgency while the watchers laughed and talked or stooped to encourage it. If there was any betting on the side I was too concerned with my ultimate decision to notice.

At the point on the driveway opposite the pool, fifteen or twenty feet away, the fish turned at a right angle. It darted through the *canna* border and began to sprint across the grass toward the pool. If the interest of the crowd was now <u>intense</u>, my situation was <u>more</u> tense, for I was about to become a very unpopular spoil-sport.

I looked at the mess of mud on the lawn, and knew that if the fish got back into the pool, we were in trouble. It would take another whole day's work to locate it buried in the mud, to replace the mud, replant the lotus, fill the pool with water, and another day's wait for the mud to settle. That could mean a two-day delay in which the *Gambusia* might die.

"Poom," I commanded the gardener who was standing by, "Catch it, quick! Don't let it get into the pool!" And deaf to my husband's urgings - he wanted to see it jump the low coping into the pool – I shouted, "Hurry! Hurry!"

The gardener made a dive for the fish and – just in time – scooped it up in his *pa kow ma,* his body scarf of many uses, and disappeared toward the kitchen. At once the crowd quietly and good-naturedly dispersed in the manner of the Orient.

This time it looked as though my *Gambusia* might have a fighting chance to survive.

Mary sitting on the edge of the pool

38 - Bandits and Lawlessness

There was general lawlessness those first years in Taptieng, and the Siamese government was having a hard time managing this province because of it. All government officials had to be bribed to come to the province with a *bea kandan* [jungle bonus]. They were not compelled to accept appointment to this isolated post, because of the difficulty of travel and also because the people and the dialect were so different. For a Bangkok Siamese, it was like going to a foreign country.

However, the principal reason for the region's unpopularity was its organized banditry, notorious throughout the entire kingdom. Many governors refused to take on the risk.

For generations the mountains and jungles had been a hideout for bands of outlaws who would swoop down and carry off their booty, unmolested. It was a medieval sort of warfare with strange rules. A wealthy householder might find a warning nailed to his dwelling that he had been chosen for attack. Weeks or months might pass.

Then one night the band, garbed in black and hooded, would come by moonlight or with torches, post lookouts while they spiked all paths leading to the house with deadly sharp bamboo points, then calmly set to work questioning the family and searching the thatch and bamboo posts for hidden money and jewelry. If the find was not up to expectation, prodding with torture was the order and not infrequently some resisting member of the family would be silenced forever. Some who were wounded by sword or knife were brought to the hospital.

In 1929 both Con's parents died and he returned to the States alone for an extended leave. The rice crop was poor because of excessive rain. The resulting poverty drove many to gambling – men and women gambled away their very clothes. Those who could get their hands on rubber latex made crude rubber sheets to be sold for a good price in Penang. Then *dacoits* made attacks night after night. Daily greetings of friends meeting on the road amounted to "Who was robbed last night?"

All that year I was alone with the children. I slept uneasily with the revolver under my pillow, listening for strange sounds. Stormy nights were terrifying because I imagined bandits ripping off the lattice wall beside the front entrance. Yet not one single incident happened to person or property on our compound.

One night I was awakened by the screams of women and the sound of a huge fight. Robbers had tunneled under the wall of our Chinese neighbor's house. Like all the Chinese houses in the area the floor was hard earth. The owner waited inside with a great beam which he wielded on the heads and shoulders of the would-be entrant.

Another night, down the road from our house, a dog barked. When the housewife went to call the animal inside, she was stabbed to death in her doorway.

Around this time the bandit leader who had terrorized the area for years was finally captured. The man had boasted, and the people believed, he had a charmed life. But women were his undoing. The police who had been foiled time after time patiently waited. They knew the outlaw, with a wife in nearly every village, would eventually give himself away.

The police received a tip that two women were quarreling over him. The police surrounded the house where he had come to sleep for the night and demanded his surrender. When this notorious robber realized he was trapped, he plunged a knife into his heart. Officials proclaimed a three day holiday and all the region rejoiced. The robber's body was kept on exhibition and photographs were sold to hundreds of people who walked long distances to celebrate and witness the corpse with their own eyes.

After Con returned, we had a mild experience with robbers who made us a visit straight from robbing a Chinese merchant in the town. One of the four was our Malay *syce* whom Con had found dying by the roadside of dysentery, cured and then hired. He must have known I kept my wedding silver in a small trunk in the bedroom. He entered by the bathroom window with a pal while two others kept watch below. They missed the shotgun in my dark corner within a few inches of my head, as well as the revolver concealed among Con's socks and shorts in an open shelf. They were taking no chances in a house with guns. However they found the key ring and some jewelry and my sewing basket on the dressing table and were starting off with the trunk when Con sprang after them with a heavy cane he kept handy in his corner. They fled, strewing the contents of my sewing basket over the compound. We learned later the *syce* was an opium addict, which probably accounted for his behavior.

Losing our trunk and suitcase keys was a nuisance. There was no locksmith nearer than Penang so the pins had to be knocked out of the hinges and unsightly hasps nailed backside. Knowing an enemy possessed the house key was an uncomfortable feeling, for Con was often away over night or for several days. When we got a filthy note asking how much the keys were worth to us, my answer was to have target practice with the revolver out on the tennis court knowing word would be spread across the peninsula that the *"Mem"* would shoot to kill anyone entering the house unlawfully as surely as if a tiger were to come into the compound.

The home of a well-to-do Christian widow adjoined the Dunlap's compound. A Malay courted her in his own tempestuous manner, and when she refused to marry him, he and his cronies set fire to a tall woodpile against her house, thinking that would so fill her with fear that she would consent. They also spiked the path leading to the Dunlap's house. The Chinese cook ran to put out the fire and was injured by the bamboo spikes, but Mr. Dunlap and the other servants succeeded in preventing further damage to the house. Mr. Dunlap also sent the Malay a strong warning about molesting the woman further, and that was the end of the affair.

Siamese Christian matron

39 - The Charming Imposter

I was standing in my doorway enjoying the garden when a portly European turned in from the road and walked up the long drive. A dozen thoughts flashed through my mind. Who can this man be, walking up from town? Impossible. They are always driven up with a flourish. A white man dressed in long khaki trousers and coat, could not be an Englishman or an American. Strangers usually just go to the hospital first. There was only a hedge between our house and the hospital, and he had passed its two broad entrances. I wondered if this meant a *tiffin* [lunch] guest, and tried to remember what we were having to eat.

As he turned into the *porte-cochere* [roofed extension over driveway] he saw me watching. He pulled off his hat, breathed a dramatic "Ahh!" and with a flourishing bow remarked, "A white woman in this wilderness! They told me there was a doctor in this town."

"How do you do. Will you come inside? Excuse me for a minute." I turned and called out toward the back door, speaking in Siamese, "*Boy*, tell the doctor there is a visitor." I knew this was Con's busiest hour in the day, but I didn't want to entertain this man alone.

We sat in our downstairs reception room conversing. In a very few minutes Con came in, looking preoccupied and slightly impatient at being called.

The stranger handed him a card, apologizing that it was soiled but was the only one he had with him. He explained that he was a surgeon studying tropical diseases. He had made a great deal of money from quinine in Sumatra during the war and was traveling around the world. He was a bachelor. He had sent his heavy luggage on to Bangkok, and had come on the coast steamer from Penang, where he had left his suitcase. Con invited him to stay with us until the next express to Bangkok and after lunch he took him back with him to the hospital. In the afternoon Con drove him to Kantang. This was Friday.

249

Margaret, one of our circle, arrived on the morning train the next day from her vacation on the island of Puket. At *tiffin* conversation turned to church and I told about my difficulties with the organ. Doctor Jay (as he called himself) said he had lots of experience and could take them apart and could put them together blindfolded. I told him he could have the job. He agreed. (I tried to believe the organ was improved. Months later we found the tremolo box had been glued tight.)

Dr. Jay made himself one of the family. He was a charming storyteller and entertained us all with tales of his boyhood in Holland, his war experiences and travels.

We were puzzled. Margaret and I laughed and joked about our strange guest, but another neighbor, Mrs. Knox, was suspicious of him. At Sunday morning service he had asked to sing a hymn solo. We were astonished at his operatic voice. She asked him where he had sung. A Fifth Avenue church. Which one? He couldn't remember. I felt sorry to see him on the spot and suggested the Madison Avenue church. Oh yes, of course.

Con had received a letter from the American doctor in Nakawn, asking if he would come to perform a certain operation on the following Wednesday. Con said to Dr. Jay, "You are a surgeon, this is old stuff for you. I would be glad to watch you do this operation."

Dr. Jay said he had already changed his mind about going to Bangkok on the Monday night express. He would like to see something of Meikong and Tung Song Junction if we would be so kind as to give him introductions to our friends in those two places. By Sunday night he decided that Trang was an attractive spot for writing his book on tropical disease. Why should he not do it in our neighborhood? No doubt Con could arrange for him to have one of the government guest cottages. He would go to Bangkok first, arrange with a bank, get his principle luggage and return.

He was full of enthusiasm over our hospital and the wonderful work Con was doing, although it was so very primitive, since we had to use kerosene lamps. He would consider himself a happy man if he might be allowed to spend part of his fortune for a dynamo to furnish both the hospital and our house with electricity. It seemed strange that a great surgeon should speak so glowingly about our poor little hospital. Something was fishy, but he had agreed to perform a very difficult operation.

Monday Margaret left us to return to her school in Bangkok, assuring Dr. Jay she would be glad to introduce him to people there and give any help within her power.

Monday night we were in the upstairs living room waiting for the gong to announce dinner below. Con, Dr. Jay and I were standing under a bright lamp conversing. A beetle of some sort flew onto Dr. Jay's coat sleeve. Lively theatrics and excitement followed. "It has poisoned me," he said, grasping his hand in great agony. "It is already swollen. What shall I do?" It *was* swollen. It must have been a very dangerous beetle. Strange we had never encountered one before. "What do you suppose it is?" "Let's look in the encyclopedia." "Poisonous!" Con bandaged it and put his arm in a sling as Dr. Jay insisted. "You must do everything to get it well by Tuesday."

When the gong sounded Con went downstairs ahead of us. He reappeared shortly with a sphinx-like face. At the time he said nothing. He was perfectly polite and apparently interested while our guest kept up a lively comment interrupted by exclamations at the inconvenience of eating with his left hand, etc. I thought Dr. Jay must have had a good deal of pain to justify such a reaction. Later Con told me that he had captured the beetle which Dr. Jay had thrown out and tried to make it bite him, with no success.

We discussed our schedule and decided Dr. Jay should take the morning train to Tungsong to see our friends, join Con on the evening train to Nakawn, spend the night with Dr. Dunlap and his wife, and be ready for the morning's operation. Tuesday morning Con took Dr. Jay to the train, his hand still bandaged, and he himself went on the late afternoon train.

When Con returned from Nakawn, on the Wednesday evening train, I drove the Ford to the station to meet him. "Tell me all about it. Did Dr. Jay do the operation?"

"No, he seemed to feel his hand was not fit."

"I suppose that you did it, then?" A nod of affirmation.

"What did Dr. Dunlap think of Dr. Jay?" No comment.

"Was he jealous of all the grand things Dr. Jay is going to do for your hospital?"

"I don't think I told him."

"Where is Jay now?"

"He is staying with the Baker's again and will take the morning local train north."

"How is he able to do that slow three-day trip when he says all his clothing and money are in Bangkok?"

"I lent him a hundred *ticals* for his expenses."

"Con," I exploded, with my first uneasy feeling that something was wrong.

"Oh, that's all right. He gave me a fine stopwatch as security. See?" He handed it to me.

I didn't think much of it, but I was speechless.

I found it difficult to settle down. So Dr. Jay had spent two nights at the Baker's. How I would like to know what happened there. I would write to her. No, I would visit. It was my turn. The week went by. I sent a telegram, "Coming Thursday if I do not hear to contrary."

I told Ah Sim and Ah Sam (the children's *Amahs*) that I was going to visit Mem Tungsong and they beamed in approval. All my friends were known to them by the cities they lived in: Mem Ronpibun, Mem Nakawn, Mem Lampeh. Cook and garden *coolie* and water carrier were also like members of our family. All had been with us for

Ah Sam, Mary, Ah Sim with Peggy, born 1924

many years and they were used to sudden trips and I could know that there would not be the slightest deviation from routine. Nothing alarming had ever happened in my absences.

Anna Baker met me at the station looking pretty in her flowered voile. We were both bursting with exciting news and curiosity. I asked, "What did you think of Dr. Jay?"

"Thank you for sending him to us. He has a magnificent voice." They had sung until after midnight. Anna had a concert voice and they ended up by calling each other Melba and Caruso.

"But Daddy thinks he is – well, be careful when he comes home to lunch what you say." Our tongues flew. I told of Dr. Jay's promise to return and set up an electric plant for the hospital and then live at the government park while he worked on his book. She told me that he was arranging to have his New York house ready for them and he had asked if he could show his gratitude for his happy visit by making a gift to them of a steamship passage from England across the Atlantic so that their two lovely daughters could meet them in New York. I knew the Bakers were planning a trip to England via the Pacific and across the States.

"Oh, Edna, if you could have heard him enthuse over your husband. He was thrilled about the operation and says Con is a very fine surgeon." I wondered. Con had long been away from any modern medical center, and Dr. Jay's praise did not ring true. I asked her what Dr. Jay told them about himself.

Anna continued. "What do you think he borrowed? The gift manicure set you gave me. He's going to use it on the trip and I'll get it back when he returns. I only wish he had not taken the hypodermic syringe with him. We borrowed it from Dr. Dunlap and I only hope he doesn't lose it or forget. I haven't told Daddy yet. He would be frightfully put out. Why do you suppose he needed it?"

She paused a bit and then said, "But don't be silly, it must be all right. He has a divine voice."

I began to feel more skeptical. We talked about nothing but Dr. Jay until noon when Anna's husband walked up the railway track with a stranger. Since the Bakers were the only Europeans living there at the time, it was an event. The stranger was a young Dane by the name of Neilsen from the Danish lumber company up the peninsula. He was on his way to Con's hospital for a checkup. As was customary with Europeans in the interior, he had gone straight to the bank where Mr. Baker was manager and was invited to lunch. After introductions, Mr. Baker said, "Mr. Neilsen has just seen Dr. Jay at Baudon."

Anna exclaimed, "Oh, tell us about it. What did you all think of him?" Neilsen told us they entertained him several days. When Dr. Jay learned that one of their elephants was having serious eye trouble, Dr. Jay had offered to cure it. Asked about his fee, said he would do it for a thousand *ticals*. The manager thought it was too much and decided to go on with the native treatment. Pressed for more news, Nielsen said Dr. Jay planned to stop over in Petchaburi on his way to Bangkok, that being the only town with European residents.

Nielsen then remembered that the assistant manager at Baudon was so impressed with Dr. Jay's personality that he lent him his very valuable camera.

At that I burst out, "He borrowed a hundred *ticals* from my husband, something from Dr. McDaniel in Nakawn, something from Anna and now a camera from a man in Baudon. I wonder what he will get in Petchaburi?"

Anna said reproachfully, "But he is coming back. He's going to settle down and write his book."

"I wonder," I said. "I feel something is not quite right."

When I got home the next day, there was a letter from Margaret saying *she* had lent Dr. Jay a hundred *ticals* and set him up in one of the missionary homes which was currently vacant. She said Dr. Jay had conducted a prayer meeting and had made a very good impression.

In the meantime, on the strength of Nielsen's information, Con wrote to the American consul in Bangkok suggesting that he keep an eye on Dr. Jay, find out whatever he could. The consul replied that the very day he tried to contact Dr. Jay, the man had left on a tramp steamer for Saigon, having borrowed from several people and taken valuable books from the house where he was staying.

As months went on and friend visited with friend, we pieced together more of the story. The next episode for us occurred one evening far from home on a mountain top south of the Malay border below Penang.

We knew several of the Methodist missionaries in Penang and were invited to join a group at their hill bungalow in Taipeng.

Instead of taking the international express across the peninsula and arriving in Penang at night, we took the small steamer from our river port enjoying the scenery at sea. We reached Penang in time for the morning express.

After a quick lunch in Taipeng we were on our way four thousand feet up Maxwell Hill, in chairs on poles carried by four Chinese. Two extra men for each chair walked behind to rotate. This being my first experience, I was much interested in the way these two could step under the poles in motion and take the burden without a jolt. The trip took six hours with brief stops when all the men would sit around on the ground.

Two of the half-dozen bungalows, each on its own hilltop, belonged to the British government for the High Commissioner and the Resident.

The mission bungalows had a permanent staff of Hindu servants, managed by a competent cook whom we paid by the day. Our companions were Mr. and Mrs. Sullivan from Singapore, who had recently moved to Ipoh, Ruth Brackett from Ipoh, who was engaged to a young Englishman, and Martha Bond from Penang.

The night before we left to return to Trang, we all gathered at the lookout *sala*, to watch the sunset across the water.

I had been fascinated at the vista from our balcony of seemingly hundreds of miles of mountain jungle stretching to the east and south. There was not a sign of life, although I knew tigers and the *Sakai* [primitive jungle tribe] inhabited the area.

At the *sala,* however, the scene was intensely dramatic. Four thousand feet below spread the whole plain, from Ipoh to Penang at the edge of the Straits of Malacca, shining gold in the late afternoon light. In nine different "pools" of water on the plain were nine tin dredges looking like tiny toys. As we sat in the *sala* watching them while we waited for the sun to go down, we spoke of the hard life of the men on the dredges. The managers had fine houses and club and social life, but the "white" foremen who worked with the native *coolies* were quite beyond the pale. I had felt a great pity for some of these lonely men I had met. Mostly Australians, many had the stamina to keep fit, while for others, their only recourse was drink and native women.

After dinner we sat around an open fire in the huge living room and conversation turned upon the inevitable experiences we must all have with people of every nationality under the sun, turning up for our hospitality on some pretext or other.

Martha told about a hare-brained spinster who settled down at her school in Penang with some wild ideas about how to teach "natives."

Ruth told about her difficulties with an old man traveling through the Orient selling a patent medicine, who was brought to the hospital where she was a nurse-assistant.

"How about you," Mr. Sullivan asked my husband.

"Not very many leave the ports for the interior," Con replied. "A Latvian was brought to the hospital by police from a tin mine where he tried to murder his native woman. He stayed five months."

I spoke up. "A Dane, who represented himself as a writer, walked three days crossing the peninsula, sent his *Boy* to the hospital for a liniment and something for his upset stomach. He drank the liniment by mistake, and after he had been treated, insisted on being brought to our home, late at night, as it was."

"I suppose you meet a great many interesting people in Singapore?" Con asked.

"Yes and no," Mr. Sullivan answered. "We have a stream of visitors from ships stopping in port on world cruises, but we are seldom inflicted by the hobo type, who stay near the waterfront in the native quarters."

"How about that man from China who fooled us all?" Mrs. Sullivan reminded her husband.

"That's right. Brown was his name. Mentioned the names of one or two missionaries in Foochow whom he knew and had worked with. Asked if he might stay with us a few days." He turned to his wife teasingly, "Madge was quite impressed with him."

She laughed, "Well, he was rather distinguished looking and quite charming. He won the children with his story-telling. They became quite fond of him during the several months he stayed."

"We let him have a room in the boys' school and have all his meals with us," Mr. Sullivan explained. "The Chinese head teacher looked out for his comfort at the school."

Mrs. Sullivan continued. "Mr. Brown became almost like one of the family. Then one afternoon he came in at teatime when I had a visitor. 'Come in and join us,' I said, 'Mrs. Selby is from Foochow. You have probably met.'

"There was a pregnant moment of astonishment on Mrs. Selby's face, and of embarrassment on Mr. Brown's. Each murmured vaguely that they had met. He flushed awkwardly for a moment, recovered, then said he merely came to let me know that he had a dinner engagement.

"When he had gone Mrs. Selby told me, quite shocked, that 'Brown' had another name in Foochow. He was born in Hong Kong, was a dope fiend and was wanted by the police for passing forged checks. She and her associates in the mission only knew him as a disgrace to all Europeans, a rather unsavory character who 'spoiled the white man's prestige' in the words of the British. I could hardly wait to tell my husband what I had learned. I wished I could have questioned Mrs. Selby further."

Then Mr. Sullivan took up the story. "At school the following day at the mid-morning recess Seng Saa, the head teacher, came up to me and said, 'Brown asked me to take him to a dispensary, so I went with him to Seng Lee's. You know, he is a member of our church. While we were talking, Mr. Brown left us. I am sorry to tell you, sir, that Seng Lee has been to see me since to say that there is no doubt at all that Brown took away a supply of heroin.'

"I took him into my confidence. 'Seng Saa, I'm afraid Mr. Brown is not at all what we thought he was. Mrs. Sullivan and I took him at his word, but, if he is a drug addict, he must not stay here longer. Could you plan to go to the cinema tonight and take a few of the older boys, and invite Brown to go with you, so I can search his room?'

" 'Yes, Mr. Sullivan, I will do that. I think it is wise not to have him here longer.'

"As I feared I found a hypodermic syringe and a quantity of heroin among Brown's few things. Before breakfast next morning he appeared with his suitcase and thanked us for our gracious hospitality and said that he was leaving for Penang where he was assured of work at a famous rubber estate near there. 'It is splendid, the model estate of the entire Malay States. A regular city and very attractive and comfortable, I've heard.' "

At this point Mr. Sullivan got up to stir the embers and put another log on the fire.

Con looked at me significantly, then asked him, "Did you say he was a Dutchman?"

"Yes, although he said he was an American. But for an American, he had an unmistakable accent."

Con was coming alive. "Was he rather large and blonde and good looking?"

"Yes," said Mr. Sullivan, then turning to his wife, "what would you say, Madge?"

"Oh yes, he was very good looking, and very engaging in manner. He talked well and had a fine singing voice."

Con asked calmly, "Have you heard of him since he left Singapore? Do you know where he went?"

Mrs. Sullivan answered quickly, "Yes, indeed. We know that he was arrested in Penang for having the assumed name of Wren."

I felt a mounting excitement, convinced that Brown or Wren was our Dr. Jay. Con turned to me. "The description tallies. To think that we should piece out his story up here in Taipeng." He proceeded to tell of our encounter with the same man, known to us as Dr. Jay.

A year or so afterwards Con saw a notice in a Bangkok newspaper about a European found dead from an overdose of opium in a cheap hotel in Singapore. He wrote to the police there, asking for a description of the man and something of his history on the chance it might be Dr. Jay, or Brown, or Wren. The answer confirmed that he was our charming imposter. We never learned whether the dose was suicidal or accidental.

40 - *Semang*

When I was living at Wang Lang I went to the opening of Wat Benjamabopet, the beautiful marble temple. It was a great occasion lasting a week. King Chulalongkorn was there, followed by a small negrito boy dressed in a bright scarlet coat with shining brass buttons. I had seen the boy sitting up proudly behind the King in his carriage.

The school girls told me that this *Semang* boy had been captured in the Malay Peninsula and presented to the king as an unusual gift, and that the king secretly enjoyed watching proud officials squirm as the boy delivered some message in his vulgar, slave idiom.

Little did I dream then that interest in the lad's people would follow me through the years.

Once each year the very tribe to which the young Negrito belonged, would come down from the high mountain range, backbone of the Peninsula, to our village on the western side. After being given rice and tobacco by the shopkeepers, they would spend the night at our hospital, sure of a welcome, a place to sleep and two good meals before they returned to their hideout fastness in the dense mountain jungle.

These *Semang* are one of the most ancient races of mankind living today. There are only a few in Siam, some more in the Andaman Islands off the west coast of Burma, and a few in the Philippines and in the interior of New Guinea. They are similar to the African pygmies, no more than four feet tall.

Young Semang

During the Neolithic Ages they covered the whole of Farther India. Their polished stone ax-heads, flint tools and weapons were periodically being unearthed. Pathetic remnant of a vanishing race, they are as shy as the Argus Pheasant whose haunts they share in the mountains. Harmless, suspicious pagans, without written language or tradition, they constantly move from place to place in the mountain jungle with their bamboo blow-guns and arrows tipped with poison made from the sap of the *Ipoh* or *Upas* tree, used now only to kill birds and small animals for food.

Years later I learned more about the boy when a Thai prince and his wife and sister were our houseguests for more than a week. The prince's consort, Khun Ying, was the daughter of one of the highest nobles in the realm. She had been with her father thirty years before on the expedition which effected the *Semang* boy's capture. She described how the lure of a scarlet coat with shining brass buttons, spread out on a stump in a jungle clearing had been stronger than fear of the unknown to the curious child and proved a successful snare. Khun Ying added that the life at court and the climate of Bangkok destroyed his constitution [health] so that he did not live long after reaching manhood.

I told Khun Ying of the *Semang's* awe and bewilderment the first time I took a group of them through our house – their first glimpse of a civilized household. Their only shelters were crude leafy structures put up in a few minutes for a few hours or days. Few foreigners had seen them in their haunts.

The British Curator of Taipeng Museum camped out at the foot of the mountains and was able to study some of these people who were bribed to come down, but again and again when he hired native guides to take him to their camp he found only a few scarcely cold embers. After a second entomologist's visit, the *Semang* were not seen for many years, having been frightened by something that was said by the scientist's interpreter.

Their return to town was dramatic. I had driven my car across the Peninsula to meet two California girls arriving on the International Express from Penang. They were breaking their round-the-world tour for a between-ships visit. As we crossed the mountains I spoke of the

Young Semang woman

"wild people" of the mountain jungle, and was surprised to learn that they had read about them.

As we drove under the *porte-cochere* of our home long after dark, there, seated in a circle on the ground-floor reception room, were ten *Semang*, men and women, calmly eating rice and curry in the light of a single kerosene lamp. My household cook, Boy and *Amah* had staged this surprise as a welcome to our guests, realizing its significance. None of us will forget the kinky heads turned toward us, the ten pairs of eyes watching as we entered the room from the car, and the short, black bodies sitting on their haunches.

On their first visits to town in the early days there were no women with them, ever. Then gradually, each year there would be one woman, always a different one, until in time several would make the trip with the group. But they never brought a child with them. Since none of the *Semang* knew more than a few simple words of Siamese, and those were spoken so gutturally as to be almost unintelligible, conversation was impossible. When we inquired about their children, as we always did each time they came down to town, they would reply, *"Mai Mi"* (No have) or *"Chep"* (sick). When we begged to care for them and make them well, or asked to educate them, they shook their heads as if they did not understand what we were saying. Having had several children stolen, they were taking no chances.

So it was year after year. The race is dying out and there seems to be no way to solve the problem.

41 - Con's Rogue Elephant Story
Written by Con

I was interested the other day when a Siamese man came in from over west, halfway to See Kow, with the story that an elephant was doing a lot of damage to their rice, and was chasing people, etc. They were afraid and were in much trouble. They asked me to come. I went to see the governor, and after some consultation with subordinates, he said, "Yes, go and shoot it."

"Come too, and help," I asked hopefully.

"Sorry – too busy now," they replied. "You try first, and if you don't get it, we will come in a few days and you can come with us."

So I went alone, and found that the elephant had wrecked five houses, killed one person, and run others up trees. I had my Army 30-aught-six – too small, everyone said.

That night we heard that it was eating in a rice field, so we sneaked out into the field and up onto a *hang* or high nest. It was not a good place to stroll around in at any time. But at night, with all sorts of trees and stumps and whatnot hidden in the rice field to stumble over, and with a cross elephant after you, it was even worse. So we sneaked up into the *machan* or watchers nest, built high up in a tree. For deer and smaller game, they may make them with poles, but where elephants are involved they are careful to find good stout trees. Rather interesting, a lot of extra men came along to watch, more than were necessary, including a priest! About a dozen of us crowded into the *hang* – meant to hold only two or three – and into nearby trees.

We could see the elephant dimly, and better with a torch, but not good enough. Since it did not seem worth while to shoot at that point, we shouted and hoped that it might come nearer, but it went away. So we came down and went with the priest to his *wat* nearby, where we slept. The next morning we started tracking very slowly and gingerly, watching sharply, because we could see nothing until we were up close.

Suddenly, rounding a clump, we came right on the beast, about fifteen yards away I should say, facing us with ears forward, looking alarming enough. You couldn't say what it was going to do. The men all broke for the trees. I backed off too, keeping on the ready, but glancing around hard for a tree I could dodge behind if it seemed advisable. But none seemed good enough, and, I really felt very lonely being there.

The other gun had disappeared somewhere, and the beast seemed threatening, advancing perhaps. So I tried for its brain which was not so easy to locate. Perhaps I went a trifle too high or low. But it was enough of a shock to turn it. The elephant did not want any more. It gave a fearful trumpet, wheeled and was gone. I doubt if a shot to another part of the body would have turned it away.

My men appeared from here and there and one of them took the second gun (my fifty Winchester, which they thought was by far the better gun, my Army 30-aught-six being too light.)

We tracked along for a while when suddenly we heard a most alarming trumpeting and squealing just ahead, and loud tramping. It seemed certain that the elephant was charging, and desperate. It was not a happy feeling I had. Same tactics as before, but this time nothing to shoot at. Then all was quiet, and we sat down to consider. When we heard it so angrily trumpeting just ahead, we all began to wonder whether we had some more important business elsewhere!

We stopped to have a powwow for a few minutes. Perhaps we did not exactly have cold feet, but they weren't awfully warm, and some good excuse to do something else would have been welcome to several of us, I think, but no one would suggest it. Well, we finally decided to keep on its tracks, and likewise keep a rather sharp lookout, you may be sure. Perhaps the rest of the men weren't so keen about it, but at least the other gun and I went on, and we didn't see any of the rest until a long time later, about noon.

To make a long story short, we finally heard a very faint noise just ahead and my companion said, "There it is!" We separated and sneaked around till I saw the elephant facing away from me. I then shot for the back of its knee, which is said to be good. It wheeled and I shot for its head. It went down but in an instant was up and I shot again, in vain, as it cleared out. No support from the other gun (my fifty Winchester) which I had expected, and which the Siamese thought was much the better gun – my Army 30-aught-six being too light.

We followed again and separated. I met the elephant head on about twenty yards away. A bullet above the eyes, and it lay down with the barest quiver. Soon my companion came up and I led him near and said, "Shoot! Shoot!" which he did in the shoulder but was rather chagrined to find he was shooting something quite dead.

When the rest of the men caught up with us there was a great lot of talking, you may be sure. The elephant could not be touched, they said, until officially reported to the authorities. Some men were immediately appointed to watch till permission came. They built a perch in the trees for the night, for there was real danger of other elephants coming, but in this case none came.

We should not have done it, but one man did cut off the tip of the trunk as a charm; also we pulled the hairs from the end of his tail - unfortunately very few and short. Also I cut off the tip of his tongue, to try to eat it, thinking that at least that would be tender.

Then I cleared out for home which was about three hours walking and stiff bicycling, some of it through waist deep water. I thought of going back the next day to photograph it and the houses it had attacked, and also help cut it up, but it rained and the water was deeper so I gave it up.

Then the next day a letter came from the official saying that they had been waiting for me before cutting out the tusks, so it seemed that I ought to go in spite of the rain and water. It meant wading to the armpits, and the pictures were no good, too dark, etc. You have no idea what a job it is cutting out the tusks, buried very deep in muscle and bone – especially the under tusk, as the elephant lay on one side with one tusk buried deep in the ground. Unfortunately the tusks had to go to the government.

I had a foot skinned out, which is interesting. Also I took a four-foot slab of skin from the side – quite a work and quite a weight, and now as stiff and heavy as a plank – not that I can think of any use for it. The tusks are interesting because one is shorter – the point had been broken on a rock as the elephant jabbed it into the ground, killing a man. It was Thanksgiving Day when I got the elephant, and I certainly did give thanks, that it had not got me instead!

42 - U.S. Trip (1930)

Mary: There were no schools in all of Siam for the children of missionaries. In 1925 Mother and Father decided to send Dorothy, who was then ten years old, to Kodaikanal School in southern India. It was a boarding school to which a few other missionaries in Siam had begun to send their children. Because of the expense of sea travel back and forth, Dorothy stayed in India with a missionary family over the holidays for two years. Dan started there a year later and Dwight a year after that.

Father had gone alone to the States in 1929 when both his parents died. The following year, Mother decided that after seven long years since their last furlough, she needed a change. Leaving Dan and Dwight to continue on at Kodai School and then live with Father in Trang over the holidays, she and Peggy, then 6, accompanied by a shipment of wild animals Father was sending to the New York Zoo, picked up Dorothy and me from Kodai for the trip to the States.

The animals provided endless diversion on our ship, the *S.S. Chinese Prince*. A baby elephant was the favorite. It was tied on the open deck, and everyone wanted to pet it or have a picture taken with it. People stayed clear of the cages of the black panther and other wild animals however.

Con's nephew John L. Cox II wrote:
When Uncle Con was in Siam, he came back to the states on Sabbatical about every seven years and often brought animals for a zoo here. One time he sent a baby elephant (probably about seven months old, but close to 1000 pounds). We met the freighter when it docked in New York and were allowed to open the elephant's cage and parade him around the deck. But when it came time to put the elephant back in its cage in order to swing him ashore (with some kind of a crane) he would go in only three-quarters of the way; then he'd back out again. We tried again and again — about six of us — all pushed

The baby elephant, Uncle Ned, Mary, Connie, Peggy, in New York

and pushed that elephant, but he'd go in just so far, then back out again. The Captain was getting furious. We were holding up progress. We even thought a swack with a two-by-four might help, but that had the same results. By now the Captain was swearing and telling us to get that blankety-blank elephant into the box – or else! It was then that Jack Janeway, who must have been about fourteen at the time – came to the rescue. At the exact psychological moment, as we all pushed for all we were worth – Jack twisted the elephant's tail! 'Eek,' said the elephant as it jumped forward the two more feet we needed! And that's how you get an elephant into a box!!

We arrived in New York on June 30th, picked up Katharine and Constance and visited briefly with Con's brother Ned.

"Can you help me buy a car, Ned?"

"You really won't need a car for New York, Edna. It's so easy to get around the city," he replied.

"But I want to drive to California."

"California! Why on earth would you want to go out there?"

"I want to show them my home state, my roots. Katharine is ready for college and she has chosen Pomona College in Claremont, which is about 35 miles east of Los Angeles."

"That's a long way from Sacramento, isn't it? The Alleghenies are far enough for me, maybe even too far."

"Maybe you should broaden your horizons, Ned. Anyway, since living in Siam, 500 miles isn't such a distance."

"Yes but traveling clear across the country with five girls is quite a responsibility,"

"Yes, I know, and I'm not afraid. Katharine will help me drive."

"Well, you always were stubborn, Edna. I know I can't change your mind."

He was perfectly true about that, but he helped me buy a used Model A Ford in perfect condition. The rest of the relatives looked askance at the adventure too. In spite of their fears, the five girls, ranging in age from six to eighteen and scarcely knowing each other, and I, set off on a trip which would take us 25 days.

Katharine and I took turns driving. Our first stop was in Washington, D.C. We spent three days in the home of a motherly lady who took in tourists. She was much concerned about our not having a man along for the trip.

Katharine and Constance kept wanting to sidetrack to see famous places, and each time I said, "The biggest sights are out West. If you wait you won't be sorry!"

We went due west from Washington over Mount Storm and the Ford met its first test. There was a five-mile grade and we thought we'd never get to the top as we coaxed the car in second, then in low gear and finally had to stop short of the top for the radiator to cool off.

Well on the other side of the mountain range in late afternoon we came to a park with a swimming pool. The girls begged me to stop, and I finally gave in to their pleading. I left them there and made for an abandoned farm cottage near by. It had been requisitioned for the summer and we were the first to try it out. There was the ubiquitous "out-house" as there was no inside plumbing, and the added adventure of a well with a pump. The early morning cold discouraged any loitering as we packed for the new day.

Instead of going straight to Clarksburg we turned south through some lovely hills and woods to the Ohio River and continued along its bank all afternoon. We found a good camp at Huntington and the girls enjoyed a few hours at a carnival close by after the days' confinement.

The girls cleaning the car, "Pegasus"

It became routine to start the day with breakfast at a cafe, have lunch as we drove or picnicked along the way, and have a hot meal when we stopped for the night. We stayed in quite a variety of auto courts, some very primitive with only the barest essentials. Occasionally one had a stove or ice box, and had two rooms. It was extremely hot some days. One time we stopped by a stream flowing over smooth rocks and I let the girls soak in the water to cool off. Katharine especially relished it, as she had contacted some poison oak and had the itchy rash all over her legs.

Modern gas stations with rest rooms were few and far between, so we had to look for convenient bushes in lonely spots along the road. There was also very little traffic. Whenever a car with a New York license plate passed us there would be wild hand waving back and forth, as if we were friends or long lost relatives.

There was one major adventure. As we were going through Kentucky one morning, I was relaxing in the back seat when I saw a boy running behind a cow which was coming toward us. At home, I thought, I would slow down, not knowing what might happen. Suddenly the cow broke from the boy and charged the car, smashing the headlight. The impact lifted the cow in the air before it crashed to the ground. Katharine's reflexes were quick and she turned off the ignition. As we all got out the boy reached us. He was scared stiff and

Clockwise from left: Mary, Dorothy, Katharine, Peggy, Edna and Constance - Claremont, 1930.

stammered out his apology while he looked at the damage. Meanwhile the cow got up and walked off. We accepted his apology and drove on. I remembered one time when Con had hit a cow on a country road in Siam years ago, he had offered to pay the value of the cow, which had broken a leg. How fortunate for us this cow was apparently unhurt. Luckily a farmhouse was near by. We filled the radiator which was cracked by the impact, we discovered. That enabled us to get to the garage in the next town for repairs. This was the most costly event of our coast to coast trip.

Eventually we reached Claremont which was a quiet, shady little town of about 3,000 with the distinction of having three colleges: Pomona, Scripps College for Women and Claremont Graduate School, plus a private boys' school. We settled in a house on College Avenue just a few blocks from the entrance to Pomona College where Katharine enrolled. Constance and Dorothy attended the high school and Mary and Peggy the grammar school.

A year later I found suitable homes for the older girls, and returned to the Orient with Mary and Peggy on the *S.S. President Polk*, jokingly called the "Slow Poke". We spent beautiful lazy days on the voyage, the girls enjoying the swimming pool on deck. After a stop in Manila and again in Hong Kong we arrived back in Siam and Trang, and rejoined Con and the boys. Life went on as before, with Dan, Dwight, Mary and Peggy in school at Kodai for three more years.

43 - The 1932 Coup

*Edna recorded her impresstions of a coup d'etat
she witnessed on a trip to Bangkok.*

The year 1932 was important in Thai history for two events,
which although totally different, were related. The first was the
celebration of the completion of the first traffic bridge across the
Menam. This united the two halves of the great city of Bangkok. The
second was the culmination of political seething, started by a group
led by one young man sent to Paris by the government. Their "bloodless
revolution" disrupted the country with far-reaching consequences.

We were still living in Trang in the Malay Peninsula, and I had set
my heart on being in Bangkok for the bridge opening. I had a
presentiment that it might be the last great kingly show. A Thai friend
told me during the bridge construction of an old prophesy that the
present dynasty would survive but a century and a half. The main
object of the bridge celebration was to glorify the 150th year since the
founding of Bangkok by the Chakri dynasty. The project seemed daring
to say the least.

For several weeks before the date set in April, various government
officials tried to dissuade me from my intention. "Don't go, *Mem,*"
they told me, as I met them playing badminton or tennis at the club.
"Better not go to Bangkok, *Mem.*"

"Why shouldn't I go?" I asked, puzzled by their concern.

The Chief Judge answered, "April is the hot season, and it would
be bad for you."

"You know I do not mind the heat. What is behind all this?"

"Oh, the Chinese are restless and might have an uprising."

I knew they did not believe that or expect me to believe it, but
they wanted to convey something important that they were pledged
not to divulge.

I assured him, "No matter what happens, I want to be there."

The look I received when I said that, told me they felt they had
done their duty. Although I was free to go, they – the officials – were
forbidden to leave.

Arriving at the capital, I was struck by the change that had taken place since my first drive through the city nearly thirty years earlier. It had more than trebled in population and extended incredibly in every direction. Bangkok could now be reached from Singapore and Penang by the finest train service in the entire Orient, over a railroad bridge north of the city into a splendid terminal. In the old days, we had had to cross the river in *sampans* above Wang Lang, then drive down by *gharry*.

Another railroad went north over the high mountains to Chiengmai. A stream of tourists traveled to the eastern border by rail and on to Angkor ruins and Cambodia. Travelers arrived daily by British, French and Dutch passenger planes flying between Europe, Australia, China and the East Indies, landing at a model airport. Many fine hotels took care of them all. One was the former palace of a king.

A university and a large government hospital were named after King Chulalongkorn. The Rockefeller Foundation now occupied the Wang Lang property and the hospital behind it. The school had been moved to a larger property on the north side of the city and renamed Wattana Witiya Academy. The Pasteur Institute, where Con had sent snakes, attracted throngs to its snake farm to watch attendants enter the enclosures and extract venom from the fangs of cobras, banded kraits and other snakes. The former palace buildings of the Second King had become a famous museum.

I was taken to dine at a popular Chinese cafe in the cooler atmosphere of several stories above the street. Steaming lavender-scented towels were passed around before the first course. Then we visited the most beautiful cinema in the Orient, built by King Prajadhipok. When shopping in Sampeng we relaxed in the booth of a Chinese tea shop that advertised American ice cream.

While there were many miles of broad, tree-shaded roads, New Road was little changed. It was still narrow and exciting, with the same tram cars, crowded and casual, and rickshas darting in and out of traffic. Bicycles with sidecars added a new note. Carriages in all stages of shabbiness still came by, but no longer the shining equipages of private owners or the smart traps driven recklessly by young Englishmen. Instead, we saw a bedlam of cars and motorcycles, while

Downtown Bangkok

jaunty Thai policemen stood at busy intersections, courteous and efficient as they directed the traffic.

On the day before the bridge ceremony I learned that a revolution was brewing, likely to happen on that very day. Apparently the radicals planned to capitalize on the old prophesy!

We were up long before daylight. King Prajadhipok was scheduled to review the troops at eight o'clock in the morning, then unveil the monument and cross the river. At six we began to work our way through the dense crowd on the last stretch of the street leading to the bridge, to where it opened onto the circular concourse. Along the entire line of march from the royal palace to the bridge, thousands of people were gathered. Every window, wall and housetop was a vantage point.

As we neared the open space of our objective, our party became separated. Only three of us reached the end of the long road. Mrs. Gill, the wife of the only American dentist in Siam, was frighteningly pale. Not only was the heat intense but the press of bodies made breathing difficult. The people who sat on the curb were the only fortunate ones, and they had probably arrived during the night. No ropes or police guards were needed to hold the crowds from encroaching on the narrow street. No shouting or ugly looks or wisecracking marred the four long hours we stood there. On this day the usually carefree, happy, witty, and fun-loving Thai people had an attitude of almost hushed reverence that made a lasting impression on my mind.

In all probability, never again will any parade in Bangkok display all the ancient insignia, costumes and relics shown in that long procession. When King Prajadhipok passed by in the throne-*palanquin*, as motionless as any of the Buddhas in the temples, one sensed the drama being enacted. His Majesty stood alone high on a platform, out in the open to review the marching troops. I admired his courage and prayed silently that he might be protected.

That day all knew that at any moment a shot might ring out to cause death and pandemonium. However, through foresight – in which the two-hour delay figured – a revolution was postponed a few weeks. It was then in the nature of an anticlimax because of the calm reasonableness of King Prajadhipok. The 150 year rule of the Chakri dynasty had ended. Siam became a Constitutional Monarchy as the king handed over power to a legislative assembly.

In January, 1934 I was at the royal landing at Bangkok when the king and queen left for Europe, ostensibly for him to receive treatment for his eyes. A year later the king abdicated his throne. I was sad that the Siam I loved had changed so much that its king was no longer wanted. [He was in England when he died, the end of May, 1941.]

44 - Memories of Our Childhood
As told by Katharine, Dorothy and Mary

Katharine: In Petchaburi we lived in a two-story house high on a bank above the river, with a wooden deck partway down, and steps going on down to the wide river. We could sit on the deck and watch the boats go by. Father's hospital was right next door to the house. We had a neighbor who was always good to us children. He treated us to hot chocolate with marshmallows. We kids all slept in a big veranda upstairs, dormitory style. We had a lot of monkeys there, and I remember them chasing us around and around inside the house. At one time Constance was bitten on the finger.

Dorothy: The house in Petchaburi had a broad front veranda where Mother had her afternoon tea, often with friends. Father had a motorcycle, by which he could make house calls or go tiger hunting. He kept it at the other end of the porch by his office.

Katharine: I have a vague memory of being on the tracks when a train came and having it go over me as I lay between the rails.

Dorothy: Above the river was a landing with a bench. I had a picture of three little girls dressed identically in white party dresses with big bows in our hair sitting together to be photographed. A hundred feet downstream a railway trestle crossed the river. When the weather was good Father would take us walking, and one vague memory was of walking across the trestles of that bridge, holding tightly to my father's hand and feeling scared seeing the moving muddy river so far below.

Katharine: I went to a Siamese school for awhile in Petchaburi. We wrote on slates with a slate "pencil." I did all right with arithmetic. . . . Siamese was my first language and I was fluent in it. But Mother taught me a lot at home. I was always curious, and loved to read, and she encouraged me.

Mary: I remember attending a Siamese kindergarten in Trang, learning with the Siamese children how to speak English! How I wish

Siamese girl's school

I had learned more Siamese, rather than Pidgin English with its smattering of Chinese words. I did learn to crochet and made a little pouch purse, and that was about the extent of my schooling in Trang. I was eight years old before I was considered old enough to go to school in India with Dorothy and my brothers and then was put into the first grade, catching up to my age level a few months later, when we went to the U.S. in 1930.

Dorothy: I attended the American Mission Girls' School, run by a Siamese teacher. Children all sat on the floor and recited their lessons out loud and in unison. I remember sewing and embroidering doll clothes with my Siamese playmates. Mother also taught me at home. She had me make a floor plan of our house. I measured everything exactly, placed the doors and windows with the correct lines to designate them, lines to indicate which way the doors open, and so on. I did a lot of it over and over to get it perfect, and didn't resent the corrections, as I enjoyed doing it. This was before I was 10 years old. Mother was a self-taught artist in pastels, creating beautiful pictures of flowers, scenery and miniature portraits. She was a self-taught pianist, too, playing anything by ear which she had recently heard.

Mary: I remember one picture Mother made with the entire sky pink. Later I had to explain to people that, yes, sometimes the whole sky was really that color.

Dwight, Edna with "the surprise," Peggy, Dorothy with Mary, Dan, 1924

Dorothy: Early in 1924 Dan, Dwight and I were told separately to keep a big secret: that we would be having a baby sister or brother. Not until Peggy was born on July 31st did we find out that the others also knew the big secret and we had all kept it! She was named Margaret Cornelia.

Mary: Our two-story house in Trang was set back from the road behind a high hedge, with a circular driveway around Mother's garden to the porte cochere and entrance. To the left of the house was the side yard and a well, and a very high hedge, completely shielding us from whatever was beyond. To the right of the house was a walkway to the hospital, just beyond a low hedge. A tree festooned with animal skulls stood beside the hedge. The back compound extended several hundred yards to a jungle-like area with a stream running through it. The area closer to the house was terraced with a sod tennis court and badminton court. The back of the house had a wide concrete breezeway which led to the kitchen, a separate building where my Amah, Ah Sam, lived with her little girl, our playmate. The breezeway was where the monkeys and other pets were kept, and where we spent a lot of time.

Back yard of our house at Trang. Note badminton net.

Dorothy: In Trang there were a number of *frangipani* trees on our compound with five-petaled flowers and a heavenly scent. One tree near the front gate, farthest from the house, was especially good for climbing, with remarkably strong and resilient branches. We would climb way out on the branches to swing and bounce them with all our energy, shouting or singing at the top of our lungs. No branch ever broke. Another favorite tree for shade and beauty was the "flame of the forest."

Mary: Mother was an accomplished hostess, and she set a beautiful table for guests with white damask tablecloth and napkins, silver-plated napkin rings and finger bowls. A brass, many-tiered candelabra which we children helped take apart and polish meticulously was centered above the large round table. The heavy cut-glass crystalware used on company occasions included pitcher, decanters, cruets and different sized bowls. The place settings were of blue willow ware. My favorites were the dessert plates. Each plate in the set of 12 was unique and hand-painted with different flowers in delicate pastel tones. The tea cups, which we were not permitted to use, were of the most delicate eggshell fragility. The hot chocolate cups, gold-rimmed

Dwight, Dorothy holding Peggy, Dan, Mary

and richly embossed, were sturdier, to be handled with great care. The monogrammed sterling silver flatware must have contained at least 72 pieces. In all my years there I never questioned how they came about having such beautiful things on a missionary salary, but then I hadn't the faintest idea about their financial situation. My guess is their families in the States gifted them over the years, to supplement their meager missionary salary.

Dorothy: Nai Choi was our cook. What wonderfully tasting meals he could prepare! Mother would translate a recipe from her cook book, and *Nai* Choi would concoct it to perfection. Mother put on elegant dinners for important guests, and very nice ones for missionary friends. Various Siamese curries were of course tops. There are many varieties of indigenous rice grown in Siam, and *Nai* Choi had standing orders to buy any that appeared in the market, and serve it during its short season. One, called black rice (really dark purple) was cooked with lotus seeds as a dessert and served with thick coconut cream poured over it.

Mary: One of my favorite company meals was chicken *pilau*. *Nai* Choi was an artist with this dish. An enormous platter was mounded with seasoned white rice with raisins. Covering it was a thick layer of artfully arranged sliced chicken. Around the border were overlapping slices of cucumbers, scored so the edges were scalloped. Beaten egg fried and thinly sliced was sprinkled over the whole platter. To add to the palate of colors I am sure there was probably some pimiento on top. So delicious! Another favorite dish was a sweet-sour stew made with venison and cucumbers and onions.

Dorothy: Mother served a company dessert which I rarely tasted, made from very young coconuts with just the right thickness of jelly-like coconut meat in the shell. The cook shaved off most of the husk, then cut a slice off the top of each fruit. He made custard using the coconut water, and probably additional coconut cream, sweetened with palm sugar and poured back into the shell and baked. There was a whole small coconut for each diner, and the gods of Olympus never had such nectar! This company dessert was only for important guests, perhaps the Governor of the Province, or other dignitaries. We children had our supper early [usually milk toast when we were little], and were banished to the upstairs. We'd sneak a peak through the banisters at the arriving guests, never daring to be seen or heard.

It must have been after a daytime dinner that I remember two rituals, since I certainly was asleep long before the evening affairs were over. The first one was for removing stains from the linen table cloths. *Nai* Choi was directed to bring a kettle of boiling water and a lot of saucers and plates. These were put under each spot that was found, and the cook poured a stream of boiling water on the spot from a height of about 12 inches while rubbing the spot with a silver spoon. In this way Mother kept the table linens pristine white. The other ritual was to count each piece of sterling after the washing, and

back: Edna with Peggy, front: Dan, Mary, Dwight, Dorothy

tie them up in their individual pockets of flannel. No time was allowed to lapse before these important tasks were completed.

Every third day through the year was Market Day. If I were out early in the morning, I was sure to see many pairs of men with a pole between their shoulders from which was suspended a squealing pig tightly trussed in a basket. A bullock cart might come along piled high with large round basket crates full of squawking chickens. People of all ages, dressed in their colorful sarongs wended their way from all directions, often with large loads on their heads with whatever they had to sell.

The market place itself was crowded and noisy. A thatched roof on poles gave protection from sun or rain. We'd find tall stalks of sugar care arranged teepee fashion. On each side of the long aisles, right next to each other, were vendors squatting by their wares – earthenware pots, toys and knickknacks of celluloid, glass or wood, flowers, bamboo furniture, hand-woven materials. A candy-maker cooking his sugar confections right before our eyes. A man selling soap and perfumes. A woman making baskets. An iron monger.

The butchers always caught our eye, for chickens in huge baskets squawked and fluttered incessantly and pigs enclosed tightly in fitted baskets squealed continually. Carcasses of pigs and beef were hung from the rafters and the butcher cut the piece requested by the customer, all for one price. *Nai* Choi usually did the marketing. He frequently brought home a whole sirloin at no added cost. But all the meat was cut off the bone. Mother wanted pork chops one time, and even explaining it to the cook with the help of pictures, he couldn't get it. But when a missionary lady visited from another town, with her better command of the language, we were able to buy some big thick ones, and *Nai* Choi stuffed them to perfection.

The most penetrating and characteristic smell was of *kapi*, a paste of fermented shrimp – quite a delicacy among the natives and by some non-natives also. It was usually shaped into round purplish black balls stacked up in a pyramid. It by no means concealed other odors however: livestock, pungent incense, sickly sweet perfume, clean fresh basketry, the earthy smell of pottery, and fragrant flowers. It was all part of the festivity, as were all the sounds – the shrill bartering, the squealing and squawking of the animals, children laughing and fighting, the women gossiping, the clang of an anvil.

When *Nai* Choi returned from the market with his purchases and an itemized list with their prices, he went straight to Mother's desk, and recited each item with its price while she carefully wrote it all down in the expense book. She explained to me, that although custom allowed the cook to make a little percentage on his trip, she felt she could keep it to a minimum by careful tabulation.

Although Mother had at least four servants around, we children each had work of our own to do, taking care of our own things and

Chinese funeral parade

feeding the pets. Sometimes we would be interrupted by the weird fluting that announced a funeral. We would grab our hats and rush out to the front gate to watch the procession. We stood quiet and awed as the wailing mourners passed. At a Chinese funeral there would often be a wildly prancing brightly colored paper dragon which fascinated us. When the last of the mourners had turned the corner we would collect the "paper money", cheap paper daubed with silver and gold paint, scattered along the way to appease the spirits.

Our chief sorrow in each day was the two-hour afternoon nap – imperative because of the enervating heat. There was never any question about it. The large screened sleeping porch allowed more air than the old stifling mosquito nets. The rain on the corrugated tin roof drowned out all other sounds and lulled us to sleep.

It was customary to clean up every afternoon after nap, whether we had any plans or not. In the rainy season, when the tank on the roof of the surgical division of the hospital next door was filled, we had running water. The rest of the year we used water from an earthenware jar or *ong*, filled by the gardener from one of our wells. To bathe, we dipped water from the *ong* to splash over ourselves. It was not uncommon to find little wrigglers or polliwogs in the *ong*.

We'd be amused by guests, unfamiliar with this way of bathing, who sometimes climbed into the *ong*, and needed help to get out of the small opening.

Katharine: Mother was always particular about her appearance. She never wanted Father to see her unless her hair and face looked nice and she was dressed. No, they did not share a bedroom. In fact they were at opposite sides of the house.

Mary: Afternoon tea at four o'clock was a daily ritual Mother never deviated from. Sometimes we children had hot chocolate with a marshmallow in it and sometimes we had "real tea" – maybe a fourth of a cup – filled up with warm milk. If fresh hot bread was delivered from town on time, we'd be treated with the crusty end slices, because the soft doughy middle section was considered indigestible for us youngsters.

Dorothy: If there were no guests we went barefoot in the afternoon and played badminton, or played with our pets, or climbed trees, or otherwise hung around while Mother tended her garden. She had a lotus pond and many varieties of cannas and hibiscus, roses, flowering trees and vines. Many species of gorgeous orchids were nailed to posts, tied to trees or planted in hanging baskets along with maidenhair and other ferns. These all grew luxuriantly in the hot damp climate.

When electricity came to Trang the generator ran from 7 to 11 p.m. for lights only. We didn't have a refrigerator, so everything was eaten fresh. Ice could be bought in town for immediate use, so Mother bought a unique ice cream maker in Bangkok. It made one dish at a time in just a few minutes and was a big treat. Ice and salt were put in a cylinder about 6 by 8 inches, the cover with handle screwed on tight. The cylinder rested by end pegs on depressions in the sides of a rectangular metal container, about 8 by 12 inches. A scant cup of homemade ice cream mix was poured into this curve-sided container and the matching cover applied. The handle, was turned slowly until the ice cream was frozen onto the cylinder. The cover then was removed, and a reverse turn of the handle scraped off a scoop of ice cream from the cylinder. After a quick slide into a waiting dish to be eaten immediately, the next dish was prepared. Oh, it taught you patience.

Mary: There was a small spring-fed lake just outside Trang, which had been made into the loveliest of parks with a number of *salas* along its shore. One of them was very large with a long walkway out to it over the water. It was probably built sometime when minor royalty visited the area. We loved to walk out to the *sala* and also to picnic at one of the smaller ones at the edge of the lake. One day we were driving slowly along the edge of the lake. I was seated in front, hanging on to the door when I suddenly found myself swinging out in space. My mother grabbed me and pulled me back in. I must have been five or six years old.

Another time my little sister Peggy was in the back seat probably hanging onto the door as I had, and she fell out of the car onto the dirt road. Mother didn't know what had happened and she kept on driving. Meanwhile an angry little Peggy jumped up and started running after the car and shouting until Mother realized what had happened and stopped to pick her up.

In 1929, the year before I went to Kodai, King Prajadhipok and Queen Rambhai Barni made a tour of the provinces and visited Father's hospital. A broad red carpet ran from the entrance, down the steps, clear out to the road. Peggy and I were coached on how to behave on this auspicious occasion. Mother put a pendant around my neck which had the Queen Mother's insignia on it. We were seated on a bench just outside the door leading into the hospital. As the King and Queen came up the steps, we were to stand and curtsey. When the moment came, we were glued to the bench, paralyzed.

King Prajadhipok came up to me, picked up the necklace around my neck and said, "Oh, I see you have my mother's insignia. Would you like to have one of mine?"

The gold pendant

Without waiting for an answer from me, fortunately, for I couldn't have said a word, he beckoned to an attendant, took two small boxes from him, and handed one to Peggy and one to me. We discovered the pendants he gave us were of solid gold, in the shape of the king's tiered headpiece. Mine had the number one stamped on the back, Peggy's had the number two. He gave out many silver pendants, we learned, but not many gold ones.

One of Mother's endearing habits found us all scrambling and competing with each other to see who could be first to get whatever she was asking for. She'd say something like, "Oh, I need my scissors on the dresser upstairs," and she'd run through all our names, "Katherine, uh, Constance, or Dorothy, oh, Danny, hm, Dwight, ah. Mary, um, Peggy – would you get it for me?" We were off like a shot before all the names were out, up both staircases, to see who would be first to return with whatever she wanted.

As a child I was probably the most submissive, dutiful and obedient of all Mother's children. I remember Dan would willingly say, "I'll do it, Mother" but end up forgetting or having to be reminded. Dwight would obstinately say, "I won't!" but would soon comply.

When guests came for tea with Mother, Peggy and I were brought in and introduced. One of her frequent guests, Mrs. Britten, would invariably say, as she pinched my cheeks, "Isn't she a good little girl," while I inwardly seethed, impatient to be dismissed.

Mother and Mrs. Britten.

45 - More Memories

As told by Katharine, Dorothy, Dan and Mary

Dorothy: Father's medical practice was a busy one. Patients came from far and wide, on foot, by bullock carts, or by car. He saw them all and did what he could for them, including pulling teeth, usually the shiny black ones acquired by years of chewing betel nut.

The hospital, raised up on 8 foot pillars, was perhaps 70 feet long and 40 feet wide, including a wide veranda, where patients' family members spent their days. They would squat on their haunches, feet flat on the floor, for hours at a time, chatting. Patients slept on wooden benches or beds, each one bringing his own grass mat from home. Their relatives brought food and prepared it in their own pots over small charcoal stoves, on the ground. Consequently there was no control over their diet.

Every hospital day began with a short religious service, conducted by my father or one of his assistants. His chief helper was Tien Hua, a

Hospital staff with Dr. Bulkley seated left.

Chinese, who started in the early days and was taught to diagnose every tropical disease that came along. His seven children – Irene, William, Goodliam, Sweetliam, Rootliam, Yerene and Yee Yee were among our playmates.

I was fascinated by the hospital, and loved the smell of the disinfectant. Occasionally Mother sent me over on an errand. I wanted to linger, but was sent home promptly.

From an early age I wanted to be a doctor, but such was the communication among us that my parents never knew until many years later when I mentioned it at a reunion. My father said he would have done anything to have made it possible for me to realize my wish, if he had known. The same thing happened to my brother, Dwight. The sad consequences of practicing the old adage that "children should be seen but not heard."

Dan: Sometimes, as a special privilege, Father took me along when he had to visit a patient close by. We would be offered *cha* (tea) from a pot brewing on a little stove, and Father would allow me to drink it, since he considered anything boiled as safe.

After he returned from a more distant emergency visit to a patient, Father told us how he had caught a train – by bicycling toward his destination until he heard the train's whistle. Then he sat squarely in the middle of the tracks with his bicycle, forcing the train to stop, so he could get on it with his bicycle. That got him to his patient in time to handle the emergency. He was very resourceful.

Mary: Family prayers. I don't think family prayers were ever skipped. Every morning, breakfast dishes cleared away, we knelt beside our chairs around the big round dinner table. Father's prayers were interminably long, covering every facet of our life and naming all the distant family as well as local people and issues needing God's help. As a little child it was hard for me to know how that was accomplished, for every sentence seemed to end in an unintelligible mumble. It took patience to sit through those prayers.

Dorothy: Sunday was always different. We dressed properly in the morning and wore shoes and stockings and attended the service at 10 o'clock. Church was a rectangular building with large arched

The church at Trang

windows along both sides, which seated 150 to 200 people. A raised platform at the end held the pulpit and some chairs. The organ was at the left. Mother played it, (with a schoolboy plying the bellows) and led the singing of hymns – well-known tunes with Siamese words – and the Siamese pastor usually preached. Men – usually wearing white linen coats over white shorts or their native *panungs* – and boys sat on the right of the wide center aisle, and the women and girls on the left.

The school girls from the Mission school attended *en masse*, dressed in their prettiest sarongs and blouses; their faces speckled with white powder, patted on with wet fingers. I didn't pay much attention to the sermons, but I didn't mind the time spent because my thoughts were my own, and the view of graceful coconut palms outside the window, swaying with every little breeze was always restful. The devotional quiet was broken only by the gentle swishing of mat or palm branch fans, which were never still.

Khaki shorts and coat, and short sleeved cotton shirt was the everyday garb for non-native men, with knee length socks, preferably wool, because it absorbs the sweat. Our temperature, at 7 degrees north of the Equator, varied from about 72 to 96 degrees Fahrenheit.

Father kept a meticulous record of highs and lows for most of his 30 years out there. On Sundays he wore white duck shorts and a jacket with a military collar, stiffly starched and impeccably ironed. Either the "Boy" or the Amah did this, first sprinkling the garment by skillfully blowing a fine mist from the mouth. The heavy large iron had a hinged top so it could be loaded with glowing charcoal.

After our Sunday dinner, Father saved the afternoon for time with us children. In the rainy season, we sat in his workshop in the house and he read to us. I remember Bunyan's *Pilgrims Progress*.

Dan: Father collected the string from every package that was ever sent to us and had it hanging from a nail in the corner. He'd bring the bundle down and we kids untangled it as Father read, then rolled it up into neat balls. Dwight and I were also given the job of straightening bent nails so they could be reused. We got to be pretty good at it.

Dorothy: In good weather we would go for a walk. This was the most companionable time we had with Father, because he was usually stern or aloof or preoccupied.

The family in 1928-29

Mary: At the beginning of our walks, we would each choose a cane from a large collection of canes by the front door. Some had carved ivory or brass animal heads. When Peggy was little, she would ride on Father's shoulders. From the earliest age we learned absolute obedience to stop instantly when

On a walk with Father. Beach house on stilts at Nong Khae.

Father said, "STOP." There could be a poisonous snake on the path. If there was, he would pin it behind the head with a forked stick which he carried, so he could pick it up to examine it.

Dorothy: We would start down the road, swing off onto the railroad tracks, follow them for awhile, balancing on the rail, then turn onto a path among tall evenly-spaced rubber trees in a plantation. Depending on the season, we might see natives making the gouges in the bark and inserting a half coconut shell to catch the dripping latex. In certain seasons, the inedible nutlike fruit would be ripe – three of them enclosed in a pod similar to a walnut. When ripe the pods split open with a loud pop, almost like a pistol shot, which widely scattered the seeds. It was nerve-wracking at certain times of the year to hear these pistol-like pops.

Maybe we would come upon a dwelling at the edge of the grove, and be invited up to visit. These houses, on six to eight-foot poles, often had walls of bamboo matting, and narrow strips of bamboo tied together for the floor, so kitchen scraps could fall through to be scavenged by the pigs and chickens below. The Siamese are lovely, hospitable people, and made us feel welcome, often serving teas and goodies. Father was careful that we didn't eat anything contamin-ated. Lucky that many of their confections were wrapped in pieces of banana leaf, fastened with a toothpick, then steamed. Some are packed inside big rounds of bamboo, and steamed. Combinations of rice and coconut, or various ways of using bananas, were always delicious and we could be sure they were safe.

We had endless places to visit – walking along rice paddies, or through nutmeg groves, the small dense trees festooned with tangerine-sized green fruit. To harvest the spice, the fruit needs to be quite ripe. But the half-inch thick flesh that covers the nutmeg itself has its own uses. Like a hard, dense apple, it makes a beautiful red jelly. It is also eaten raw. Sliced into very thin segments, they were strung onto a bamboo skewer, and sold in the market. I once nibbled on a slice. What a strange combination of flavors – sweet, sour, salty, bitter, and astringent. The nutmeg that you grate is the innermost part. This is covered by a thin shell. Clinging to it is an eighth-inch veining of red stuff. This is the spice mace.

One walk took us to a distant hill, whose summit was graced by

Mary and Peggy with leopard skin

a Buddhist shrine. It had a beautiful big footprint of the Buddha in gold, green and red, under a fancy awning. Buddha was such a perfect man, ac-cording to their legends, that his feet were exactly sym-metrical – all toes the same size and shape, the right and left foot identical. Our feet are lopsided, since we are imperfect humans. The priests were glad to let us see the footprint, but kept us out of the inner room. There were many small hills like this one, each of limestone formation and all having caves.

Almost every cave of any size was also a shrine containing one or more Buddhas in niches here and there, sitting in the lotus position, reclined, or standing with palms together and fingers pointed upward.

Father's trophies at head of stairs

With garlands around his neck, pungent incense burning and thanksgiving offerings of food and flowers before him, his half-smile and inscrutable eyes seemed to benignly bless his devotees, century after century. Exploring some of the caves was always an adventure. To be sure we found our way out, we took a flashlight and candles, and would tie a string at the entrance.

Dan: One time while exploring caves in the area, we found a tiny opening we hadn't seen before. We excitedly squeezed through it, being sure to tie a string at the opening so we could find our way back. We were sure we would discover a brand new room, an area that hadn't been explored before. But instead, we found a cigarette butt on the floor.

Dorothy: Father was interested in the natural history and ecology of everything in the country. The natives, hearing of this would bring him rare animals which they found. We would see them being brought to the hospital, often tied by the feet and slung from a pole between two men, or else in a crude cage carried the same way. Skulls of large animals were hung from a tree between the house and the hospital, (we didn't climb that tree as often), or decorated the landing around the stairwell in the house.

There was excitement of a kind one year – an epidemic of rabies! Father's solution was to shoot every dog that wandered into our compound or the hospital's. A rifle was within reach at either place, and one shot would drop the critter, rabid or not. Then a servant would drag the animal to the back of the compound where the turkey vultures would do their thing. We never played there anyway, and now it was a place of revulsion.

Dan: During the filming of the epic movie *Chang* by Cooper and Schoedsack, the directors stayed at our house. Their script called for a huge python to come down from a tree and attack a person below. They had to chloroform the snake to get it up into the tree, then wait until it woke up to be enticed down. Father offered to chloroform it, but they insisted they could manage that, and ended up giving it too large a dose. It never revived. They gave the carcass to Father and he skinned it. We had that skeleton, its full length draped above the hospital veranda for all the years we were there.

Many live king cobras were brought to Father over the years and kept in cages fronted with chicken wire. We were always told not to get too close to these cages in the hospital compound, because the cobras would try to strike through the chicken wire and become bloodied in the process. When Father had three cobras he would ship them to the snake farm in Bangkok where the venom was extracted from their fangs. It would then be injected into horses to produce an anti-venom to treat people who had been bitten. Over the years he shipped various poisonous snakes to that snake farm, which is still in operation.

One time he was brought two king cobras and kept them in cages on the hospital compound, awaiting shipment to the snake farm in Bangkok. Somehow, one of them got out of its

Five kids in a tree

cage and was in the hedge between the hospital and the house. Father got a long forked pole and managed to pin it behind the head so that he could grab it safely. Then he took a picture of it with me and three Siamese holding it stretched out at full length – around 10 feet. That was exciting.

People all over town knew Father was interested in animals, so they always brought them to him first. If he wanted to keep the animal, he gave them a fair price. If not, he at least paid them a little for their trouble. We ended up having lots of pets. There were always monkeys: long-tailed little gray ones, larger red-faced brown ones, black monkeys with white faces, white monkeys with black hands and faces. Some made wonderful pets and some were more dangerous and had to be chained at a distance from others.

Mary: One of my favorite activities was climbing trees – especially the tree in the front corner of the compound. How I loved climbing way up high where I could survey my whole world. I would imagine how a monkey felt, swinging from branch to branch. Monkeys were always fun.

Mary, Dan, Peggy, Dwight and Dorothy on and by
"Isabel" or "Jezebel" depending on how it acted.

We always had many pets. The number fourteen sticks in my mind as the most that we had at one time – cats, dogs, monkeys, moosangs, birds, pang pangs. The last year I was there a white moosang was my very favorite pet. It was fluffy and cumbersome-looking but could move like streaked lightning. It was so huggable. It would curl up in my lap and go round and round, clawing and making strange purring sounds.

Katharine: I remember being at the beach at Nong Khae and having a picture taken sitting on a huge sea turtle. One time I caught cold and was coughing a lot. Father said, "Stop it. Stop it. STOP IT!" in rapid succession. I did, and the coughing stopped.

Mary: For whatever the offense, we all remember Father saying "Stop it. Stop it. STOP IT!" to us.

Dorothy: We undoubtedly took many interesting trips, but the only one I remember was going to Chong. This was a vacation for ten days, and what a flurry of packing, for we had to take everything, including food, as well as the cook and Amahs. Though it was only about ten miles away, the drive took almost three hours, all of it exciting in spite of being crowded in the small car.

Mary: Chong was one of our favorite places to go when Father could get away for a few days. We stayed at one of several little Government bungalows. Some of the area was park-like, but it was also like the jungle. After walking through that area, we always carefully checked our legs for leaches. We hated picking them off. If you weren't careful, the head was left in. There was a wonderful wide stream cascading over the rocks and we loved swimming in the pools and sliding down the rocks.

We were especially aware of tigers in the area. One night, from the safety of our bungalow, I remember seeing two eyes glowing in the darkness like two hot coals. We knew it must be a tiger.

Katharine: Father was a very strict disciplinarian. We'd be spanked with a hairbrush when we sneaked downstairs to peek at their dinner parties but somehow that didn't keep us from doing it again.

Chong cascade

Mary: I remember one time – I had been particularly naughty or said something bad – I had my mouth washed out with soap. That was a lesson learned the hard way. For all Father's gruffness, we always had a big bear hug from him before going to bed, and I remember his whiskery kisses as he rubbed his face against mine.

Dwight, Peggy, Dan, Mary

Dan: One time we discovered that some coconuts had been stolen from our back compound. I woke up one night when I heard Father's voice yelling, "STOP! Stop or I'll shoot" and heard several loud shots. Then more voices and more shots. We ran out to see what was going on, and found out that several of his hospital assistants had also gone out there and fired their guns. There weren't any robbers. Father was just making sure that word got out that he would shoot if any robbers did come around again. And it worked, because we had no more problems with robbers.

46 - School Years at Kodai
As told by Dorothy, Dan and Mary

Mary: As children of missionaries in Siam reached school age, they were either home-schooled or sent back to the U.S. There were no schools available for the non-Siamese in the early years. Mother and Father decided to send Dorothy to a boarding school in Southern India where a few other missionaries in Siam were beginning to send their children.

Kodaikanal School, familiarly called Kodai, had been founded in 1901 for schooling the children of missionaries in India. It was situated at an altitude of approximately 7,000 feet in the Palani Hills, above the plains of Tamil Nadu in the Western Ghats, with Madurai the nearest large city about 90 kilometers to the southeast. Over the years it drew Caucasian children from as far east as Hong Kong and as far west as Kuwait and the Arabian Peninsula. Most of them were from missionary backgrounds, though some parents were in government or oil, or other occupations.

Dorothy: January 26th, 1925, was my tenth birthday. Plans were made which changed forever my familiar, carefree childhood. New clothes were sent for, more were made at home, and name tags stitched in. But I have no recollections of any of it, except one: Mother got me off alone, and with embarrassed clearings of her throat, gave me a bundle of diapers, and instructed me about the "facts of life", of growing up. It was years before I needed them, but better too early than too late, I guess.

In the middle of May, Father and I boarded the train for Penang, Malaysia, then embarked on a steamship for Madras, India. My only memory of the trip is the crowd of natives on the lower deck, steerage passengers, Malay or Tamil, going to seek work elsewhere. While watching them disembark, I was shocked to see the bare brown breast of a young woman whose sari slipped off her shoulder as she was being assisted into the lighter.

I am dismayed at the dearth of memories of incidents. During my adult life I often mentioned the facts of my life as a child, and never felt any emotion about it. Then in 1982, I was visiting with my eldest daughter in Alaska. One of her daughters was ten. I suddenly began to *feel* what it might be like for a child that young to be wrenched away from all that was familiar, taken by her "strange-father" (for he was always, or mostly, distant and punitive), to a different country with odd customs, people, and language. Suddenly there were many other children to learn to play with, and other adults to be wary of. Did I feel bereft and lonely? Did I ever cry with homesickness? I don't recall! Did I shut it all down to encapsulate the pain? At the age of 68 I wanted to cry.

The ship landed at Madras. Then we took a train journey for a day and a half to the foot of the Palani Hills. There we boarded

In front of Boyer Hall, the girls' dorm. (front) **Peggy B***. Betty A.* **Mary B.***,
(back) Frances S. Janice L.* **Dorothy B***. Faith S. Justine F. — (1930)*

a bus. The seats were across the middle, the sides were open. The road was worse than you can imagine, and the native driver scared the life out of us as he raced around the hairpin turns, disregarding all traffic, whether man, beast, or motor!

After three or four hours we arrived at the school compound. We were 7,000 feet up, in a warm temperate climate. The school was perched on a hilltop above a lovely lake. I don't know where Father was put up, or how long he stayed. I was given a room in Boyer Hall, the girls' dormitory. It was here that some of the girls told what happened between married couples. I was shocked!

One of our housemothers made marvelous fudge including marshmallows and peanuts, and told scary ghost stories before bedtime. Another one, British and portly, was a strict disciplinarian with some unusual ideas. Every single morning, after the wake-up bell, we had to strip to the waist and line up, wash ourselves, brush our teeth and hair, and dress. Then we had to perform what we all considered the most unnecessary, useless, time consuming, pointless exercise imaginable! We had to strip our beds down to the mattress – folding each item over a chair – and leave them to air until after breakfast. Then we had to turn the mattress and make up the bed. After that we lined up for inspection and she checked us over before we left the dormitory. Many's the time we were cleaning one nail with another one, and hoping the quick rub of each shoe on the back of the other socked leg would suffice for polishing. The breakfast bell demanded that we race up the hill to the Main building to eat.

We had many wonderful outings to scenic spots for picnics, swimming or camping trips. Scattered far and wide over the Palani

The School Orchestra — Dorothy, Dan and Dwight all played instruments.

hills were *sholas*, stands of tall straight pines, planted in rows to provide masts for His Majesty's sailing ships. Each one had a *godown* or shelter where the *coolies* had lived when they were planting – six or eight attached mud-walled rooms with a single window opposite the door opening onto a covered veranda. In good weather we could sleep in the open on thick mattresses of springy pine needles, or move into a *godown* if it rained.

We never saw any dangerous animals at Bear Shola, or Tiger Shola. One nice aspect of our long camping trips was that *coolies* carried all our equipment, and even the food for picnics. Several varieties of Eucalyptus trees, an import from Australia, graced the landscape. Tree ferns and maidenhair abounded in the lush woods, and fragrant violets.

The lake, a dammed stream, lay just across the road from the school. We learned to swim, and to use canoes, rowboats and punts at the boat house. The punts, paddled like a canoe, were fun to laze around in on a hot afternoon.

Sunday afternoons, the little kids gathered in the big living room or adjoining veranda to write letters home. The shared ritual made it easier to complete the onerous task. When a child had a birthday that week, the whole school was treated to a taffy pull. The cooks boiled up a sugar goop, poured it into pie tins and scored each into six equal sections. We kids lined up at the end of school, got our hands buttered and received the warm soft mass of sweet stuff. Pulling commenced right away as groups fanned out across the compound, for an hour or two absorbed in the ritual. Some candy was pulled until glistening white, some to intermediate stages, and some eaten quite promptly.

Another birthday tradition occurred at Sunday Chapel. While we sang a song, all the students filed to the front of the room and each dropped an *anna* (about a penny) in the collection plate. I suppose it went to charity.

Every so often, for reasons which I never concerned myself with, some Indian businessman would treat the whole school to a rice and curry meal. It would be served in the middle of the day, on a lawn with us sitting on the grass. We ate our food from torn pieces of banana leaf, using our fingers. Ah! what a treat! There would be special condiments to accompany the spicy hot food, and always *poppadums*. They might be compared to Mexican tortillas only because nothing else remotely fits, but of course they're nothing like them. When the fried bubbles burst, they make a little suction which sticks your tongue to it!

Rice and curry were served once a week in the regular dining room and we could eat with our fingers here too. This is quite an art, and done properly, is not at all messy. The food is rolled into a small ball with three fingers and thumb of the right hand, barely touching beyond the first joint. The thumb gracefully propels the food into the mouth, and you're ready to prepare for the next bite. Very satisfying, indeed. Then you'd excuse yourself to wash your hands.

My first winter away, Mother arranged for me to stay with the Scudder family. My brother Dan was brought to Kodai by Mother the next May, and the following winter, we both stayed with friends in India. The following May, Father brought my brother Dwight, to the school, and the next two Christmases a teacher chaperoned the three of us home.

Our school year at Kodai started in February. It was nippy cold at 7000 feet in the Palani Hills, with an occasional white dusting of frost. The whole month of May was vacation, and the "Season" for the adult community which included an English Club, a Catholic School, and on a distant hill a Lutheran Boarding School. May was the hottest month on the Plains where the Missionaries had their stations. As many as could, certainly most of the women and children still at home, came up to Kodai, the Hill Station for some relief. They owned, or rented homes and took their school kids out of boarding. There were always one or two like me, whose parents lived too far away and we remained at the school. One year the school nurse and her two children lived at the school and I was included in all their outings.

School commenced again in June, and the children returned a few at a time as their parents went back to the plains. November was the end of the school year, and the time for packing and tearful good byes. We took the rickety old bus down that horrendous road, and at a certain place, we gave a resounding cheer because we were safely away from the hated school. On the trip up the *ghat* [mountain pass], at a certain place we would let out the most awful groans because we were returning to that terrible school. What fictions kids like to create. It was a wonderful life and we loved it.

Mary: My recollection of dormitory life was that the "big girls" (those who had started menstruating) were housed downstairs in Boyer Hall, while the younger girls were upstairs. There were always whispers among us when one had attained that status and was moved downstairs.

I also recall the whooping cough siege. We were quarantined in a cottage inside the front gate. No one seemed to be seriously ill, so it was a time of fun and release from classes. But we missed a Gilbert & Sullivan performance and tried to sneak a view from a distance without being caught.

I loved climbing trees and had special little hideaways where several of us formed a little club and played together.

Kodai student body, 1926

Dan: One year Dwight and I managed to smuggle a little gray, long-tailed monkey and a white *moosang* on to the boat, hiding the pets in our jackets. Somehow they escaped notice, or maybe the officials looked the other way. In any case we succeeded in sneaking food for them during the two-week boat trip, the two-day train ride and the bus up the *ghat*. At the school we were permitted to keep the pets and a cage

Dan and monkey

was built for them. One of the teachers, Miss Marshall became so enamored with the monkey that she carried it around with her, powdered and perfumed.

Dwight and I played in the band and had a lot of fun on hikes and overnights. One time Dwight fell on the concrete floor in the shower, passed out and got "water on the knee." He had knee problems for the rest of his life.

Dwight, moosang and monkey.

Mary: I was permitted to take piano lessons the last three years I was at Kodai. My teacher was Miss Page. She spoke little, was meticulous and patient. I don't remember that she particularly encouraged or discouraged me, but I do remember that she had the bluest eyes and always wore blue.

Kodaikanal International School is now an autonomous residential school with a broad college-oriented curriculum rooted in spirituality. Approximately 98% continue toward a college degree. Many of its graduates are outstanding in their fields. The school recently celebrated its centennial.

47 - Back to the U.S. (1934) & Beyond

Edna: By 1934 we had begun to feel the Depression to such an extent that it was difficult to continue to keep four children at school in India. Each year it meant their leaving home early in January two hours before daybreak to motor across the Peninsula and its mountain pass, to entrain for Penang. Then it took ten days to two weeks to reach Madras on the coast of India by boat, stopping at several other ports on the way; then a night on the train and a fifty mile bus trip up to Kodaikanal.

Each year it meant leaving the school in November for the long return trip to Trang. Tuition and railway and steamship rates had increased while our salary was reduced. America and its public schools seemed the solution. To join the three older children already in the States and make a home for all seemed imperative.

Mary: In May of that year Mother picked up Dan, Dwight, Peggy and me at Kodai and we began the long trek from the Orient to New York for the last time, this time via Europe. Mother was glad we children were old enough to enjoy and appreciate our European experience – traveling by boat down the Rhine, seeing castles on the hills, the Cologne Cathedral encased in scaffolding, but I was in my bunk suffering from tonsillitis and missed the castles.

Mother bought a car in New York, and she and Dan drove the five of us across the States. When we reached Claremont, Connie and Dorothy joined us and the seven of us lived in a four-bedroom house outside of Pilgrim Place, an area for retired missionaries.

A few years later Mother bought two lots on Mills Avenue south of town. She designed a home, made of concrete blocks, where we lived for many years.

Father came to the U.S. in 1936 and our entire family was together under one roof for the first and only time in our entire lives, and that only briefly. He returned to Siam shortly after and continued with his

The house on South Mills Avenue, Claremont that Mother designed.

life work at the hospital. In 1940 Dorothy and her husband Roy Bucknell went to Thailand (as it was called after 1939) to work with him. When the Japanese invaded the country they had 40 minutes to get out with their five-month old baby Anore before the border was closed. [See the next chapter for their story.] Father chose to remain at his hospital in Trang.

During the Second World War Dan and I served in the Navy, and Dwight and Peggy in the Army. Dan and Dwight both ended up in different branches of the Office of Strategic Services [the O.S.S., the forerunner of the C.I.A.], the intelligence unit responsible only to the Joint Chiefs of Staff. They were both assigned to a unit in Ceylon, then in Rangoon, and were preparing to parachute into Thailand.

Dan: We flew over Thailand ready to jump, but our reception "team" of natives on the ground didn't give the signal, meaning the Japs [sic] were onto our landing site and were waiting for us, so we flew back to Rangoon. We [flew over and] were all ready to jump again, sitting in the chute. All we had to do was to put our feet together and slide out, but no go. They had dropped our gear the night before, so I guess the Japs got all our gear. We were set to try again two nights later, but someone saved the day for us by dropping the atomic bomb – and that ended my career as a parachute jumper.

The whole Bulkley family together for Christmas, 1936. (back) Dan, Kay, Connie, Father, Mother, Dwight, Dorothy, (front) Mary and Peggy.

A short time later they flew all of us into Thailand to help with post war activities of the surrender. I had one interesting experience when the Graves Registration Team sent me into the back country with a couple of Thai officers to locate a U.S. bomber that had been shot down. I retrieved the ashes of the crew which the natives had saved. The trip included two days on an elephant – the second day's ride took 14 hours – the longest day of my life!

When I was with the O.S.S. in Bangkok, the King, [Ananda] and his younger brother, Bhumpibol were very interested in our activities and asked to see one of our training camps. While there, the young king tried out one of our rifles, and also a 45 pistol, which we gave him. Later he and his brother were playing with it in the bedroom, and I am sure the gun went off accidentally and killed the king. Although the story went around that he had been assassinated, I feel sure that it was an accident – that his brother did not kill him. In any case Ananda's younger brother Bhumpibol then became king. Ananda had become king when he was only ten, before his mother took him and his brother to Switzerland for school. A regent ruled during the intervening years. When he came back to Thailand in 1946 he was only 19 years old. I don't remember any ceremony of his being crowned king, though he actually did reign for a short time until his death.

Jim Thompson was a major in the army with the O.S.S. in Bangkok. When the war ended, he was decommissioned in the States and went back to Thailand and started a weaving industry in the north. He had a number of weavers in the area who wove material for him. He also collected 3 or 4 Thai houses

Peggy, Edna and Mary, 1945

from different parts of Thailand, brought them to Bangkok and put them together as one big house – his own. He was very anti-communist.

One night, while on a vacation trip at a hill station in Malaya, he went out for a walk and never came back. Simply disappeared. People searched and searched and never found a trace. They thought he might have been grabbed by a tiger, but then they would have expected to find some remains. Some thought he might have been kidnapped by the Communists because he was so violently anti-communist, possibly for ransom, but no claim was ever made. He just disappeared off the face of the earth. To this day no one knows what happened to Jim Thompson. His industry is still going. There is a Jim Thompson store in Bangkok which sells the cloth his weavers still make for him. His house – the four separate Thai houses he put together – is a museum now – a very fascinating place.

The Free Thai were mostly students in this country going to school when the war broke out. They didn't want any part of what Japan was doing to Thailand, so they started the Free Thai Movement, and the Regent became part of their group. He was ostensibly cooperating with the Japanese but in reality was an American agent, you might say. All our O.S.S. communication went thru the Regent, and he made sure it got through. One of the first O.S.S. men infiltrated into Thailand, Howard Palmer was the son of one of the U.S. missionaries in Bangkong, who also attended Kodai school. He had many narrow escapes and harrowing experiences before the war ended. He was captured by the Japanese and put in jail, but because of the Regent and the Free Thai or Underground which were sympathetic with us, He was permitted to use his radio in his jail cell and thus was able to communicate with the O.S.S. in Ceylon. During the whole war the Regent was part of the Underground. Most people didn't know about it. You hardly hear anything about the Free Thai or underground war that went on in Thailand during the war.

Rhonda Bulkley: [Dwight's daughter-in-law, in a memorial booklet after Dwight's death in 1998]: .... Dwight, being fluent both in reading and writing in the Thai language, was put in Research and Analysis, interviewing P.O.W.'s, etc. During Dwight's time in the service, he ended up as a spy. A lot of what he did couldn't be put in his scrapbook, but there were some interesting things that were found. He received a Certificate of Merit in the Strategic Services Unit, many letters of recommendations and honors, and an appointment as Vice Consul to the American Embassy in Thailand after being discharged from the service.

In one of the Certificates of Merit it read:

> ... Through brilliant achievement and utterly devastating frustration within the orbits of Army confusion with respect to just distribution of credit through rank, he emerges bowed but not humbled, crippled but triumphant ....
>
> As witness of achievement, I, the undersigned, testify that the above named, during 19 months of service with the Office of Strategic Services was foremost intelligence expert on Thai affairs outside of Washington, D.C.

Instrumental in shaping facets of international relations, [he] has professional contact in the line of duty with 169 officers up to and including an Allied Chief of Staff, a Foreign Regent, Premier, Cabinet Minister and other dignitaries, and was two weeks distant of being a Master Spy in an enemy-occupied capital city at the time of cessation of war in the Pacific. September 18, 1945.

As Vice Consul, Dwight spent several years in Thailand (along with his wife Virginia). He accomplished many good things, but finally resigned in frustration, because higher-ups in Washington were more or less ignoring his intelligence reports, which he got from the horse's mouth so to speak. Although he could speak the language and read the newspapers, they preferred to rely on second hand information from unreliable sources.

Mary: In 1947 Mother chose to return to Thailand alone. After a year in Bangkok she settled in the northern city of Chiengmai and opened a guest house. Dwight visited her there several times. [He wrote about her experiences in chapter 49, page 327.]

48 - Dorothy's Escape From Siam

by Dorothy Bulkley Bucknell Anciaux

Dorothy returned to Siam in 1940 with her husband,
Roy Bucknell. Here is her story as she wrote it.

Somewhere along the way, after Roy and I were married, we got the idea to go to Siam. Years before, my grandfather had purchased a Purities Baker Bond for me and each of my two older sisters. It matured on my twenty-first birthday, but I hadn't used it yet. In 1938, five hundred dollars paid for our San Juan Islands property in Washington State. The second half paid for our trip to Siam. We would work for my father in his Mission Hospital for a nominal salary and have a great adventure. We decided to go in September, 1940. My mother warned us that war was coming to the Orient, but that didn't deter us. We got our passports and visas, and our shots, and booked our passage on a Swedish freighter, the *Dagmar Salen,* whose principle cargo this trip was to be gypsum for Bangkok. There were four staterooms.

Roy, Dorothy and Con

311

We arrived at Bangkok on October 13th, 1940, then took the train down the peninsula to Tung Song Junction where my father met us. We changed trains and took the spur line to Trang.

Trang, the biggest city of the south, was still a small town, but now it had electricity. Father's house was much as I remembered it eleven years before, without the feminine touches my mother gave it. She had a flair for interior decoration, a sore point in their marriage since she spent more than he deemed justifiable. He was quite spartan in his tastes and needs.

The hospital was much as I remembered it. But now, across the street from it, was an imposing cement hospital built by Tien Hua who had been Father's chief assistant in the early days. After some thirty years Tien Hua had acquired enough learning, equipment and medicines to go into practice independently. His wife, Khun Chine, meaning Chinese Mother, was a midwife and did the obstetrics.

Nai Choi, the same cook that mother had trained, was still fixing superb meals. Many foreigners had tried to woo him away but he remained loyal to my father. He could fix any American dish you might ask for, and excelled in fixing Siamese food, which we always loved.

Soon Roy took over the lab and learned to do the tests required. He had worked as an orderly in Surgery at Harborview Hospital in Seattle while in pre-med studies at the University of Washington. He also started following the auxiliary staff around, one by one, to see what they were doing. He laughingly intercepted their unauthorized leaves and convinced them that eight hours pay meant eight hours on the job. Roy had the knack of getting a laugh with them about any situation, which oiled the transition from laziness to competence.

We had no newspaper, so international news came from rumors. In January 1941 Trang had a big parade. Everyone in town donated a cloth sack of supplies for the soldiers fighting on the Indo-China frontier, such as canned food, towels, soap, toothbrushes, etc.

One day Trang had a blackout trial. Dark cloth "mufflers" were made to set above each light to be dropped down quickly. Bicycle lights also had to be muffled. Conjectures as to the possibilities of war were widely discussed. The British Consul in Singora expressed his belief that the crisis would subside without any major incident.

Nevertheless all British women were sent out to New Zealand or Australia, since it was impossible to return to England.

Two and a half months went by before we got return mail from the States. In each letter we begged for international news, specifically as it dealt with the possibility of war. We had a radio full of static which we listened to every night, then talked over what each person thought he heard, and what it meant.

I became pregnant while on the *Dagmar Salen,* not surprising with all that time, and the moonlit ocean! I continued working at the hospital until the end. When the time came, the midwife arrived and we had fun getting acquainted and making preparations. Labor started around midnight, and Anore was born at 4 a.m., weighing just under 7 lbs., on July 18th, the day after Roy's birthday. No anesthesia and no tear. Our letters home about the baby were effusive in our delight and wonderment at her perfection and precocity. I hired Ah Sim to be the *Amah,* so I could go back to supervise at the hospital. Ah Sim had been Peggy's *Amah* when she was an infant 17 years before, so I was especially pleased to find her. I thought she was old then, but she was still competent and loving. The hospital was right next door, so I could run home frequently to look in on Anore and nurse her.

In September, 1941, a cable – probably from my mother – came urging us to come home immediately. Roy reasoned that we were safer on land than on the sea, and that the British would rush in to protect Siam if the Japanese invaded!

Dorothy and baby Anore

An exciting prospect loomed ahead. Roy had gotten a position as Assistant Dredge Master with the Tongkah Harbor Tin & Dredging Ltd. It would be in Ronpibun, northeast of Trang, and pay three times the salary my father could afford for both of us. We would live in a beautiful house in their lovely compound across the peninsula with cool sea breezes. A gardener provided, light and fuel paid, and even an allowance for the baby! Roy was told that he was not to lift a finger to work, even to pick up a bolt! Every bit of manual labor was to be performed by the Malayan work force. We were to start January 1st, 1942. But because of ensuing events, we were notified "We regret position is no longer valid due to existing conditions" – a mild statement for the chaos which followed.

Another event I missed was a chance to go to Chiengmai in the north of Thailand with Father for the Mission meeting. This was the end of November, 1941, and the Japanese had made preparations in Indo-China, everyone guessing whether a push would be on the Burma Road or into Thailand. Roy decided that I should not go, for it would be easier to escape from Trang if such a move was necessary.

December, 1941. Speculations and news about impending war filled the air. We packed a trunk with our clothes, and a wooden box with our valuables – my silverware, Roy's cameras, souvenirs we had bought. Father gave Roy his Colt automatic, just in case. He had resolved to stay with his hospital. We continued our work at the hospital. Kru Tamada and I had completed our preparations for a diet kitchen for the hospital, and were unpacking the bowls and spoons we had purchased. At seven o'clock on the morning of the 8th (because of the dateline, the 7th) the Chinese pharmacist came running up the stairs to our living quarters – an unprecedented liberty – gasping excitedly that over the radio, the Thai government had announced that the Japanese had entered Thailand without contest, and that all foreigners were to be under house arrest.

What to do? Breakfast was ready, so we went down to eat. Neither Roy nor Father did more than pick at their food. I, a nursing mother, my stomach never tied to my emotions, ate my eggs and toast. The Britishers in Nakon had assured us that we were included in their escape plans. As we talked, a Ford truck drew in under the *porte-cochere*. A Britisher jumped out and demanded, "Where's

Klong Teng?" My father had meticulously mapped each area he had been to. Father's maps were requested by the British War Office as there were no others as complete. But he had not heard of Klong Teng. The closest he could come to in sound was Kantang. It was reasonable, up from the mouth of a river, and only twenty-six kilometers from Trang.

Hasty goodbyes while our boxes and bags were thrown into the truck, and two men, a woman and a baby roared away down the narrow red earthen road to Kantang. Half an hour later we were in the village, sitting in the shop of a Chinese businessman, friend of Father's, with many helpful people. The Britisher did not find the 18 tin miners or a British shore boat as expected. He returned to Trang to look for another river mouth further north. A Station Agent came to inform us that the Japanese had just arrived at the junction of Tung Song. The train, with the troops, would be arriving in 40 minutes! The mail boat, a small diesel lighter was at the dock ready to embark for Puket, a Thai island just off the coast, a 21 hour trip.

It was decided that we would go, and we left at 3:20 p.m. hurriedly for the dock. The captain lost no time in pulling away. We slept as best we could. Some time in the middle of the night, we arrived at a Customs outpost, where the officer thought he should detain us as per orders. The boat captain and I argued that since Puket was Thai, we weren't really leaving the country. My story was that some missionaries there (we weren't asked their names, fortunately, as I didn't know any) had invited us for a visit and it just happened at this time. Finally he decided in our favor, and we chugged away. We arrived at noon. Thai Customs confiscated everything except our personal luggage, including the cameras and Colt, promising that we could have them when we left the island. We were taken to a home where eleven British tin miners lived. These men had just returned from a 30-hour excursion up a river to meet the 18 men from Nakon, who never showed up. Apparently none of them escaped.

Dinner that night was champagne and boiled potatoes, and a song fest. We were kept under armed guard all day and night. The Thai Governor said it was to protect us from 100 Italian sailors who were wandering about town after scuttling and burning their three ships a week before. Or was it, we rumored, to keep us from damaging the airport and other facilities before leaving? Thai officials displayed two different attitudes: one of personal respect and interest in our safe evacuation, and the other, dictated from Bangkok following the treaty with Japan, which demanded that they arrest us and confiscate our belongings. In the end they chose to follow the former, which allowed our escape. I hope they suffered no consequences.

At 5:30 a.m., Friday, December 12th, we saw our code signal flashed from the armed merchant ship outside the bay. Its tender, heavily armed, soon docked and took us all aboard. Because of mud-shallows, an outgoing tide, and too heavy a load, the tender wouldn't budge. A minimum crew, the baby and I stayed aboard, the rest of them splashed and swam to deeper water along a submerged breakwater, bought a sampan from a near-by junk and met the tender in mid-channel. Anore received a hearty hand clap from the 112 evacuees when we took her aboard. Throughout these three days of travel by truck, motorboat, and now the ship, the *Mata Hari,* she ate and slept and smiled. She was a week short of five months. We were to disembark in Penang, but it had been bombed and strafed the night before. As we sailed by we could see the sky still lit up by the fires.

Five days later, with only two Singapore warning "alerts", both from British planes, we arrived in Singapore at 3 a.m. We had only our hand luggage and a pocketful of worthless Thai money, but were alive and healthy with our baby. We were sent to the famous Raffles Hotel where we luxuriated for a day and a half. Then we were safely ensconced in a fine house owned by the Goodyear Rubber Company, seven miles out of town. All our expenses including food and servants were taken care of through the Consul General's Office. We used an air raid shelter there once, and Roy wrote home that "Anore spent the half hour with her thumb and four fingers in her mouth. She has a nonchalance we can't help but imitate. . . . We haven't been more comfortable and complacent for years."

At the Raffles Hotel after a group of men had been standing around telling of their escape experiences and present plights to each other, an elderly man drew Roy aside, and said, "You'll be needing a bit of spending money while looking for work here. Let me offer you – say

$150 payable without interest in the next few decades, or later if you wish." His name was Matthew MacGregor Jack, a Scotsman, which stops us from ever joking about their tightness with money.

Roy registered for Ambulance and First Aid duty, signed on at Man Power Bureau, and at the General Hospital for fracture and cast work, skills he had learned at Harborview Hospital. He wrote home that "if at all possible we will remain in the East. Don't worry." Most of the people in Singapore believed what we had been told: Singapore was the Gibraltar of the East, and Britain would never let her fall. Meanwhile the High Command knew that with the conflict in the Mediterranean and Africa, they could not wage war on both fronts, and Singapore was going to be sacrificed. Some people guessed – we heard that wealthy Chinese were making their exodus.

We lived in a false paradise. Roy wrote: "It's an unexplainable fact that being in or fleeing from a war zone is not nearly so frightening as sitting by an American radio listening to reports of the bombing of London or Hawaii. In fact we've had no other feelings than a business-like practicality in what we should do and how. . . .So don't worry."

An American dentist and his wife from Penang were sent to live in the house with us. They came away with nothing but the clothes they were wearing, leaving behind a lifetime of savings in equipment and belongings. At least they and we had a fine Christmas with a tree, a turkey, plum pudding and candy. Also a large roast, pork chops, and plenty of fruits and vegetables. It was Anore's first Christmas and one that Roy wrote "we won't soon forget." I don't recall a single thing about it!

Roy asked his sister to send a penny post card to everyone we knew to apprise them of our whereabouts and safety, but not to write for awhile as mails were uncertain. The Singapore Post Office did not know, or would not say, by what route his airmail letter would be sent. She did receive it and saved it for us.

Roy wrote: "Anore has been a perfect evacuee. Always calm and collected – and wet. Dubs has her trained to a strict schedule and we hardly need our wristwatches. During our "trip" she didn't miss a meal. We managed to bring hot boiled water in a thermos, canned milk, oranges, prunes and boiled egg yolks. Diapers constituted a major headache. I washed them for the first time while aboard the *Mata Hari*, using salt water. Worked fine."

Singapore, "Gibraltar of the East", defended to the teeth from assault by sea or land was now being bombarded from the air. Japanese planes from 30,000 feet up were making sorties over the Island and hitting their targets. They were sporadic and intermittent at first, and soon increased.

We were ordered to leave, but Roy chose to stay, still believing that Britain would come to the rescue and the war would be over soon. The money was good, and he would send for Anore and me. Our idyllic tropical life would go on as planned. A Dutch freighter, the *S.S. Peele Telle*, was taking refugees, but wouldn't say to what destination. West to Ceylon and on to the Mediterranean, or South to Australia? Baby and I had a small stateroom to ourselves. We sailed West to Palenbang up a river on the Island of Sumatra. We took on oil at the huge refinery, then continued around the south end past Merak.

We set anchor at a dock in Padang harbor, about half way up the huge island, for two weeks. The ship's holds were filled to capacity with rubber, tin, and quinine. Get the cash crops out! I don't know how many passengers she had, but we were mostly women, wives of businessmen and officers, and missionary couples. First night out, a ship's officer with a gramophone played music on deck. We all settled ourselves on the improvised seating afforded by a cargo ship while Beethoven's Ninth soared into the warm night sky. Never again has it been so uplifting.

Miriam King, another American, and I discovered that we had more in common than with either the businessmen's wives or the missionaries. Miriam was married to a British officer with General Wavell's high command who had to stay behind. She had two boys, three and five years old.

We heard of a swimming hole about a mile from where our ship was docked, and going there by bicycle taxi with our children became a daily activity. The swimming pool was a beautiful natural rock basin fed by a high-drop waterfall. Giant tree ferns and other tropical plants covered the cliff, while towering trees festooned by liana vines shaded us from the fierce equatorial sun. The boys splashed and played, Miriam and I talked and swam and watched them and Anore. Two weeks passed happily by.

One morning a small group of airplanes flew overhead. Japanese, we were told, 30,000 feet up. A little shiver of alarm went through us, but there was nothing to do about it. The next morning, I had just finished bathing Anore in the tiny bathroom with porthole securely shut for blackout purposes. Since it was beastly hot anyway, and no air in there, I was wearing only a sunsuit and no bra. She only had a diaper on – it was too warm for a shirt. I had put my watch back on, and was wearing my wedding ring when we heard the thud of bombs. We all scrambled to the dining room and ducked under the tables.

A ship's officer poked his head down the broad stairway and shouted, "You have about three minutes to get off the ship!" I grabbed a large square diaper to cover our heads from the sun, did *not* grab my handbag hanging at the foot of the bed, and ran with the others up the stairs and off the ship to the road. A ditch had been dug along the side and we just had time to scramble in and duck our heads. Bombs hit our ship, a sheaf of them right through my cabin area.

Then we ran again along the road about a thousand yards to where the hills rose abruptly. I had only a seven months old baby to carry. Miriam carried her 3-year old, and dragged the five-year old, while able-bodied men ran past her. Finally someone picked up the crying boy.

We crouched under the small trees among the big rocks of the hillside for about an hour while the planes, still small specks in the sky, made repeated circles and bombed every ship in the harbor, then flew away. They didn't aim any at the land.

People from the Dutch Red Cross came from the town of Padang in buses and took us back for shelter. We were housed in a convent for a few days. I vaguely remember the high-ceilinged rooms, food served cafeteria style, people milling about, being given clothes, and lying awake at night inside my mosquito net hearing the continuous hum of a multitude of the buggers as they searched for our blood.

I had time to regret not grabbing my handbag which hung at the end of my bed on the ship. The passport and money could be replaced, but not the heavy gold chain – my grandfather's watch chain – which

I loved to wear as a choker. Also my mother's ruby ring which she had loaned me – I loved it with a passion – and a medallion on a gold chain with the Queen of Siam's initial done in gold and red enamel, given to my mother when she entertained the royal couple.

There are few roads on Sumatra. One led from Padang over the mountains and almost to the coast. The bus system was rudimentary. Hotels along the way were spaced about a day apart. Refugees were being sent in groups determined by the availability of transportation and accommodation. We waited our turn patiently, taking care of our children, whiling away the time.

The trip took several days. I vaguely recall gorgeous jungle scenery, and huge wood houses with curved roof lines. At each rest stop there seemed to be something to do for my baby, such as changing and feeding so that quite often there wasn't time for me to eat. Anore ate whatever anyone provided, bless her heart. There were assortments of canned baby food sometimes, more beets than anything else, which was her least favorite. Also cereal and milk. Fresh bananas and oranges, of course, and I don't recall what else. One night, Miriam and her two boys, Anore and I all shared one huge bed. There were no other beds.

The bus trip ended at a town in the midst of rubber plantations. The rail line began there and continued to the coast, ending at Merak at the very tip of Sumatra. At the station a British family on a rubber plantation heard that a British officer's wife was aboard. Immediately Miriam was offered a place to stay, and I was included. What a haven of rest! A huge home, many servants to keep it immaculate, marvelous food, a gorgeous garden, and a feeling of safety.

Miriam's younger boy had come down with diarrhea. She took him to the local hospital, but after observing the conditions, brought him back and nursed him to health in the few days we had there. Our hostess had a darling two-year old girl. She gave me many baby clothes for Anore.

The train, like the buses, could take only so many passengers each trip. Other refugees were put up at the railway hotel, and elsewhere. When the little boy was well enough, our turn came. We were packed and summoned to breakfast. There was something special

– scones and jam. We relished our food, and sat around the table talking. Our hosts were too polite to say, "We must hurry", and we were too unaware to notice that they were getting anxious, until finally in desperation, they did urge us to get going. They drove us to the station . . . and the train had left! There are no words to describe the feelings among us. (Or maybe too many words would be needed.)

After all their wonderful hospitality we couldn't impose on them any more, so we thanked them and took a room at the railway hotel for one night, and left the next day. I do not recall much about the train ride to the Southern tip of Sumatra, nor the boat trip across the narrow Sunde Straits to Java, which we would go through subsequently under even more stressful conditions. At Customs, Miriam phoned the British Army High Command and learned that her husband had left Singapore and was with General Wavell's headquarters at Bandoeng, high in the mountains above Batavia. She was to meet him there. She turned to me and said, "You come too!" I had no business doing so, but it was so nice to be looked after that I gratefully accepted.

I thought Batavia the most beautiful city I had ever been in. Broad boulevards lined with graceful trees, handsome buildings, and elegant shops. Beautiful, friendly people going their unhurried way created an ambiance of serenity. We saw it briefly, then were driven up into the mountains. We stayed at a cottage-type hotel, and once again relaxed into an illusion of safety. However, the war was drawing ever closer.

One day, Miriam's husband returned from a trip to Batavia with orders from the British Consul to send his wife and children to the city immediately. He had reported my presence to the American Consul and brought the same orders for me.

Anore and I were put up at the posh Hotel des Indes for one night. Dinner was the famous *Ris Tafel*. Our long table with twenty-five or thirty people at both sides were served by a retinue of servants each with a different spicy condiment to add to our bowls of rice. Ecstasy of flavors! Next morning we were dispatched early to the waterfront where boats were waiting.

These were small vessels meant to ply the inland waters between the myriad islands of the great archipelago. There were twenty-two cabins. As I came up the gangway with babe in arms, a young woman greeted me, invited me to share one of the cabins. We went below decks to the cabin. One narrow bunk filled the six-foot width below the porthole which was securely blacked to let no light in or out. Another bunk took up one side. Another woman and her baby was in there also. Three women and three babies, crying, in a six by ten foot hot, airless cubicle? I moved out immediately, and plopped my few bags on a bench in the dining room. Subsequently I was assigned to one of the two hundred mattresses, thoughtfully sent from a hotel to spread out on the decks for that many passengers.

My place at the stern of the vessel, over the engine room, was near the broad stairway leading to the women's washroom below. That was the fortunate part of an unfortunate location. The pitch and toss of the stern, the fumes of the engines, and probably other factors made me sicker than ever before in my life. Seasick, and more. I hardly got off my bed except to run below. Someone must have looked after my baby, because I wasn't able to. A crew man was recruited to wash all the diapers. I don't know what food was served, or where. I didn't eat for a number of days. I guess I recovered before the nine days were up and we chugged into the harbor of Bunbury, West Australia.

Perth was the only city of any size on the west coast of Australia. With war in the Mediterranean and Europe, it wasn't safe to send ships with refugees in that direction. There was nowhere else to go but south to Australia. Perth had received so many people that our ship was sent ninety miles south to the town of Bunbury. I found myself sharing a hotel room with a Mrs. Duyndam and her nine- or ten-month daughter Deirdre, or Deedee for short. Our ship's doctor volunteered to take the train to Perth, and report our arrival to the American Consul. He returned with the instructions that all of us were to take the train leaving at midnight which would arrive in Perth at seven a.m.

Meanwhile Roy was working in Singapore for the British Government. His job was to buy food, rice particularly, and all other staples to stock up all the hospitals. He lived with a group of men doing various jobs, becoming special friends with Tommy, an Australian. The bombing came steadily closer, finally with daily raids on Singapore.

Roy saw plenty of casualties. The British men decided to stay with their duty, but Tommy and Roy felt no need for such loyalty. They began planning for escape. One of their group, offered them his sailboat, anchored in the harbor. He guessed he wouldn't be needing it.

They supplied themselves with a dozen hard-boiled eggs, a bottle of brandy, and some potassium permanganate to darken their skin, and pulled out of the harbor without chart or compass. As they reached open water, planes flew high overhead. The men looked back and saw a sheaf of bombs strike the water in the Yacht Basin where they had been a half hour before. That was February 11th, 1942.

By a miracle, they arrived at Pakham Baroe a week later. Roy saw the burned-out ships, and sought out the town Burgermeister, who said: "We heard that most of those people got off all right," while he kept exchanging glances with his secretary. This made Roy more anxious but he could get no more information about the bombing of the ships, which occurred almost a month before.

Some British destroyers had arrived in the harbor, and Roy and Tommy were among a group wanting to leave Sumatra. To satisfy British Navy protocol, each of them had to register as a member of the crew. Roy was a medical technician. A couple of days later the destroyer steamed into the harbor at Tjalatjap, on the south coast of Java, about in the middle of the island. From there he cabled the Consul in Batavia and received a reply a week later with the good news that the baby and I were in good health en route to Australia.

Then came frustrating days trying to get away. They would be apprised of a sailing, arrive at the dock only to find that the ship had left hours earlier. Every movement of ships was kept as uncertain as possible to foil enemy attacks. One such possibility was a British passenger ship, the *City of Manchester.* It got away without them. A few days later they were able to board a small interisland vessel comparable to mine, carrying 200 Australian soldiers who had deserted, and been caught, and were being returned for court martial. Shortly after, everyone on board heard a tremendous Boom! off in the distance, and learned subsequently, that the *City of Manchester* had been torpedoed with the loss of all lives.

Roy's trip to Australia was unpleasant too. For food they had only corned beef, ship's biscuits, and tea the entire seven or eight days. They arrived at Fremantle, port for Perth, on March 9th, 1942. At Custom's he asked how he might learn of my whereabouts, and was motioned to a large stack of typewritten pages. Each one had lists of names of the refugees who had disembarked there. He scanned all the pages, and near the end, came upon a Bucknell - but it wasn't Dorothy. He phoned the American Consul, who kidded around a bit before telling him that I was OK, and what he was to do next.

Meanwhile Mrs. Duyndan and I and our babies caught the train at midnight. When the train arrived at Perth, we were waiting in our compartment for instructions. Suddenly I heard my nickname "Dubs!" There at the window was Roy.

Mason Turner, the American Consul invited us to stay with him for a couple of weeks. He had recently sent his wife and children to the States, and was lonely. It was a wonderful two weeks, as Roy and I – resting, loving and eating (I had lost a lot of weight) – shared our stories of the nine weeks we had been apart.

On March 23rd, Mr. Turner put us aboard the *Island Mail,* an American freighter, bound for San Francisco. The limited number of cabins were assigned to women and children, while male passengers bunked with the crew. My roommate was another American woman who had had to say goodbye to her Dutch husband in Java, not knowing whether she would ever see him again. She had been the premiere ballerina with the San Francisco Ballet Company, and she also had a small daughter.

We sailed south from Perth, clear around Tasmania, and far east of the usual route because of the danger of enemy planes, so it took about a month to get home to California. The captain told us we sailed close to Pitcairn Island, where the *Bounty* mutineers settled.

We were back in Claremont the last week in April, 1942, eighteen months after leaving for our "Siam Adventure." I had my twenty-seventh birthday without celebration, and Anore was nine and a half months old, having traveled between 25 and 30 thousand miles.

Con conducting church service for fellow internees at the prison camp.

Mary: After leaving Father in Trang in December, Dorothy and Roy had no further contact with him. Not until they reached Claremont in April did they learn that he had been interned in a Japanese prison camp since that fateful day in December. He was actually well treated in camp, partly because of his long friendship with the Thai people and also because of the medical services he could provide his fellow internees. He was repatriated to the States on the Swedish vessel the *S.S. Gripsholm* in July, 1942.

The lack of focus and the inactivity after so many years in the tropics seemed to have taken a toll on him, yet he still beat me at a game of tennis, and walked up th 150 or so steps from the cove at La Jolla beach without stopping, when he visited me. He stayed with various family members for varying lengths of time, and he briefly worked on an Indian reservation near Gallop, New Mexico, and at a leper asylum in Louisiana.

He and Mother had been going their separate ways for some time, and he was living with his daughter Kay and her family in Niland, California. He died of a stroke on January 21, 1949. Mother had returned to Thailand in 1947 and was in Chiengmai when he died.

Edna Bruner Bulkley (July 14, 1883 - March 25, 1962)

49 - Jungle Grandma
by Dwight Bulkley (1950)

Her jungle hotel, deep in the northern interior of Siam, was called *Faharam* or "Bright Skies." She used to sit, a little white-haired old lady, in its riverbank tea house and watch the elephants break up teak-log jams.

For color, there were great masses of bougainvillea – eight different shades, she used to boast – which she herself had trained over the trellises between the house and the river. Wild orchids clung to the Lamyai trees. Purple-sheened kingfishers darted over the warm brown water.

Her missionary days were brought to a close by the war, and her doctor-husband has since passed away, but there was no stopping this jungle grandma. Siam was her adopted home, and the seventeen million Siamese living in a tropical paradise the size of California, her adopted people. She could talk politics with the best of them.

I paid a few visits to *Faharam* in 1947. If it hadn't been for a tumor, she would have been there longer and the place overrun with touring authors, Royal Siamese Princes, British lumbermen, U.N. officials, and whatnot. And all because of a little old lady with grayish white hair who was just as full of life and interests as she was when she pulled up stakes in Sacramento to go, all alone, to Siam as a missionary in 1903.

But it's finished now. She had to fly home to California, undergo an operation, and cut her activities down to begin writing a book about her life in Siam, and doing research into the ancient history of the central tribes of the Indo-Chinese peninsula. Some people just never grow old.

She wasn't content with the raising of seven children in the jungles of Southern Siam, getting them all safely married. She wasn't content with settling down after forty years of packing in enough adventure for three lifetimes. But at the age of seventy, she had to set up a jungle hotel in Chiengmai in the north of Siam which became a byword in

Bangkok. Nor did the operating of a hotel keep her from an incredible trip into the wilds of the Shan States [in Burma], or a week-long journey in a houseboat down the rapids of the Meping River accompanied only by one other white lady. Sometimes I wonder at this fantastic mother of mine.

The house at *Faharam* was built by a wealthy Chinese businessman during the war as an evacuation retreat – there were occasions when our Eastern Air Command had bombed the railway terminus at Chiengmai to hinder the Japanese supplies on their way overland to Burma. It was built of sturdy teak in two stories, with three living-rooms downstairs and six bedrooms above. On the south side, or rear, of the house, were the quarters for her staff of five servants and the kitchen and laundry. In the area of the circular driveway she had planted smaller species of palms, some hibiscus, cannas, and a flame tree. The electric supply from the power plant in the town a mile down the river was adequate for all practical purposes.

For transportation she had purchased an old German Adler. The Siamese folk used to be amused to note her white hair streaming in the wind as she drove on her way to the airfield to pick up some new patrons vacationing from Bangkok or other points East or West.

"Why don't you charge a more reasonable rate?" I used to ask her. "Every single one of your customers would not only be willing but expect to pay more than a mere three and a half dollars a day. And you feed them like kings. You don't save much of a nest-egg after spending a life as a missionary."

"But they're not exactly 'customers'," she would explain. "Every one who comes here is a friend, or a friend of a friend. Why, they are really just paying guests. Besides, I like the company." And she certainly did. But she laid down one fundamental rule. She wouldn't have any guest who felt that they had to humor her. No, sir, she was leading her own life, doing her own writing, and they could do exactly as they pleased, come and go whenever or wherever they wished. If they wanted suggestions for sight-seeing, she would help. She could tell them where to go to see the famous old temples, or the girls painting designs on umbrellas, or the men hammering out elaborate silver bowls, or where the teak forests were. She would help plan trips to waterfalls or to rural silk-weaving centers, but no pampering, please.

So, after her guests had seen all these sights, and returned to their homes elsewhere, they were filled with memories of Mrs. Bulkley, having found that the most interesting aspect of the vacation was a personality. They couldn't understand how this little old lady had done so many things.

It wasn't long after I had returned to Bangkok when I received this telegram: "Twelve day trip into Burmese Shan States successful, five days in Kengtung, but hectic strenuous traveling crowded busses often nearly all night. Have brought back one Kengtung Princess for a visit. Bulkley."

Couldn't anybody stop her? Rumor had it that the Shan States were in imminent danger of falling into Communist hands. A thriving business was being conducted across the Siamese border because the Shan territory was cut off from Rangoon and the rest of Burma due to the civil war there. Many businessmen in Bangkok had made every attempt to secure visas for travel but had failed. No one had done it. But Mrs. Bulkley did.

Packing a few light bags, she had joined a visiting German lady, and these two, traveling alone and without passport or any other official documents, had merely taken the local commercial trucks and traveled four hundred miles through a country notorious for its bandit opium traffic. In Kengtung, the capital of the Shan States, she had stayed in the guest villa of the ruling Chief or Sawbwa, and according to later accounts, had a wonderful time.

She had one complaint, however. That was the odor of the putrified prawns which was part of the cargo of one of the trucks in which she traveled. The Siamese immigration officials at the border were so dumbfounded at the innocent request of the two lone white females to cross over, that they waived all formalities. They thought it was an immensely humorous situation.

One adventure which Mother had long dreamed of, was shooting the rapids down the Meping River from Chiengmai to Raheng. At the age of seventy she finally did it. But not during the height of the flood season. That would have been too easy. Several other parties, including that of the Prince Regent of Siam went down on comfortable rafts during the month of December. Most of the river is then quite navigable.

She waited until late in January, and then with the company of a young English lady, engaged a typical river-boat to make the trip when the water had receded enough to reveal the treacherous rocks.

She admitted that she was scared on one occasion. The river narrowed down and rushed in a zig-zag of six hairpin curves, where shear rock cliffs towered two hundred feet above on both sides. But the steersman was clever and each time the vessel was obviously doomed to a thirty-mile-an-hour head-on collision with the solid rock, a flip of the pole brought it safely around the bend.

She told of one evening when the boat was tied to the shore and the crew were asleep in their pup-tents on the bank. She and her partner awoke simultaneously and peered into the darkness on the river side, thinking they had heard some sound. Nothing seemed amiss, so they went back to sleep. In the morning there were the deep imprints in the sand of three sets of leopard paws. The papa leopard's measured four inches across. That's a large leopard. They could have reached over the side of the boat and touched them, they were that close!

Another evening, sitting around a campfire, Mother induced the men to tell the old tales of the river, the legends of the ancient days, of kings and princes and princesses. One yarn had to do with an ancient capital city which modern historians insist does not exist. She had heard of it previously in Chiengmai, and was convinced of it's logic. Now she had a bone to pick with the historians.

On her round-about return trip, she herself hiked some miles through the jungle, climbed a mountain, and from it's top, looked down on temple spires choked in a matting of creepers and vines – surely an ancient city – and spread over an area of over a square mile. And it wasn't even mapped! Just before leaving Chiengmai for this trip she had mentioned the possibility of locating these ruins, and had been told by an authoritarian British teak-man that he had worked for years through that general area, and had never seen any such city. But what he didn't seem to realize was that the Siamese are superstitious of ruins, and in every likelihood deliberately gave him a wrong steer whenever he was too close.

Then there was the time when she made a trip to the famous ruins of Angkor Wat in Cambodia. That was a week-long journey round-trip across the border into French Indo-China. It was during the time of revolutionary struggle between Cambodian guerrillas fighting the French for their independence. She was with a party of Bangkok officials, accompanied by about eighty French troops with arms. It took three days to hike from ruin to ruin, climbing pyramids, crawling through and around tangles of vines which had grown over many of

Edna at the ruins of Ankhor Wat

the ruins, through the total area of at least twenty square miles. It was on the last day, when the group was passing through Phra Khan, that they suddenlly noticed that Mrs. Bulkley was missing. After a frantic search back through a mile of ancient temple palaces they found her at last, calmly sistting beside a jungle path, studying some ferns.

"Twenty-five miles of hiking has done me in," she said, "I just couldn't go any further, and I knew someone would come back to find me all right."

"But you should have called out, or something, before we were all out of sight. There's a war on here, you know."

"Oh, pshaw!' What would Cambodian guerrillas want with a little old lady like me?" She hadn't been worried. "I've been thinking about the architectural similarities here compared with what I've noticed in some of the oldest temples in Chiengmai. You know, these historians have been deliberately playing down the age of the Siamese civilization. They all say there was nothing much before 1200 A.D. They want to attribute so much to the *Mons. . . .*" And she was off into other historical thoughts.

After she was back in Chiengmai, I heard that she was planning a bang-up Halloween party for the local Siamese government and other officials, missionaries, etc. There never was a dull moment for anyone around her.

Mary: While living in Chiengmai Mother began to have health problems. A tumor was discovered and she returned in 1950 to the States for surgery. After recovering her health, she lived in Claremont for several years and began writing her memoirs. Before long, the urge to travel returned and she moved to several locations near Chapala and Guadalahara in Mexico, even in a former governor's palace. She was delighted to find she could live inexpensively there, renting a house with servant help for as little as $100 a month for everything except clothing. In order to maintain her U.S. citizenship she was required to cross the border to the U.S every six months.

The year she was 76 she took a 7600 mile trip by Greyhound Bus to visit each of her children. She traveled up the California, Oregon and Washington coasts as far as Seattle to visit Dorothy, and back by way of Arizona to see my family.

A year later she was settled in a small house she bought a few blocks south of the home she had built in Claremont. There she pursued her research into Thai history and continued writing her memoirs. To the end of her days she was captivated by anything to do with Thailand, her adopted country and knew its history and culture intimately.

She died in Claremont in 1962 at the age of 79.

Postscript

In 1953 Edna Bulkley wrote how this book began.

Fifteen years ago, when I was 55 years old, my college son [Dwight], was home for lunch one day. During our conversation I remarked, "Polo and playing the harp are two wishes that eluded me. I guess I'll have to wait until I get to heaven!"

He looked at me thoughtfully, then burst out enthusiastically, "Just think, Mother, you still have thirty years ahead of you – free to do all sorts of things!"

I must have looked blank for he broke off suddenly and it was about time for him to leave.

I had built my home and lavished all my love of color inside, and I had landscaped the grounds around it. Before that I had tired of painting and was not very interested in the clubs I belonged to.

Into this sort of vacuum shortly after my son's remark, I had an accident that laid me in hospital with nothing to do but think. An idea presented itself and marked the day of convalescence. I had enjoyed a very full life with years of travel and living in a foreign country. I would write about it! And immediately I was full of enthusiasm, deciding on a title and the beginning chapter.

Fifteen years I have been at it – discarding, expanding, rewriting, learning. It may never reach a public but has been invaluable as a creative interest, and I can't bear to think how different my life might be but for that inspired idea.

Appendix - I

Reflections on My Family Hstory
by Edna Bruner Bulkley

Grandfather Ashley Bruner of the German-Swiss Von Brun family, settled first in West Virginia, then married Henrietta MacDonald and raised a family of five sons and two daughters in Zanesville, Ohio. In 1856 the family sailed around the Horn and settled in the Santa Clara valley, south of San Francisco. To him, I am told, goes the honor of founding a college, I believe the first Protestant college [California Wesleyan College in San Jose] on the Pacific Coast. It later moved to Stockton and was renamed the College of the Pacific. His son, Elwood Bruner, my father, and his three brothers all graduated from its school of law, and three years later my father was on the California Supreme Court. My father eventually left my mother and went to Alaska, where he practiced law. [Elwood married Lillian Flint in March 1880 in Sacramento, California. Lillian gave birth to four girls. Edna was the oldest, followed by Gladys, Bernice and Leslie. In 1904 Elwood moved to Nome, Alaska and practiced law there with his two brothers. He was elected to the first Territorial Legislature for Alaska in Juneau. He died in California Jan 15, 1915.]

I barely remembered Grandmother Bruner. She died when I was six years old. All I knew of her is that in her young days she corresponded with her first cousin, General Arthur MacArthur. His son was General Douglas MacArthur of World War II fame. My father's sister kept the letters among her treasures.

Thoughts about Destiny always reminded me of my maternal grandfather, Daniel Sivarsey Flint, of New Hampshire. As a very young man he put all his belongings on a ship in Boston, bound for San Francisco, but missed the boat! Not until he reached San Francisco on a later ship did he learn that his belongings had been lost by fire at sea with all on board. That was in 1852.

Two years later he left his bookkeeping in San Francisco long enough to return east and marry seventeen-year-old Mary Ellen Russell of Crown Point, New York. She must have had a lot of spunk for that time, for at one point she had run away from the Female Seminary she was attending because she didn't like the food.

Those were rough pioneering days in San Francisco. Grandmother lost her firstborn. My mother Lillian was their second child. They lived around the corner from the mansion of the governor, before the capitol was moved to Sacramento. Their group of friends used to meet regularly in one of their parlors and sing to the pitch of a tuning fork.

When my mother was six months old Grandmother got homesick for her family on the east coast. Since some of their friends were planning a trip to the east going by boat down the coast and across the Isthmus of Panama, she decided to join them. The party crossed the peninsula on mule-back – Grandmother with her six-months-old infant in her arms! Apparently when he decided she had been gone long enough, Grandfather Flint went East to bring her home overland. Along with his luggage he brought a coffin full of hops grown in England where it was used for making beer. He hoped to introduce hops-growing into the States. When they returned, the Flint family moved to Sacramento, which became the site of the future Capitol.

Grandfather bought his first "Pioneer Ranch" on the Riverside Road south of the city and went through two floods before the levees were built high enough to protect the property. The land was fertile and as he experimented with growing the hops and drying them over the kitchen stove, the time came when he had enough to carry a pillow-full of hops to San Francisco. It created a sensation. Roots from his plants started hops-growing in the Napa Valley of California, in Oregon and in Washington.

The year he sold four thousand pounds at a dollar a pound he built his fine, large home in the city. Then he bought other ranches and raised fine horses while Grandmother raised seven sons and two daughters. When they were grown she took up lessons in oil painting. In her sixties she organized a whist club of a dozen old-timers who called themselves the "Giddy Girls."

In the 1880s they went to Europe and traveled from the lakes in Scotland to the canals in Venice.

Appendix - II

Bulkley Descendants
Compiled by Mary Bulkley Stanton

1. **Katharine "Kay"** [05 Jan 1912 – 08 Sep 2001] married John Woollett, a Baptist minister in 1934. They had four children: Ted, Charlotte, Kathie, and Peter. They served with the American Soul Clinic and the Conservative Baptist Foreign Mission Society in Japan for 24 years. After retiring in 1975, they returned to Japan as independent missionaries for another nine years. Until her death, Kay continued to minister to others in a retirement home in California.
• **Edwin " Ted"** [25 Sep 1935 –] earned a PhD in plasma kinetic theory. Before retiring as full professor at 63, he taught astrophysics, plasma physics, relativity, elementary particle physics phenomenology, and computational physics. He authored many books. He lives in California with his wife Kathleen. • **Charlotte** [30 Oct 1936 –] and husband Bud Kroeker, have been missionaries with the Biblical Literature Fellowship in Belgium since 1959. They publish, print and distribute religious materials in over 65 French-speaking countries. Their six children are bi- or tri-lingual: Rosalie married an Italian; Caroline an Ecuadorian; Yvonne a Dutch/Frenchman; Phil an American; Steve a part Russian part Chinese girl; and Esther a Belgian. They have 14 grandchildren.
• **Katharine "Kathie"** [22 Jun 1939 –] became a teacher and taught 32 years in California, with interim teaching in Okinawa and Germany for the U.S. Department of Defense. She married Peter Woelper in 1993. She has traveled, alone, with other teachers or later with Peter throughout Europe, the Near East and Far East – more than forty countries. • **Peter** [11 Sep 1943 –] attended Northwestern Medical School after Naval service and pursued a medical career in Hawaii, where he managed a hospital emergency room. He and his wife Lynda sailed to Tahiti and other South Sea islands in their custom built yacht.

2. **Constance "Connie"** [12 Nov 1913 – 27 Jul 1977] married Philip Madison and had two children: Tony and Janet. After her divorce, in the late '60s, she signed on as crew member of a sailboat bound for Hawaii, worked on the waterfront, then for the Cancer Research Center in Honolulu until she developed breast cancer, returned to the mainland

and lived with her daughter.

• **Philip Anthony "Tony"** [20 Nov 1936 –] was an engineer with Boeing Aircraft until moving east. • **Janet** [25 Sep.44 –] was a Licensed Psychiatric Technician for twenty-three years until a disability turned her to real estate. During a trip to Thailand, she visited her grandfather's hospital in Trang. She now lives in Thailand with her father and her partner Karen Bone. They have been accepted into the Thai community and are teaching Thai children English and selling real estate on Koh Samui where they all live.

3. Dorothy [26 Jan 1915 – 09 Aug 2000] became a nurse and married Roy Bucknell. They had four children: Anore, Don, Jimmy and Susan. They lived for a while on an island in Washington State. After her divorce she became a licensed midwife and eventually was married to Baldwin Anciaux for 28 years. Her varied interests included: belly dancing, cabinetry, alternative healing, gardening and marketing her edible flowers and herbs. They traveled extensively around the U.S. and Canada in their VW bus.

• **Anore** [18 Jul 1941 –] attended the University of Alaska, and was the second white woman to climb Mt. McKinley. She married Keith Jones, and raised two daughters, Willow and Arunya, an adopted Inupiat infant. They lived 23 years above the Arctic Circle. They now oversee a ranch in the foothills of the Sierras in California. In 1983 Anore published a book on the traditional Inupiat use of local plants. She is currently working on a sequel, *Iqaluich Nigingnaqtuat, Fish That We Eat*. Arunya has five children. • **Donald "Don"** [18 Apr 1943 –] graduated from the University of Washington with majors in Russian and History. After U.S. Army service, he lived in rural Alaska, crafting dogsleds, boats and houses. Currently he lives on the island he grew up on, where he has run a small sawmill for ten years. • **James "Jimmy"** [18 Mar 1945 –] spent most of his life on the same island, with interims at school and odd jobs in Seattle and Alaska. He raised his daughter Tierra (Ibn) on the island and ran a sawmill. He is a gifted woodworker and has a wood products business. Tierra is married to Gary Harris and is involved with him in two businesses: internet development and general contracting. Malina and Garrett are their children. • **Susan** [04 Oct 1950 –] worked on tugboats and commercial fishing vessels for some years. More recently she worked for the state of Alaska, coordinating advisory committees in northwest Alaska to give local input on fish and game regulations. At present she's taking a year off.

4. Lucius Daniel "Dan" [04 May 1917 –] is a sportsman. After serving in the Navy and the O.S.S., he was a teacher/coach in Oregon for 30 years. He married Vicki Germaine. They had two daughters: Dani and Connie. After Vicki's death he married Marjorie Boyer in 1983. At 70, he began competing actively in track and field events world-wide and has accumulated hundreds of medals and ribbons. He is a National Champion in various U.S. track events, and still holds world records in many 70, 75 and 80 age group (Masters) track and field events, plus skiing and badminton.

• **Dani** [13 Oct 1949 –] and her husband Bert Hinkley have been teachers in New Hampshire for 27 years. They have traveled extensively in the U.S. and Europe. On sabbatical in 2001, they spent seven months in Slovenia, assisting teachers of English. Their daughter Erin, married to Adam Shaffer, is pursuing graduate work in counseling. Their son Jed was on the U.S. Team in the 2002 Olympics as a Nordic Combine (jump and cross-country), and is training for the 2003 Olympics in Italy. • **Constance "Connie"** [11 Oct 1953 –] is married to Jerry Deady, an attorney. They have a daughter, Mary.

5. Dwight [15 May 1919 – 12 Aug 1998] served in the Army in World War II, ending up with the O.S.S. in Thailand. He was a Vice Consul in Bangkok, with his wife Virginia. After his divorce he worked as a Marine Biologist on a Russian ship. He later married Miriam Wilson and had a son, Brian. In Seattle he founded the Seattle Institute for the Life Sciences and focused on research in electromagnetic biology. He was calling for a major paradigm shift, a revolution in biology, and published numerous papers and monographs on the subject. His published book *Psycles* documents how traumatic events trigger accidents.

• **Brian** [13 Jul 1954 –] turned his love for surfing into a thriving international business of building surfboards, based in California and Spain. He has a son Taylor and four "adopted" children of his wife Rhonda. She has her own wholistic wellness center where she specializes in cancer and auto-immune diseases.

6. Mary, [08 Feb 1922 –] was a WAVE (women's branch of the Navy) during World War II. She married Clyde Good and had two sons, Ron and Alan. After her divorce, she married Jack Stanton. They were associated with the Frank Lloyd Wright Fellowship for 10 years. That marriage ended in the early '60s. Mary started several sales and promotional businesses, and from the early '70s she was involved with non-profit groups in Colorado, at the Findhorn Community in Scotland,

and in California. For the past fifteen years, she has lived in Washington State, and with her interest in nutrition and alternative healing she runs her whole food supplement business.

• **Ronald "Ron"** [29 Jul 1948 –] was a Vietnam war veteran and father of Katrina, Chelsea and Ryan. He was a Harley-Davidson enthusiast, skilled in building and altering many motorcycles in his own business. He has a grandson, Cody, by Katrina. • **Alan** [02 Feb 1950 –] was in the Marines, married Sharon Ann Gaucher and has a daughter, Heather, now a veterinary technician. He worked for many years in New Hampshire. While with the Naval shipyard, his work involved the overhaul and upgrade of nuclear powered attack submarines. He married Luanne Hanson in 2001 and currently works with the government's last non-nuclear submarine, in Southern California.

7. **Margaret "Peggy"** [31 Jul 1924 – 12 Dec 2001] served in the Army, married Jack Maechtlen, and had five children: Jay, Lynn, Mark, Curt and Ann. They grew avocados and citrus on a ranch in Southern California, and raised horses. After her divorce Peggy took a round the world trip, with major stops in Australia and Thailand to visit where she was born. During her last three years she settled in Nevada and was an active volunteer.

• **Jay** [30 Nov 1950 –] served in the Army in Germany, then took up Mechanical Engineering. He married Susan Marie Coad. His work-related travels took them to Japan, Italy and Connecticut. He's been a tech writer since 1982, with other businesses on the side. They have one daughter, Katie. • **Lynn** [02 Jan 1955 –] has had horses all her life. Her career path included nearly 20 years in the foundry business. She has also sold jewelry, fences and insurance, and run a boarding stable. She helped put on the first PRCA sponsored rodeo in San Dimas, CA. She and husband Dan Paul are long-distance truckers. • **Mark** [26 Aug 1956] joined the Army, served at the White Sands Missile Range in New Mexico and in West Germany. He has been a technician, a desktop publishing assistant and has had several small businesses. He has worked as a Lab Aide the last 4-1/2 years supporting the Galex satellite and Nuviews rocket experiments. • **Kurt** [01 Jan 1959 –] has a BS degree in Business Administration, has worked in the circuit board industry, run an auto repair business with a friend, and is now active in land acquisition and development work in California. • **Ann** [11 Jul 1960 –] usually owned a horse, rode and showed them. She has been a bookkeeper, owned a grocery store with her husband Arthur Schmidt, and after a divorce became a certified massage therapist. She is now an administrative assistant in an engineering office, and offers massage out of her home in northern California.

Appendix III

Glossary/Index

Appendix IV

Five Thai Kings
Succession of the five Thai kings
who reigned while Edna was in Siam

1868 - 1910 — King Chulalongkorn (Rama V) succeeded his father, King Mongkut, who was popularized by the musical "The King and I". He did much to continue the modernization of Siam started by King Monkut. He ruled for 42 years.

1910 - 1925 — King Vajiravudh (Rama VI) was educated in England. During the first World War he declared war on Germany. Thai troops fought with the Allies.

1925 - 1935 — King Prajadhipok (Rama VII). The 150 year absolute rule by the Chakri dynasty came to an end with a coup d'etat in June 1932, and a Constitutional Monarchy replaced it. He abdicated his throne less than three years later due to ill health.

1935 - 1946 — King Ananda Mahidol (Rama VIII) succeeded King Prajadhipok, his uncle, when he was about ten years old. Was educated in Switzerland and a Regent ruled until he returned at age 19 and reigned briefly though he was never crowned. His death in 1946 was never fully explained, though it was believed it resulted from a gunshot wound. (see Dan Bulkley's explanation in Chapter 47, page 310.)

1946 - present — King Bhumibol Adulyadej (Rama IX) Ananda's brother, he is the longest reigning king in the world today. He is responsible for the stability which has endured in Thailand, and he and Queen Sirikit are much loved and revered.

SIAM WAS OUR HOME
ORDER FORM

	U.S. Price	CN Price	Total
m War Our Home	$19.95	$26.95	
Shipping & Handling			
00 for orders in the US/ $7.50 for Global Priority			
Sales tax, (WA state residents only, add 8.9%)			
Total enclosed			

ne Orders:
800-461-1931
our VISA or
Card ready.

. Telephone Orders:
free 1-877-250-5500
your credit card ready.

Orders:
5-398-1380
l out this form (or a copy)
d fax.

ostal Orders:
Hara Publishing
P.O. Box 19732
Seattle, WA 98109

E-mail Orders;
harapub@foxinternet.net

Methods of Payment:

—— Check or Money Order

—— Visa or MasterCard

For credit cards fill out the following:

Expiration Date: _____

Card # _____

Signature:_____

Name_____

Address_____

City_____State_____Zip_____

Phone (   )_____ Fax (   ) _____

Quantity discounts are available.
Call 425-3679 for more information.
Thank you for your order!